A FELLOWSHIP OF DEFENDERS

A FELLOWSHIP OF DEFENDERS

The World War II Veterans, First Baptist Church, Marietta Georgia

Ruth Wagner Miller, ed.

Copyright © 2003 by Ruth Wagner MIller, ed..

ISBN :   Hardcover   1-4134-1262-9
           Softcover   1-4134-1261-0

Compiled By: Harland B. Armitage
                  George Beggs
                  Marcus McLeroy
                  Charles W. Miller
                  Ruth Wagner Miller
                  Ernest J. Wester

All rights reserved. No part of this book may be reproduced or transmitted in any form or by any means, electronic or mechanical, including photocopying, recording, or by any information storage and retrieval system, without permission in writing from the copyright owner.

This book was printed in the United States of America.

To order additional copies of this book, contact:
Xlibris Corporation
1-888-795-4274
www.Xlibris.com
Orders@Xlibris.com

CONTENTS

ACKNOWLEDGMENTS 13
PREFACE 15
INTRODUCTION 17
OUR WORLD WAR II VETERANS 21
SIGNIFICANT DATES
    AND EVENTS 25
        European Theater 25
        Pacific Theater 26
JAMES ALLEGOOD 27
HARLAND B. "ARMI" ARMITAGE
    And Katherline Armitage 32
THOMAS ASKEW
    With Katie Askew and Eddie Askew 39
LUTHER WILLIAM "BILL" BARBER 41
W. LAYTON BARRETT 47
LACY GILBERT "BUDDY" BISHOP
    With Bertha Bearden Bishop 51
HERBERT BLACK 54
HARRY JAMES BOLZA
    With Louise Bolza 59
BILL BORDERS 62
RALPH BOYD
    With Margaret Boyd Roach 67
KENNETH EARL BRAMLETT 71
WILLIAM CLYDE BRAMLETT
    And Marian Bramlett 78
ROBERT BRAWNER 86
GEORGE W. BROWN
    With Reid Brown 91

HORACE ELWOOD BROWN
  And Dorothy Brown 95
J.W. BURNS 101
LORAN BUTLER
  With Ann Butler 106
SHERMAN CLINTON "S.C." CAGLE 111
WILLIAM HOWARD "BILL" CAGLE 114
BRANTLY CALLAWAY 119
WALTER CAMP
  And Virginia Camp 124
GRIFFIN CHALFANT 126
FORREST LEON CLARK, JR.
  With Sarah Clark Goff 132
RUFUS CLOPTON 134
WILLIAM E. COLLINS
  And Marjorie Collins 141
JAMES A. COLQUITT
  And Betty Medford Colquitt 147
DENVER CORN
  With Ann Corn 152
MERRILL CRISSEY 154
JACK PERCY CUMBAA
  With Lillian Cumbaa 157
WILLIAM RALPH DAVIS
  With Ruth Richardson Davis 160
THOMAS J. "JACK" DAWS 164
ROBERT DELOACH
  With Greg DeLoach 171
KELLER H. DORMAN, JR.
  With Virginia Dorman 173
WILLIAM "BILL" DOUGLAS 177
CECIL DUDLEY
  `With Elizabeth Dudley 180
VERNON DUNCAN
  With Ann Duncan 182
LEON DURHAM

    With Joyce Durham Barber 186
WILLIAM EDWARD "ED" EADS
    With Dale Eads 188
HENRY ELDRIDGE 192
WILLIAM FOWLER
    With Ann Tillery and Kay Elliott 196
EUGENE M. FUNDERBURK 199
ROBERT GARRISON
    With Lorene Garrison 203
EUGENE WESLEY HAGOOD
    With Ruth Hagood 208
GEORGE BARNETT "BARNEY" HAGOOD
    With Christine Bramlett Hagood 211
HARRY JACKSON HAMBY
    With Elizabeth Adair Hamby 214
HARRY OWEN HAMES
    With Margaret Delk Hames 218
HOMER McCOY HARRISON 222
JAMES DAVID "BLINK" HARTSFIELD, SR.
    With Millie Hartsfield and Jim Hartsfield, Jr. 224
FRANK HATCHER 228
GEORGE W. "BILL" HAYNES 230
OTIS CALLEY (O.C.) HUBERT 236
HARVEY N. HYATT 239
JAMES, JOSEPH, BILLY,
    AND PHIL INGRAM
    With Ellen Ingram 242
        Billy Ingram— 244
WILLIAM C. INGRAM
    With Mrs. Will Ingram and
    Mary Ingram Wheeler 250
ANDY JANSAK 252
LEE THRELKELD JANSAK 255
CHARLES B. JOHNSON
    With Kathleen H. Johnson 262
GEORGE JOHNSON

And Evelyn Stephenson Johnson 266
EMMITT CLINTON JONES
    With Lucille Jones 270
THOMAS DAVID JONES, SR. 272
SAMUEL WALTER KELLY, JR.
    With W. Joe Kelly 276
WILLIAM JOSEPH KELLY 279
DAVID KILE
    And Kitty Kile 284
HORACE KILLEBREW 291
HUGH KINARD 295
CLEVELAND KIRK
    With Janette Kirk 300
PAUL KOCH
    And Eileen Koch 304
ROBERT B. LAMBERT
    With Catherine Lambert 308
HUGH LITTLE 312
WILLIAM E. "BILL" LLOYD
    With Catherine Lloyd 315
NORRIS KEMP MABRY 319
CHARLES MAHIN
    With Pauline Mahin 324
JAMES L. "PEPPER" MARTIN
    And Dan Martin 326
JOHN H. MATTHEWS
    With Abbie Matthews 329
PIERCE "BUCK" McCURLEY
    With Martha Crissey McCurley 332
CLIFTON MOOR 334
JOE MOOR
    With Pam Moor Gomez,
    Eddie Gomez, and
    Chuck Miller 336
HARRY R. MULLER 340
THOMAS MURNER

    With Louise Johnson Murner 345
JAMES NEWSOME 348
HENRY ORR
    And Carolyn Orr 352
COPELAND J. PACE 356
JAMES PARRISH
    And Jo Waldrop Parrish 359
DARRELL PERKINS
    And Jo Perkins 365
ROBERT ERNEST PYLANT
    With Fred Pylant 371
HOMER W. RAXTER
    With Wilma Raxter 374
WESLEY C. REDWINE, JR.
    With Dwayne Redwine 376
CHARLES "PETE" REEVE 379
DOYLE ROACH 390
ARTHUR THOMAS ROBERTS
    With Dorothy Roberts 392
GERALD "ROBBIE" ROBINSON
    With Bobbie Robinson 397
REUBEN BRADLEY "BUCK" ROEBUCK 401
THOMAS ROGERS, JR.
    With Pat Rogers Anderson,
    Marcia Rogers Thompson,
    And Thomas Rogers, III 406
DALLAS RYLE 409
HENRY ELDRED RYLE
    With Bonnie Zimmerman and
    James Zimmerman 411
DONALD SCOTT, JR. 414
J. F. SHAW 429
FRED "JACK" SHIFLETT
    And Jo Shiflett 431
JACK MADISON SMITH 436
K.B. SMITH

With Ann Smith 441
MILDRED MURRAY SMITH 444
JOHN STEWART 448
WILLIAM THOMAS "BILL" SWAIN
    With Barbara Swain 451
TOM TABOR 453
JAMES CLAYTON TEAGUE 456
JAMES THOMAS
    And Katherine Thomas 459
NORRIS "PUG" THORNTON 464
WALTER UHORCHAK
    And Sarah Uhorchak 468
JAMES "UPPIE" UPSHAW
    And Eleanor Upshaw 474
MARVIN PAUL WABLE
    And Louise Wable 480
ERNEST J. WESTER 483
JAMES BRYANT WESTER, JR.
    With Amy Wester 489
SAMUEL DORSEY WHATLEY
    With Jean Whatley Baldwin 491
JAMES B. WILSON
    With Shirley Olmstead 494

DEDICATED TO:

The men and women of Marietta First Baptist Church who served both in military and civilian capacities in World War II. You have fought the good fight and you have kept the Faith.

ACKNOWLEDGMENTS

Several people have made financial contributions to help defray the cost of this book. They have done so in honor of, or in memory of, family members who served in World War II. They are:

Ellen Ingram for her brothers:

James Ingram
Joseph Ingram
Billy Ingram
Phil Ingram

Andrew and Annette Moore for the first cousins of Andrew's father:

Comer Anderson Wilson
(1907-1941), died on the *U.S.S. Arizona*
at Pearl Harbor

George Byron Lunday
(1920-1942), killed in a training accident
at Trinidad, W.I.

Walter Brantley Moore
(1920-1944), severely wounded in Europe and
died in a hospital in England a few weeks later

Also:

Herbert Black
Kemp Mabry
Ernest Wester
Several Anonymous Donors

PREFACE

It all started one evening as several members of the Church Senior Adult Committee were sitting around telling "war stories." Those of us who heard them were intrigued with the idea of preserving those stories in some permanent form. Our interest in such a project became a feeling of urgency when we realized that, nation-wide, the veterans of World War II were dying at the rate of 1500 a day. Clearly, somebody needed to do something.

With the blessing of Marguerite Borders, Minister to Senior Adults, several of us agreed to form an *ad hoc* committee to interview the World War II veterans or their survivors who are/were members of Marietta First Baptist Church. God brought to the Committee the right mixture of personalities, experiences, expertise, and dedication.

Our Committee met, established guidelines for the interviews, and publicized what we hoped to do. We thought we might have twenty people to interview. Instead, we identified more than 100 veterans and survivors. Our first goal was to record the interviews and donate the recorded tapes to the Church Library. Then, if there was enough interest, we would put the information into a book.

We soon found that the interview process, of itself, was providing a ministry. As we listened to the stories—some very sketchy, some in amazing detail, we developed friendships with some people we had not known before.

Wives said, "He's never talked about that before." Veterans and widows of veterans said, "Thank you for caring enough to listen." Over and over again, we heard them say, "I was just doing my job." We were humbled in the face of their humility. We also gained a renewed appreciation for this generation that gave of their youth and energy in defense of their country.

As the interviews were completed, Ernest Wester transcribed the tapes and Ruth Miller turned the transcripts into readable narrative. You hold the results in your hands. May it inspire future generations to love God and our Country as much as this Fellowship of Defenders has done.

The World War II Project Committee:

Harland B. Armitage, Major (ret.), U.S. Air Force, World War II Veteran, and Retired Lockheed Test Pilot

Dr. George Beggs, Lt. Colonel (ret.), U.S. Army Intelligence Reserves and Retired Dean of Arts, Humanities, and Social Sciences, Kennesaw State University

Marcus McLeroy, Former Army Sergeant, Retired Equipment Engineer, Lucent Technologies

Charles W. Miller, Former Captain, U.S. Air Force, Retired Aeronautical Engineer, Lockheed

Ruth Wagner Miller, Author

Ernest J. Wester, World War II Veteran, Retired Georgia Agricultural Extension Agent

INTRODUCTION

When first approached about collecting and publishing the stories of World War II veterans, I was appalled by the enormity of the task, and dismayed by how much I didn't know about World War II. Before we were finished I had learned more about the military than I ever thought I wanted to know. But the most important thing I learned was how it took the effort of every military man and woman, regardless of rank or assignment, to come together in defense of our freedom.

We have not set out to write a definitive history of World War II. Far abler minds than ours have already attempted that. We simply wanted to make a permanent record of what the men and women of Marietta First Baptist Church have contributed to keeping us One Nation Under God. The list of those who served is longer than the list of those we interviewed because some have already joined the Mighty Hosts of Heaven and some were not available for interviews.

Realizing that we were dealing with fifty-year-old memories—some accurate and some vague—we have taken the stories told us at face value. We have corrected a few dates and place names. Where it contributed to clarity, we have changed the syntax and smoothed out the grammar. However, wherever possible, we wanted the men and women interviewed to tell their stories in their own words. Some turned out to be born story tellers. Some had difficulty verbalizing their feelings. In some cases, a story doesn't quite "hang together." We've resolved the discrepancies as best we could and apologize to any World War II historians who may find inaccuracies. All was done with love.

Many veterans lent us their precious photographs and news clippings. Sadly, just as the fifty-year-old memories have dimmed, so have the photos. Although, in some cases, the pictures lack clarity and quality we felt it important to include them. A few simply couldn't be reproduced.

Where our interview was with the actual veteran, we show just that name. Where we interviewed someone else on behalf of the veteran we use the term "with." Where another person sat in on the interview we use an "and."

This book is a collaborative effort. All Committee members did some interviews. They also paid, out of their own pockets, for tapes and supplies. They drove their own cars—sometimes to other states. They gave generously of their time and knowledge. My thanks goes to each of them for the sweetness of their spirits. And to their wives for supporting them in this effort.

Thank you, MARCUS MCLEROY, who got it all started and wouldn't let it rest until I finally said, "O.K., Marcus, I will do it if you will help." Thank you, ERNEST WESTER, for your faithful transcription of all those tapes, for the loan of your books, and for your quiet encouragement. Thank you, "ARMI" ARMITAGE, for your knowledge of the inner workings of things military and your orderly thinking. Thank you, GEORGE BEGGS, for bringing us the historian and political science perspective. And thank you, CHUCK MILLER, not only for your interviews, but for your financial support, for your acting as our business manager and publisher, and for putting up with hurried meals and my long hours of isolation at my computer.

Most of all, my thanks to you who have shared your

stories. You are heroes, all. Because of your relationship to our Church, truly you are a Fellowship of Defenders.

Ruth Wagner Miller
February, 2003

OUR WORLD WAR II VETERANS

Henry Adams
Rev. Alexander
William Alexander
James A. Allegood
Jesse L. Annendale
Harlan B. Armitage
Thomas Askew
Walker D. Awtrey
Ernest C. Atkins
Luther William Barber
Layton Barrett
Albert Beavers
Milton Y. Benson
Thomas R. Benson
William R. Benson
Lacy G. Bishop
Herbert Black
Lynn Blake
Harry J. Bolza
Bill Borders
Ralph Boyd
Kenneth E. Bramlett
Wm. Clyde Bramlett
Robert Brawner
John R. Brooks
George W. Brown

Horace E. Brown
J. W. Burns
Joe E. Butler
Loran Butler
William A. Cagle
Sherman C. Cagle
Allen Cairens
Brantly Callaway
Walter Camp
Griffin Chalfant
Alvin Chandler
Ray Childers
Forrest L. Clark, Jr.
Rufus Clopton
Elwin Cogburn
William Collins
James A. Colquitt
Ralph Connelly
Denver Corn
J. B. Cox
Joe E. Cox
Willis R. Cox
Merrill Crissey
Jack Cuumba
William Ralph Davis
Jack Daws

William H. Dean, Jr.
Robert DeLoach
Keller H. Dorman, Jr.
William L. Douglas
George W. Dowell
Cecil Dudley
George A. Duncan, Jr.
Jack W. Duncan
Vernon Duncan
James Leon Durham
William Edward Eads
W. A. Eaton, Jr.
W. E. Eaton
Henry Eldridge
Grover Fennell
William Fowler
Carl H. Frasure
Eugene.M. Funderburk
Robert Gaines
Robert T. Garrison
Eugene W. Hagood
Geo. Barnett Hagood
Harry Jackson Hamby
Harry O. Hames
Luther C. Hames
William B. Hamner
Vernon Hand
Bennett Harbin
Homer McCoy Harrison
Willard Hasty
W.E. Hart
Jas. D. Hartsfield, Sr.
Ralph E. Hartsfield
Frank Hatcher
George W. "Bill" Haynes
Claud M. Hicks

O.C. Hubert
Eugene Hughes
James H. Hulsey
Joe T. Hulsey
R.H. Hutcherson
Harvey Hyatt
Bill Ingram
James Ingram
Joe Ingram
Phil Ingram
Ingram, Will
Raymond James
Andy Jansak
Lee Threlkeld Jansak
Charles B. Johnson
George Johnson
Emmitt Clinton Jones
Thomas David Jones
Glenn D. Jordan
James Everett Jordan
William C. Jordan
Julian Keith
Samuel Walter Kelly
William Joseph Kelly
Hollis R. Kemp
David Kile
Horace Killebrew
Hugh Kinard
Cleveland Kirk
A. Stephen Kytle
Minga LaGrone
Robert .B. Lambert
Ebbie T. Lance, Jr.
David M. Latimer
E.W. Lawrence
Julian A. Lawrence

W.W. Lee, Jr.
Fred V. Legg, Jr.
William Leverett
B. Hugh Little
William Lloyd
Norris Kemp Mabry
Charles Mahin
Elbert H. Malier
James L. Martin
John Matthews
O'Donald Mayes
William R. McBrayer
Charles M. McCollum
Hugh L. McCollum
Pierce McCurley
W.L. McDaniel
John W. McLemore
Milton L. McLemore
Marshall McLemore
Edward S. Milam, Jr.
William M. Moon
Clifton Moor
Joe Moor
Harry Muller
Thomas Murner
Hulsey C. Nash
Wade Nelms
James Newsome
H.M. Northcutt
M.D. Norton, Jr.
Henry Orr
Hugh L. Orr, Sr.
Hugh L. Orr, Jr.
William J. Owenby
Copeland J. Pace
James Parrish

J.C. Payne
Darrell Perkins
Jack Pounds
R. Ernest Pylant
Homer Raxter
Wesley Redwine
J.W. Reese
Pete Reeve
Ross N. Reeves
Reginald Regglesford
Holt E. Register
Doyle Roach
Arthur Roberts
Reuben B. Roebuck
Thomas Rogers
Dallas Ryle
Henry E. Ryle
Arthur J. Scarborough
William H. Scoggins
Don Scott
J.F. Shaw
Fred "Jack" Shiflett
George R. Smalley
Jack M. Smith
K.B. Smith
Mildred Smith
Charles C. Stanton
Maidie Lee Stanley
John Stewart
William T. Swain
James H. Swanson
Tom Tabor
James C. Teague
Martin Van Teem
James Thomas
Norris Thornton

Walter Uhorchak
James Upshaw
Marvin P. Wable
Ben Davis Walker, Jr.
J.C. Ward
Frank B. Ward
Charles N. Watson
A.B. "Mike" Webb
J.B. Wester
Ernest J. Wester
Samuel D. Whatley
Bennie L. Whitlock
James Wilson

SIGNIFICANT DATES AND EVENTS
European Theater

1933—Adolph Hitler becomes Chancellor of Germany
1936—Italy and Germany form the Axis
1939—Germany invades Poland. World War II begins
1941, December 7—Japan bombs Pearl Harbor
1942, November 8—Allies invade North Africa
1943, July 10—Allies invade Sicily
  July 26—Mussolini resigns as leader of Italy
  August 17—First U.S. bombing raids on Germany begin
  September 3—Italy surrenders
1944, June 6—D-Day, the Allied invasion of Normandy
  August 24—Allies liberate Paris
  December 16—Battle of the Bulge
1945, March 7—U.S. Army captures bridge at Remagen, Germany, and crosses the Rhine River
  April 25—U.S. and Soviet armies meet at Torgau, Germany
  April 30—Hitler commits suicide
  May 7—VE-Day, Germany Surrenders

Pacific Theater

1941, December 7—Japanese sneak attack on Pearl Harbor
December 8—United States declares war on Japan
1942, April 12—Doolittle bombing raid on Japan
June 4—Battle of Midway
August 7—U.S. Marines invade Guadalcanal
1943, May 11—U.S. troops invade Attu
1944, June 15—U.S. forces invade Saipan
June 19—The Battle of the Philippine Sea, followed by the invasion of Leyte
1945, February 19—U.S. Marines invade Iwo Jima
March 9—B-29 nighttime bombing of Tokyo
April 1—U.S. Forces invade Okinawa
August 6—Atomic bomb dropped on Hiroshima
August 9—Atomic bomb dropped on Nagasaki
August 15—VJ-Day, Japan surrenders

JAMES ALLEGOOD

Was World War II necessary? I think it was. I believed then, and I believe now, that God was on our side. We did the right thing. At that point in time, it was really special to be an American. Men and women closed ranks and did what we had to do.

My military service began when I graduated from Auburn University in December, 1942. Born in Dothan, Alabama, March 23, 1921, I grew up in Moultrie, Georgia during the Depression. After graduating from Moultrie High School and spending a year at Georgia Military College, I went on to Auburn and was there when the Japs bombed Pearl Harbor. At that point everyone had to start thinking about military service. I had elected not to go on to Advanced ROTC, so in May, 1942, I joined the Naval B-7 program. I graduated from Auburn on a speeded-up program in December, 1942. I went on to the U.S. Naval Reserve Midshipman School at Columbia University and was commissioned Ensign on June 16, 1943.

Following my commissioning, I went to the Navy Amphibious Base at Little Creek, Virginia, where I was assigned to an assault craft unit. We trained there and in November, 1943, all units shipped out to England to train for the Normandy Invasion (D-Day).

We landed on the south coast of England and trained until June, 1944, when the boats in our unit were sent to Weymouth—one of the departure points for the invasion of Omaha Beach. Both the Army people and the Navy people, in a briefing before we left for our boats, assured us that there would be nothing left alive on the Normandy beaches to stop us. We had been bombing them for weeks. What they didn't know was that the Germans had twelve-foot-thick concrete bunkers built into the side of the bluff above the beach. When our bombardments started, the Germans just took to their bunkers. In addition, two days before, a German Panzer Division had arrived there.

The Germans thought we would go into Calais because it was a short distance (eighteen or twenty miles across the English Channel), but we didn't. We came in at Omaha Beach. The weather was bad but Ike had made the decision and we were going to go anyhow. We crossed the English Channel that night on those fifty-foot boats and got to the designated area about five o'clock the next morning. From the transport ships, we picked up the demolition teams that we were to ferry to the beach, and went on to the line of departure. It was just beginning to get light.

There were 5,000 ships involved in this invasion at Omaha Beach. The battleships, the cruisers, the launchers, the rocket ships were all firing. The destruction and noise was just unbelievable. We could see the shells from the fifteen-inch guns. They were trying to avoid hitting the beaches because the troops and tanks and equipment needed to go in there and they didn't want to tear it up.

We hit the beach at 6:30 AM, about three minutes after the shelling stopped. The seas were still bad but it was magical the way we got the boats in. It was our job to put the troops on the beach then go back to the ships, get other troops and bring them in. As soon as our bombardment stopped the Germans manned their guns in the bunkers and just rained fire down on us. When the Germans came up out of their bunkers it was like they were sitting in the balcony of a theater, shooting at the stage. The firing from the Germans was not so intense at the other beaches in the invasion because the Germans didn't have the gun emplacements that they had at Omaha Beach.

The gunfire was so bad that the first two men to step out of my boat were killed right there. Then the other men wouldn't get out of the boat. We told them they had to get out or none of us would survive. A Chief Petty Officer finally said, "Come on, let's go." And they did. Then we packed up and went back for another load. I went in there three times that day. It was June 6, 1944. That stands out in my mind like December 7, 1941 (Pearl Harbor) stands out in a lot of minds. I have always said the real heroes were at Omaha Beach. There is a big cross up there and a beautiful national cemetery with ten thousand men who gave everything at Omaha Beach.

The demolition men, who were supposed to blow fifty to one hundred foot channels in the water so that the ships could come in closer, were pinned down. They never did get that done. We had about two or three hours in which to blow the beaches so that the big ships could come in with the tanks, all the equipment, and the infantry. Finally the tide came in and they were sending unmanned boats in there just to blow a channel through.

The next morning a PT boat came along side and said, "Follow me." We followed him over to the British cruiser, *August*. General Brecht, Commander of all the troops in the European Theater, and Admiral Stark, Chief of Naval Operations, came down a rope ladder and got into our boat. We took them to another cruiser and when we looked up Ike Eisenhower was standing there waiting for them. Things were going very badly at Omaha Beach and I strongly suspect they were meeting to decide whether or not to stay. However, things got better. Our soldiers were able to get that Panzer unit under control. And of course our Air Force just bombed the daylights out of them. We had total air superiority. After three or four days our troops were able to push inland and the beach appeared secure.

After that our work was done. We did some shuttle work back and forth but our unit was pretty well broken up. I was assigned to the Royal Naval College, Dartmouth, England. In

November, 1944, I was assigned to an LST—a big ship, and I was a small boat officer in communications. We transported troops coming in from the States during the Battle of the Bulge. I remember thinking that we were getting down to the bottom of the barrel because I was seeing guys just eighteen years old, and the other group in their high thirties and early forties. Some of these kids hadn't been in the Army six months and they were shoveling them up there to face combat at the Battle of the Bulge.

Prior to D-Day, the Germans were in France. They controlled all of Europe, right on up to Norway, and were getting ready to hit England. Then, when Patton got over there and went to Paris, things started going our way.

By VE-Day, we were taking occupation troops into Hamburg, Germany. Hamburg had suffered such huge casualties from bombing that it was just chaos. Then we went on to Kronlein, where German soldiers were waiting to surrender with nobody to surrender to. They surrendered to the people our troops carried in there.

After that, we picked up a shipload of U.S. Eighth Air Force guys who had been prisoners of war. We brought them back to New York. I had thirty days leave and then was scheduled to go out to the Pacific. Instead, VJ-Day occurred and I, along with a lot of others, was very happy.

I went to Jacksonville, Florida, to decommission the old LST 292. Then I went on to the Charleston Naval Yard, and was discharged from there in January, 1946. I came out as a Senior Lieutenant in the Naval Reserve, having been awarded the Bronze Star and the Navy Unit Commendation for our participation at Omaha Beach. I even got the Good Conduct Ribbon.

After getting out of the Navy, I went to work in Wilmington, North Carolina, where I met Jo. We dated for about a year and were married in September, 1947. We have one daughter and one son.

We came to Marietta in 1986, when I retired, and joined

Marietta First Baptist at that time. I had grown up Baptist. In Moultrie the only building in town bigger than the Baptist Church was the courthouse. Jo was a staunch Methodist, so when we married I became a Methodist. But when we came to Marietta, First Baptist had a wonderful choir and we liked to hear Dr. Parker so we became Baptists.

Did my faith in God help me through Omaha Beach? Well, you know there are no atheists in foxholes. You get close to God in situations like that. My aunt gave me a New Testament and I had that in the pocket of my life jacket. It was with me when I went into Omaha Beach.

Would I do it over again? In the blink of an eye. I owed it to my country. But let's admit it. The Germans and the Italians and the Japanese felt the same way. They loved their countries and were willing to lay it on the line just as we did. The difference was in their leaders and ours.

—Interviewed by Harland Armitage, November, 2001

James Allegood

HARLAND B. "ARMI" ARMITAGE
And
Katherline Armitage

I was born on a dairy farm in Spring Creek, Pennsylvania, in 1925. As I went through grade school and high school I became extremely interested in airplanes. Before my brother-in-law entered the Service in 1941, he built a glider. This got me even more interested.

Right after Pearl Harbor (1941), I served as a civil volunteer plane spotter. We would take a four hour shift, sitting out in a little four-by-four (like a telephone booth) watching for airplanes. When we heard a plane, we would try to identify it, tell which direction it was going, and phone this in to "headquarters" in Pittsburgh. I would study the charts in those little booths and soon could identify every plane I saw. In my free time I would lay out on the lawn, look up at the sky, and just know that someday I would fly one of those machines.

In 1943, at the age of 17, and without my parents' knowledge, I took an exam for an Army Air Corps Pilot program and passed. Then my biggest job was convincing my parents to let me go. After much talk and heartache they did sign the consent. I took my high school exams early and was called into Service to start pilot training in the old Army Air Corps. I had never been more than fifty miles from home but I got on the train in Erie, Pennsylvania, and went to Miami Beach for basic training.

Following basic training, we did pre-flight training and lots of testing. Next, it was on to Center College, Danville, Kentucky, for three months. From there, I went to primary training at Bennettsville, South Carolina. We flew the old PT-17 bi-wing plane and I loved that airplane. My instructor was a jolly chap, a bit overweight, and a very good instructor.

After Bennettsville, we did basic flight training at Shaw Field, Sumter, South Carolina. My instructor there was much more hard-nosed. The first day we met, he called out the four of us who had been assigned to him, looked at each one from top to bottom, shook his head and walked away. I didn't see him again until the next day. However, the training was fairly easy for me. We had four hours a day of academics and four hours of flying. We flew the old twin-engine AT-10, which they called the "Bamboo Bomber." It was a light airplane, very difficult to land. When you made a good landing the instructor cheered.

About halfway through that class, they switched us over to B-25's. That became my favorite airplane. It was our advance flight training plane. I was qualified, and commissioned as a 2nd Lieutenant with my wings.

This was just past my eighteenth birthday. For a time, I was the youngest pilot in the Army Air Corps. I must have looked like a kid. One time, at a bus station in Chattanooga, an Infantry Corporal looked at me and said, "Second Lieutenant in the Air Force. That's about equivalent to Corporal in the Infantry, isn't it?" And I said, "Yes, sir, it is!"

I then did some combat training in the B-26's, getting ready for North Africa. However, that area had quieted down, the victory was essentially won, so I was picked to go back into B-25's as an instructor.

At age nineteen and a half, I was still a B-25 instructor.

I did my best and I'm proud to say that none of my students ever crashed. I stayed on as instructor until 1945 when they almost stopped the cadet program. They had started sending back the U.S. servicemen who had been prisoners of war. Some of them wanted to stay in the Service and they had to do a refresher course. I was still instructing when I got out of the Service in 1946.

I had met Katherline while I was in Montgomery, Alabama. We dated and decided to get married. About then, the U.S. started the big push against the Japanese on Iwo Jima, just before they dropped the atomic bomb. I was on orders to go to Japan. They were planning a tremendous force of B-25's and, being a pilot, I was on orders to go. We got a short leave before going, and Katherline and I got married and took a brief honeymoon. While we were on our honeymoon our orders for Japan were canceled and I went back to instructing former prisoners of war.

During World War II, everybody suffered. Shoes, clothing, sugar, gasoline, tires, meat were all rationed. Partly, because of the sneak attack at Pearl Harbor, everybody supported the war effort. I'm not sure that people really understood, though, the depth of the sacrifice of those who went overseas. There was no television, only radio, and that was limited by distance from the radio station. The whole news media was far behind and things were often reported a week after they happened.

Families suffered. My high school class graduated in June, 1943. By November, some of the boys that graduated had been drafted, sent to Europe, and had already been killed. In six months! My own brother-in-law, the one who flew the glider, was killed doing a test flight on a C-46 in North Africa. He had offered to do the flight in order to get in some extra flying time. This was actually after the war was over and he was on his way home.

When I got out of the Air Force in 1946 I went to Auburn University. While I was there, I actually worked for Eastern

Airlines for about a year. I didn't like the seniority system because it didn't matter how much experience you had or how hard you worked, you could only be promoted when your seniority number came up.

Katherline worked as a beautician and we bought a beauty shop at Auburn. She ran the shop and I helped as I could. I had stayed in the Reserves and was flying B-29's for the Air Transport Command at Maxwell Air Force Base, and instructing at the Auburn School of Aeronautics. I would go to school half a day, work the other half day, and in the evening we would clean the shop and get ready for the next day.

The B-29 was a good airplane but we had a lot of problems with false engine fire warnings. I was with the Air-Sea Rescue Squadron and we would go out over the Gulf of Mexico or the Atlantic Ocean for a five or six hour flight. We seldom returned with all four engines running because we would have a fire warning and have to shut down that engine. You have to believe your instruments even though you think it is a false alarm. Even though it was a good airplane it had the "4360 engine" with either twelve or fourteen oil scavenge pumps. If any one of those pumps failed then oil wouldn't get to the engine, it would overheat, and you had to shut it down. But I enjoyed flying that airplane.

In 1951, during my senior year at Auburn, I was called back to active duty to go to Korea. You could not get a deferment. I was assigned to Brookley Air Force Base, Mobile, Alabama. Katherline left the shop and joined me.

We had a short time at Mobile, where I was flying in a squadron of hospital ships: C-74's, 54's, and C-47's. We would fly to the west coast, pick up a load of boys who had been wounded in Korea, and bring them back to the hospital in Mobile, and then we would disperse them to a hospital nearest their home. After a few months, they started screening everybody's records for B-25 and B-26 pilots. I had lots of experience in that area. My commanding officer called me in and said, "You will report to Camp Stoneman next week for immediate transfer to Korea."

I went to Camp Stoneman, Sacramento, California, and Katherline went back to the beauty shop. She was able to fly out and join me and we had about a week together before I went to Korea. Then she went back to Auburn.

I was part of the 67th Tactical Recon. All our missions were night missions. Our purpose was to stop the Communists from supplying the front lines. They stopped moving in the daytime because we had so many planes in the air, but they would move at night. We had C-47's we used as drop flares. We had B-26's that we used to work underneath those flares for bombing, strafing, that kind of thing. We would fly all the way to the Yalu River. Any time we could see a light on the ground, we would drop a flare and go down to investigate.

When I came back from Korea in 1953, Katherline met me in San Francisco. We bought a car, drove down the coast, and then we drove back across the country. I went back to Auburn but switched majors from Agricultural Engineering to Aeronautical Engineering. I also got out of the Active Reserves but stayed in the Reserves until I had 20 years service. After Auburn, I went to Georgia Tech to earn a master's degree and then applied to Lockheed for engineering employment.

At Lockheed, I worked in engineering, then got a job as an engineering test pilot. I spent the rest of my career testing airplanes. We had many interesting programs. For example, we landed the four-engine C-130 on an aircraft carrier. In a program to test re-supplying aircraft carriers at sea, we made more than 130 landings on the *U.S.S. Forrestal*.

I then went on to other planes that Lockheed built—the C-141 and the C-5. On the C-141, Lockheed developed the automatic all-weather landing system. Prior to that system, airplanes often had to "over-fly" the planned destination. That is, if a plane got to a destination where there was bad weather, it would have to fly to a different destination. The new system would allow us to land in any kind of weather—fog, snow, rain, anything. We made 3600 landings all over the USA in the worst weather conditions we could find. I also participated in the FAA certification of the L-1011 (Tri-Star).

On another program to develop a missile system, we designed what we called the "QB-47"—a drone B-47, six-engine jet bomber, to fly without pilots on board. We made many flights with that plane. After it was in the air they would fire missiles at it and sometimes they would shoot it down. Usually they did not and we would have to bring it back and land it without pilots on board. We built 13 of the planes and I think only one of them crashed.

We did have some disappointments. Back in 1980, when the hostages were in Iran, we were asked to develop a C-130 that could land and take off on a soccer field. The plan was to fly in and rescue the 52 hostages as they took their exercise on the soccer field. The plane definitely had that capability. Unfortunately we were rushed because they wanted to accomplish this in time for President Carter to be re-elected. We were rushed too fast and we did crash. We lost a C-130 completely. All five crew members got out successfully but it was by the grace of God that we all lived through that one. I believe we could have been successful had we not been rushed.

In summary, my career started with World War II. I have had 45 or 50 years of aeronautical experience, most of as a pilot. It has been a good career. I am proud of the things we accomplished and disappointed at some of the things we were not able to do.

Our three daughters, Kaye DeJarnett, Sheri Pender, and Lisa Liebe have given us nine grandchildren. We enjoy them all.

—Interviewed by George Beggs, August, 2001

Armi Armitage

THOMAS ASKEW
With
Katie Askew and Eddie Askew

Thomas "Chief" Askew was born January 12, 1907, in Newnan, Georgia. Soon after graduating from high school there, he went to work for Georgia Power. He and Katie were married on June 21, 1941.

Chief was drafted and entered the Army at the age of 35. He was ready to go and didn't resent it. He probably could have gotten a deferment because Georgia Power was desperately short of manpower, but he felt it was his duty to go.

Following his basic training at Fort Monmouth, New Jersey, Chief was sent overseas. He took part in nine major battles and three invasions including: Tunisia, Sicily, Naples, Foggia, Rome, Anno, Southern France, Rhineland, North Apennines, and Po Valley. He was awarded the EMMET Service Medal, and the Good Conduct Medal.

When asked whether or not he had ever shot anyone during the War, Chief replied that he didn't know. He had shot his gun some but didn't know where the bullets went. "I was too busy stringing wires to worry about shooting," he said.

One thing Chief enjoyed about his service time was

meeting the Italian people. He would give them his chocolate and sugar ration and they, in turn, would cook a good meal for him and his outfit. Chief loved playing with the Italian children. He found the Italians to be accepting and helpful.

When Chief went into the Army, Katie moved back home to live with her parents. She worked at Bell Aircraft until about a week before the end of the War. On VE-Day, Katie and a friend walked up to the Marietta Square to get a bite to eat but every store had closed. People in the various neighborhoods pooled whatever food they had in their pantries and had a community lunch.

After being discharged on July 12, 1945, at Fort Gordon, Georgia, Chief came home. The family and neighbors were sitting on the porch and Katie had gone into the house to take a bath when a taxi pulled up. Everyone started shouting for Katie to come out. She came out, gave Chief a big kiss, and told him to sit on the porch while she finished dressing.

Katie's mother gathered up all the meat ration coupons and sent Katie's sister to the market. When the young man working at the market found out that the family wanted the meat to feed a soldier who had been away for three years, he told her to pick out what she wanted and forget about the coupons.

Following the War, Chief returned to Georgia Power, where he worked for 42 years. He retired in 1969. The Askews have two sons, Tommy and Eddie.

Thomas "Chief" Askew died on November 12, 1984. Katie Askew died on July 1, 2002.

—Interviewed by Marcus McLeroy, March, 2002

LUTHER WILLIAM "BILL" BARBER

My military records will show that I am two years older than my actual age, and that's part of my story. I was born at Grady Hospital, Atlanta, Georgia, in 1927. My daddy was a cotton miller and we moved to any place that had a cotton mill—Cumming, Buford, Fulton County, Cherokee County, Gwinnett County, Forsyth County. Sometimes our moves were job related and sometimes we moved because the rent was due. Times were hard for our large family.

I remember Pearl Harbor. It was a Sunday and I had gone to the post office to pick up some mail before going on to Sunday School at First Baptist Church. Someone told me to go out to the car and listen to the radio, and I heard the news about Pearl Harbor. I had joined the Boy Scouts in 1938 or 1939, and after Pearl Harbor one of our projects was to collect scrap iron. We collected old cars, old wire, old anything. We would get fifty cents for 100 pounds of junk iron.

When I was old enough, I joined the Home Guard. That became the National Guard later. It was for young folks. We trained on weekends. We would go out on the golf course and make Molotov Cocktails. Those were fruit jars filled with gasoline and a rag tied around to light them. We would pretend we were blowing up bridges and things. It was good infantry–type training. That's when I decided I didn't want to be in the Army.

I left home about age 13 or 14. I thought I could eat

better on my own. I came to Marietta and settled down in a hotel which was above the furniture store where the First Baptist Family Life Center is today. I went to school during the day and worked at the theater at night. At Marietta High School, Ed Covington was our principal. One day he gathered up several boys and told us that since the War was going on we should go out and get a job. I got a job at Bell Bomber.

Suddenly the Home Guard was called up and made a part of the infantry. I asked the Major if I could join the Navy, so he discharged me in order to join the Navy. I quit my job at Bell Bomber and took the train to the Navy recruiting station in Macon. There was a bunch of strange boys there. Several of us got a hotel room. It cost us fifty cents each to stay one night, eight to a room.

The next morning we all went down to the recruiting station and were told that we had to have proof of birth. I had never had a birth certificate. They told me I was out of luck unless I could come up with some kind of record like a family Bible. Several of us in the same boat went to the Salvation Army to look for Bibles. The Major there was surprised and happy to see all of us looking for Bibles. I found a really big family Bible with none of the records filled in. The other boys found other Bibles. We took them back to the hotel and filled them in. Then we took them to the Navy recruiters and they signed us up. I was sixteen at the time and I was pretty sure my parents wouldn't give their consent so I just made the Bible record look like I was eighteen.

The Navy sent me to Bainbridge, Maryland. They gave me clothes and food and I didn't have to work for either one. I'd never had that before. Basic training was hard (up at 4 AM) but it only lasted six weeks. When the Navy learned I had worked in the aircraft industry they put me in aircraft training. They shipped me off to the University of

Oklahoma at Norman, for flight training. I was too young, too inexperienced, too everything. I couldn't pass those tests so they put me in aircraft maintenance. I could do that. They made me an aviation metalsmith—a "tin bender." I learned drilling, riveting, and repairing planes, and we had plenty to repair.

After my training, I was sent to Pensacola, Florida, and I stayed there the rest of my time in the service. I was assigned to Squadron 8. We flew PBY's. Although metalsmiths weren't part of a flying crew, we did fly sometimes. We flew submarine patrol off the coast of Florida. I couldn't fly and couldn't operate the radio so I was given binoculars to look for submarines. We would fly for two hours, come back to base, and another crew would go out.

When I requested shipboard duty I was assigned to the *U.S.S. Ranger*, an aircraft carrier. It was mostly a training ship but it did go out to the open seas. I never did get a shot at the enemy but lots of the airplanes I worked on came in all banged up and full of bullet holes.

I was in Pensacola for both VE-Day and VJ-Day. After that everybody wanted to go home. I didn't get out until August, 1946. My rank when I finished was Aviation Metalsmith First Class. I came home and went to the University of Georgia on the G.I. Bill. I began working for Lockheed in 1951 and worked there for 37 years.

My military service was a good experience. It gave me some good opportunities

I had met Joyce in high school before I went into the service. One day I saw this little black-haired girl at school and wanted to find out who she was. I knew another girl at school who invited me to go to the First Baptist Church. Then I learned that's where the little black-haired girl went to church and her name was Joyce Durham. One day I asked her for a date and she said no because I hadn't asked her daddy yet. When I asked her daddy, he asked me if I went to church. I said no, and he said no. I started going to First Baptist Church and joined right quick. When I went into the service, Joyce and I wrote a lot of letters. On one leave I brought home an engagement ring for her and she accepted it. We were married in 1947.

—Interviewed by Marcus McLeroy, August, 2001

Bill Barber

Layton Barrett

W. LAYTON BARRETT

I was born in Cobb County, Georgia, September 25, 1922. I have lived in Cobb County all my life. I attended County schools. I met my late wife, Frances, at some function at Crestview Baptist Church. The first time I saw her was at a picnic when she was twelve years old. I watched her until she was seventeen and then I married her in July of 1942. Next to meeting Jesus Christ, she was the best thing that ever happened to me.

At the time I was drafted into the Army, in March, 1943, I was working for American Laundry and Cleaners. I did my basic training at Camp Wallace, Texas, and within a few weeks they put me in a motor pool. I stayed with that motor pool until the war was over. After thirteen weeks at Camp Wallace, I was transferred to Fort Sheridan, Illinois, to help activate the 134th AAA (Anti Aircraft Artillery) Gun Battalion. Following several more months of training and maneuvers, in March of 1944, we went to Camp Miles Standish, Massachusetts, to board the *U.S.S. Brazil* bound for Scotland.

We landed at Glasgow, Scotland, and took a train to a little town near Birmingham, England, where we got all new equipment. Then we went down to a little resort called "Hythe" on the coast south of Dover. We stayed there until September, shooting down German V-1 buzz bombs. Later I had the privilege of meeting Hitler's number two rocket scientist who helped develop that thing.

The Germans fired those V-1 bombs from a launching pad in France. The bombs didn't have a guidance system. When they ran out of fuel, they came down. The Germans were pretty good at finding the targets and having the bombs come down in the right places. It wasn't as scary hearing the bombs as it was when you stopped hearing them because when the sound stopped you knew the bomb was coming down. Shooting them down was a tremendous sight, especially at night. They were loaded with the equivalent of one ton of TNT and if you exploded them at night they lit up everything. When they hit the ground and exploded they would wipe out a city block.

We were firing 90 millimeter guns and they were very accurate. I wasn't on a 90 millimeter. I was driving the M-4 (36,000 pound) tractor towing one of them. I had to man the 50 caliber machine gun and the turret of my tractor when we were sitting still. The Germans had those big 16 inch guns set up on the coast of France. The British would lob a little 8-inch shell and stir them up, and here would come their 16-inch guns at us.

The V-1's would go about 400 miles per hour. Once I saw a British fighter pilot come up and put his wing against the wing of a V-1 and turn it around and send it back. Later the Germans developed the V-2 rocket. There was no defense against those rockets. They were launched from a launching site and they were much faster than our projectiles. Even if we had seen them we couldn't have caught them.

In September, 1944, we went across the English Channel and landed at Omaha Beach (this was after D-Day). We then went to Liege, Belgium. We were attached to the First Infantry Division and went along with them to various places. From Liege we started moving up to the Ruhr River.

We were sent to guard the Remagen bridgehead. The infantry had found this bridge across the Rhine River intact and they tried to blow it up but they only got a portion of it. We got many thousands of troops across that bridge before it fell in. It was while we were guarding the bridge that I saw my first jet airplane. I also saw that bridge fall in. The engineers were working on it with cutting torches and welders. We were about three-fourths of a mile away, up on a ridge, and we heard this huge rumble. The bridge just fell into the water with about thirty or forty men on it. The engineers then put a pontoon bridge eleven hundred feet across the river (which had seven-mile-an-hour current). We stayed there and guarded that pontoon bridge until they got it finished. After that we just did support for the First Infantry Division.

Our unit's first Battle Star was for the ground defense of England. The second was the Ardennes Campaign (the Battle of the Bulge). The third was the Battle of Germany, west of the Rhine. The fourth Star was for the Central Germany Campaign. The only personal award I got was a Unit Citation for going into a mine field and dragging out a couple of guys who had gotten blown up.

Morale in our unit was excellent. Our leaders were outstanding and we respected them. Even though the higher grades maintained discipline it wasn't unusual for a Major or a Lt. Colonel to come, put his arm around you and ask how things were going.

Living conditions were pretty rough. We slept in foxholes, anywhere we could to get out of the weather. Under the circumstances the food was good. It was a little disheartening, though, to get your canteen cup of coffee, set it down to take a couple of bites, then have to reach arm's length into the snow to get your coffee.

Most of the time we had adequate cold weather clothing. I have to confess that the only time in my life I ever stole anything was then. They had sent me to drive a truckload of combat boots. When I got it loaded, I asked, "OK, Sarge, where does this go?" He said "First U.S. Army

Headquarters." That burned me up because I was out there in the mud and the snow. So, once I got out of sight, I stopped my truck and found a box that had my size boots in it. I opened the box and got two pair of boots.

We were in some little town in Germany on VE-Day. I remember we were very happy. After that we pulled back to an area near Kassel, Germany. We had too many points to be sent to the Pacific but not enough points to come home so they made security guards out of us. I had set up my bunk in a vacant school house and was living well. After VJ-Day our unit was disbanded and I went to the 398th Infantry Regiment. I came home with them. At the time I separated from the Army, February 3, 1946, I held the rank of Technician Fifth Grade. My brother brought my wife to Ft. Gordon to meet me. It was the first time we had seen each other in twenty months.

After Service, we resumed our civilian lives. Frances and I had two sons. We joined Marietta First Baptist Church in 1954. I was privileged to sing with the Chancel Choir for forty-five years. I worked for 42 years for auto dealers in Atlanta, fixing wrecked cars. I retired in December of 1988 and the following year I started working for my son at his marina on Lake Allatoona. I was there eight and a half years. Frances died on August 16, 1993.

I still keep in touch with my WW II buddies. Every year our Battalion has a reunion. We usually have between 80 and 100 in attendance. Most are still in good health, which is remarkable because they are in their eighties. Last time I attended the reunion I said, "The weather gets colder; the battles get more fierce, but we still win every time."

I am proud to have been a part of the WW II military service. I was a young man but it taught me a sense of responsibility that I would never have gotten anywhere else. I think ever young man should have two years of service.

—Interviewed by Harland Armitage, January, 2002

LACY GILBERT "BUDDY" BISHOP
with
Bertha Bearden Bishop

I was born in a house on Burnt Hickory Road, right at the foot of Kennesaw Mountain, and have lived all my life within six miles of where I was born. I went to school out in the country but the school is gone now. After high school, I went to work in a beauty shop.

My husband, Buddy, was born April 29, 1911, in east Cobb County. His family, the Bishops, came to Cobb County about 1850. They owned a mill and a big farm near what is known now as Bishop's Lake.

Buddy and I met over the telephone. He was working at B&N Auto Parts on Powder Springs Street, and I worked just down the street. He said I would walk down the street with my nose in the air. We had a mutual friend, Betty Benson, and Buddy got her to call and introduce us over the phone. We dated some but then we went our separate ways. He told one of our grandchildren that while he was in the service he decided that if I was still single when he got home that was going to marry me.

I remember Pearl Harbor. A group of us had been at a singing class at a Baptist church up at Atco. On the way home, we stopped at the home of a friend who had just had a new baby. They were all hovered over the radio listening to the news. Janette (Mrs. Cleve) Kirk was with us. The Kirks had come home from army duty in Newfoundland, thinking they were going to be discharged. When we got to the Kirks' house, Cleve's father came out with tears streaming down his face. Cleve, along with many others had to go back into the Service.

At that time, Buddy was thirty years old and working at Sears. The day after Pearl Harbor was bombed, he enlisted in the Navy. He never talked much about his war experiences and all his papers have been destroyed. I know that Buddy did his basic training at Norfolk, Virginia, and then was sent to the European theater. While he was stationed in England, he befriended a little girl about the age of his niece. The English girl and Buddy's niece became pen pals and corresponded all through high school.

I know Buddy took part in D-Day. He was on a landing craft that took men into Omaha Beach. Actually, he was a Storekeeper—his rank was First Class Storekeeper. They all did a lot of things when it came right down to it. Toward the end of the war, Buddy was wounded and came back to Fort Houston Naval Hospital. He was discharged from there after the war ended. He was awarded the Purple Heart medal.

Meanwhile, in Marietta, my sister, Colleen, and I worked—she at Bell Bomber and I at Marietta Beauty Shop. Because of the rationing of gas and tires, we had to double up on the transportation. Colleen had to go to her job early so I would come into town with her. They had put in a streetcar line from town right out to the Bell plant, so Colleen would ride the streetcar from town to Bell Bomber. I would sit there in the shop on the Marietta Square, waiting for the shops to open and the Square would be absolutely asleep. In the afternoon, Colleen would get a ride home with Henry Orr or somebody.

Buddy was discharged from the Navy on September 27, 1945. We had a whirlwind renewal and romance and we were married the end of October, that same year. It lasted for 47 years. We had two sons, Bill and Beau. Bill was the first person to get a diploma at Kennesaw Junior College. They did it alphabetically and he happened to be the first one.

In 1952, we joined Marietta First Baptist Church. Buddy worked with the Boy Scouts some. I am active with my Sunday school class. When our sons were young, we did some chaperoning at youth summer camps. I still live in the house we moved to in 1960, 51 years ago.

After the service, Buddy worked first at Sears, then later at the Marietta post office. He had to take medical retirement from there because of back problems.

Buddy died from lung cancer on July 7, 1992.

—Interviewed by Ruth Miller, July, 2001

Buddy Bishop

HERBERT BLACK

When I turned eighteen, I was drafted out of Lanier High School (in Macon) and sent to Camp Blanding, Florida. That place was hot! We were out in the boondocks—a bunch of shacks and lots of mosquitoes. We were in the infantry and trained with rifles, old water-cooled machine guns, and 88 mortars. I remember that our last training exercise was a night walk, about thirty miles. We had a ten minute break every hour, then up and at it again. All night, from sundown to sun-up.

The political leaders swore up and down that they weren't going to send any more eighteen-year-olds overseas, so they kept us at Camp Blanding until the election was over. Then they shipped us to Camp Checker, Arkansas, and then overseas.

We left for Europe, by ship, from New York. They sneaked us on board and we couldn't come up topside until we got out of the harbor. They didn't want anybody to know that there were troops on that ship. That was during the big U-boat scare. It took us about a week to cross the Atlantic. We landed at Marseilles, France, and were flown almost immediately to Luxembourg aboard C-47's.

That was during the Battle of the Bulge. We joined the Third Army, Fifth Division and fought our way to Czechoslovakia. I was a machine gunner and that equipment was heavy. We would have to split it up, the plate, the tube, and the tripod. Then we also had to carry our rounds of ammunition.

We encountered some small arms fire, but mostly it was mortars, and artillery.

Most of the time, we were outside of towns, in the fields. We would dig a three-man foxhole, deep enough to sit in and long enough lie down in, and cover it with whatever we found. Then we'd put a foot of dirt on top of that to stop the cold air. We set the machine gun up right outside the hole.

I have never been so cold in my life. The cold was worse than the Germans. It was the coldest winter in about 75 years. Many nights I would bump my feet together and I couldn't even feel them, they were so cold. I have never gotten over being cold. To this day, my wife sleeps with the window open and all the covers thrown back while I sleep with the window closed and the electric blanket turned on.

We lived most of the time on K-Rations. They consisted of a sealed box about six or eight inches long, four inches wide, and an inch and a half deep. They contained some cheese and crackers and some sort of potted meat. Once in a while we'd get C-Rations, with a can of something like green beans in it. Occasionally we'd get a warm meal.

Toward the end of the War, we were staying in a house in Czechoslovakia and had set up a machine gun on one side of the house. The door was around on the other side. The Sergeant wanted the machine gun cleaned. It had antifreeze in it, which they dumped out. The only safety on that old machine gun was to not load it, because as soon as you did it was ready to fire—no safety, no trigger guard, or anything. That night we had a really hard freeze. I had just come off duty and was lying down when I heard a ruckus and a big hole opened up in the roof. It seems that a couple of Germans were coming in on us. The guy couldn't get the machine gun to fire but a Browning Automatic Rifle man was there and cut the Germans down. Evidently, when they fell down backwards it blew a hole in the our roof.

The Germans had screaming rockets called "Nemo Morphus." They would start screaming from the time they were launched and scream all the way in. It made your hair stand up.

We were out on the front line in Czechoslovakia when VE-Day occurred. We had Germans coming in with their hands up. I just said, "Come on back," and they went on through our lines and kept going toward the back.

Within three or four months after the thing was over, they shipped all we new guys back to the States to pick up new equipment and to go fight the Japanese. They left the old fellows, who had been in Europe a year or two or three, in Germany because they didn't want them to have to go through another war.

I was back home, in Macon, for 30 days leave when they dropped the atomic bombs on Japan. When the Japanese surrendered, it was a relief for us. We were sent to Camp Campbell, Kentucky, where we stayed for another year. Then they sent us back to Fort McPherson and put us out of the Army there. I took the bus home to Macon.

After the War, you couldn't get a job. I went to school a summer quarter to get my high school diploma. Then I spent three years at the University of Georgia. I didn't take the summers off, so I was able to finish in three years.

I graduated in 1949 and spent a year as a sign painter at Fort Benning, in Columbus, Georgia. When Lockheed opened up, I got a job there. That's where I met my wife, Catherine. On September 8, 2001, we celebrated our 50th wedding anniversary.

While I was at Lockheed, I started doing some real estate work. Eventually, I got my broker's license. When the big Lockheed lay-off came in 1973-1974, I left and never did go back. I have been doing real estate business ever since. It's something you don't have to retire from.

How do I feel about my World War II service? Well, it was something somebody had to do and we got it done. I guess we did a pretty efficient job of it. We knew we were going to beat the heck out of them. There was no doubt about it. We didn't like being cold, and being tired all the time, but our morale was good. We always felt like our backsides were kind of half-way covered, being under General George Patton.

—Interviewed by Marcus McLeroy, November, 2001

Harry Bolza

HARRY JAMES BOLZA
With
Louise Bolza

My late husband, Harry, joined the Merchant Marines on November 23, 1944. He took his basic training on board armed ships, where he qualified in elementary gunnery positions. He served in three war zones—the Atlantic, the Pacific, and the Mediterranean Middle East. At times the ships were escorted in all three theaters of operation. Harry's last ship was a Coast Guard ship, the *Fort Mimms*.

Harry never talked much about his war experiences. He did tell about a storm at sea when he was on watch in the "Crows Nest" and had to tie himself in. He couldn't come down because he was on watch. He said the ship was rolling so badly from side to side that he could reach out and almost touch the water every time it would go over the side.

Another time he talked about a storm when two torpedoes down in the hold broke loose. Harry and two other men were sent down to secure the torpedoes, which were rolling around. They could all have been crushed.

He also told a story about turkeys. It seems they had been on the ship for several months without being able to go ashore and the turkeys had "gone bad" but they still were served every Sunday. One night, Harry and a couple of other guys threw the turkeys overboard. The next Sunday, the Captain asked the cook where the turkeys were. The cook replied that the turkeys had apparently been thrown overboard. At this, the Captain muttered under his breath, "It's about time somebody did."

Harry didn't say much about the men on board ship with him. He did say that on one ship they had several Sikhs. These are the people from India who wear the turbans. They are not allowed to cut their hair or their beards so they bind them up in the turbans. One of the other men, pulled the beard of one of the Sikhs and the Sikh killed him.

Harry was a musician. After he left the Service he played with some of the big bands in New York. He did concert work and, at one time, had his own band. He liked to tell the story of how, as a young man, he and Frank Sinatra worked together on a job at Asbury Park. Harry was accompanying Frank, and Harry made more money than Frank.

Harry and I met while Harry was visiting his brother in Marietta. He had a job lined up and was on his way to Cuba. His brother persuaded him to play for a Lions Club function. I was singing at that function. Harry never did leave Marietta. He started teaching music and did that the rest of the time, along with a few performing jobs on holidays.

I was born in Canton and grew up in northern Marietta. I remember seeing boys in class one day and the next day they were gone. They had enlisted in the Service rather than wait to be drafted. We had ration cards for everything.

I graduated from Marietta High School in 1944. When I started to Asbury College, in Biltmore, Kentucky, I had to take my sugar card and my butter card with me. Mother and Daddy had to save their gas rationing coupons a long time in order to be able to drive me to Kentucky. We could come home only at Christmas and the trains were full of soldiers. One time I was the only girl in a whole car full of soldiers. The Conductor kept passing through to make sure that I was O.K.

Harry and I married in November of 1949. We have one daughter, Debra Ann Bolza. Harry Bolza died in 1973.

—Interviewed by George Beggs, November, 2001

BILL BORDERS

Although I was born in Thomson, Georgia, I would call Cedartown my home town. That's where I grew up and finished high school. After high school, I went on to Georgia Tech but ran out of money. So I went to Georgia Tech night school and worked at Westinghouse Electric during the day.

In April, 1941, I received my draft notice and told them I wanted to go in immediately to get it over with. I was twenty-three years old. At that time, the draft was for one year. Then they kept extending it and I wound up spending five years in the Army.

Our group was the first to go through basic training at Ft. Bragg, North Carolina. The barracks were brand new; the parade field was nothing but sand. We'd get out there trying to do "about face" and be up to our knees in sand. I became very proficient at peeling potatoes while at Ft. Bragg.

After eight weeks of basic training, I went to an artillery unit at Camp Forest, Tennessee. A week after Pearl Harbor, we got orders to move. It took a week to get a train in there and our unit was loaded onto three trains—flat cars, boxcars, anything and everything. We were not told our destination. We spent a full week on that train. On Christmas Day I was able to get off the train at Green River, Wyoming, and give someone a quarter to send a telegram home. When we finally pulled into the yard at our destination we found out we were at Camp Roberts, California.

By the time we got to Camp Roberts they were getting edgy out there. The Japanese had shelled the California coast from a submarine. For three or four weeks we had to wear combat gear, including gas masks. Our unit stayed out there in California, but I left to go to OCS at Aberdeen, Maryland. I graduated from OCS as a 2nd Lieutenant in Ordinance. From then on my situation was different from that of an enlisted man in the Army. My first assignment after being commissioned was at a little place called Warner Robbins, Georgia. That would have been in 1943.

I didn't stay long at Warner Robbins. I was sent to Aerial Gunnery school in Texas and went overseas from there. We went aboard the *Queen Mary* to the European Theater. That's when I found out why it was worthwhile going through OCS. The officers traveled as passengers sleeping in staterooms (albeit twelve of us, along with all our gear, in a room designed for two) and eating in the regular dining room with waiters to serve us.

There were thousands and thousands of enlisted men on board the *Queen Mary*. They got two meals a day. They would get up in the morning and get in line to get a meal. About the time they would finish, it would be time to get back at the end of the line and go through again for the second meal. The enlisted men had triple bunks in all the cargo spaces.

I went, first to London, where I lived with an English family. We were there during the bombing of London and when the V-1's and V-2's were coming in. Every now and then we had to go to the bomb shelter across the street from our house. If we were in town we would go into the Underground (London Subway) tunnel during the bombing raids.

We were getting ready, and when D-Day came we were already on ships. I was part of an Ordinance Unit receiving and distributing ammunition to the Air Force. The first place we set up was right on Omaha Beach in Normandy.

That was about a week after D-Day but there were still a lot of gun emplacements and snipers. Later, we moved up to Belgium and were there during the Battle of the Bulge. The Germans got within ten miles of where we were but they ran out of fuel and ammunition and had to pull back. Then I went on over to southern Germany and helped set up a depot there. We stayed with the Army of Occupation for several months, even though we had enough points to come home.

Of course, everyone wanted to get back home and some felt that the Army wasn't getting them out of there fast enough. When I arrived back at my Port of Embarkation, the Tech Sergeant was complaining about having 64 points and not being able to get out. I told him I had left men overseas who had 125 points and couldn't get back to the States. I couldn't sympathize with him a whole lot. He hadn't even been out of the States.

We knew we were headed for Japan next. They had already told us to get up a list of equipment that needed replacing. Just as soon as they could, they were going to re-equip us and ship us out to Japan. We were thinking, "If we had to be the first to go in over in Europe, why can't somebody else be first in Japan."

I remember VJ-Day because it was also my birthday—August 15. I had picked up my mail and had a letter from my sister. We were in a jeep, going to a new area and could see planes flying overhead in formations that said it was VJ-Day. Our jeep was in a wreck and I wound up in the hospital. When I got to read my letter (it was covered with blood from my nose bleed), I learned that my sister had gotten married.

I was at Fort Monmouth, New Jersey, when the Army turned me loose. They gave me 90 days of rest and recuperation leave. I came home, and that's when I met Marguerite. I had actually signed up to stay in the Army but they had us sign the wrong form so it wasn't valid. I left the Service as a Captain. I think I had eight or nine decorations when I got out but I don't know where they are now.

I came back to Georgia and went back to school full time on the GI Bill, while Marguerite earned our living. I got my degree from Georgia Tech and worked for Atlantic Steel for six years. Then I spent two more years in the Service during the Korean War. When I got out, I went to work for Lockheed. After five or six years, I started working for the Navy and stayed there until I retired.

How do I feel about my World War II service? Well, I got through it. It was interesting for a country boy.

—Interviewed by Marcus McLeroy, August, 2001

Bill Borders

Ralph Boyd

RALPH BOYD
With
Margaret Boyd Roach

My late husband, Ralph Boyd, and I both grew up in Bushville, West Virginia, although I did not know him until after the war. Ralph was born August 28, 1924, in Bushville.

Ralph wanted to get into the War so he volunteered. He entered the Army at Huntington, West Virginia, and then reported to Ft. Thomas, Kentucky, on April 30, 1943. He was issued clothing and bedding, and four days later he was shipped to Ft. Leonard Wood, Missouri. There he trained with the 75th Infantry Division, in jungle fighting. In September, 1943, the Army asked for 30 volunteers to go overseas and, without knowing where they were to go, Ralph volunteered.

The next day, Ralph went by train to San Francisco, California. They had four days of training in climbing nets up the sides of ships, and in using gas masks. Then, still not knowing their destination, they boarded the *S.S. Lurline*. Ralph enjoyed the trip but when he landed the fun was over. They spent one day at New Caledonia loading ammunition and equipment. On October 15, 1943, he landed on Guadalcanal, where he joined the 37th Infantry Division.

Ralph told us several stories about his experiences in

the Army. One night while on guard duty he was opening a can of rations. He wondered how many clicks it would take to get the can open. So he began to count; "one click, two clicks" until he got to the very end. Then he heard another click. He looked up to see a Japanese sniper and realized that that extra click was for him. Ralph had his rifle in his arms and he shot first.

Another time on patrol they were walking down the beaches and had to cross a river. One man lost one of his shoes. They waved at a plane flying by. The pilot flew lower to see what was the matter. The men had written in the sand the size of shoes they needed. In about half an hour the plane came back and dropped a pair of shoes and socks. That saved the day for one man.

Once, they had to bury a dead Japanese soldier. The next morning, the corpse was on top of the ground. They buried the soldier a second time and the same thing happened. The third time they buried him, they decided to stay up all night to see how he was getting back up out of his grave. In the wee small hours they saw an alligator come up, smell the body, and dig it up.

Some of Ralph's stories were not funny. They had been told, "When you are in a foxhole, do not answer back during the night to any whispering or messages. You can get shot." Sure enough one of his buddies heard something, raised up, and was shot in the head and died. Ralph told about hurling grenades and firing into the little caves where the Japanese were holed up because they wouldn't come out. Finally the Japanese would come out all burned up and they would have to shoot them. When they went to take Manila it was just fighting and fighting, week after week, and snatching a wink of sleep when you could. With bullets flying around the walls, and the stench of death everywhere, any bullet proof building was a haven for them. There were times when they couldn't change clothes or take a bath for three months and had to have their clothes cut off them.

Ralph was wounded twice. The second time it was in an effort to capture the summer capitol of the Philippines. After four days of hard fighting he was hit in both arms and two places in his back. That ended his fighting for a while. They flew him to a hospital on Leyte Island where he spent five months recuperating. By the time he was able to rejoin his unit, they had taken Luzon and were on the northern part of that island, serving as surrender hosts for the Japanese.

Ralph received a number of awards and medals including the Bronze Star with Oak Leaf Cluster, and the Purple Heart twice. He also received the combat infantryman badge for exemplary conduct in combat against the enemy during the northern Solomon campaign, Company F. He got the Distinguished Unit Badge in December, 1943, Company F, 148th Infantry Regiment for heroic action on Hill 700 in Bougainville. He also received the greatest tribute, the Distinguished Service Cross, which is a citation from the President of the United States.

Ralph and I met through my brother while I was still in high school. After the War, Ralph decided he needed to get his high school diploma so he came back to Beaver High School, where I was attending. We began to date and we were married in 1947. When he first came home, Ralph had a lot of nightmares. He had also contracted Malaria and Yellow Jaundice overseas. He couldn't donate blood because of that.

After getting his high school diploma, Ralph attended and graduated from Bluefield College. He then got a degree in engineering from Virginia Polytechnic Institute. Ralph went to work for Lockheed in July of 1951. That's when we moved to Marietta. We joined Marietta First Baptist Church in September, 1951. Ralph died January 19, 1993.

From the time he was a Boy Scout, Ralph was a very

patriotic person. He considered it a privilege to go to war for his country. When we would see things on TV especially with soldiers, or when he would hear "The Star Spangled Banner," the tears would just run down his face. That War cost a lot of lives and took a lot of sacrifice but God brought Ralph home.

—interviewed by Marcus McLeroy, July, 2001

KENNETH EARL BRAMLETT

I was living at home when Pearl Harbor was bombed—December 7, 1941. It was late on Sunday afternoon when we heard it on the radio. To tell the truth, I didn't know where Pearl Harbor was! I was young and didn't know much about war and hadn't thought much about it. I figured that eventually I would be in it, but it didn't worry me at the time.

I was born on a dairy farm on Wade Green Road, Cobb County, Georgia, in 1922. Later, we moved to the west side of the county. Because we lived out in the country, I went to McEachern High School (8th through 11th grade). They only had eleven grades back then. After I finished high school I was fortunate enough to find a job and worked until I went into the military.

In November, 1942, when I was twenty years old, (I had to get Dad to sign for me), I enlisted in the Marines. I didn't wait to be drafted. The Marine Corps is a rugged outfit and I don't know why I joined except that I wanted to see if I could become as rugged as they were. I don't think I ever did but I made it through anyway.

I did my boot camp at Parris Island, South Carolina. I was there thirteen weeks and then went to New River, North Carolina, for communications school. The food and morale were both good. Later on, in combat, the food was mostly K-rations, not very appetizing after a week or two, but our morale was still good. We really looked after one another. I learned a few new words in boot camp: "chow" (food) and "head" (bathroom) and many I can't repeat. Boot camp was pretty rugged. We had to take orders and the only thing you could say was "Yes sir, Sir; and No sir, Sir.' I was used to taking orders from everybody at home so it didn't bother me. It bothered some people that they couldn't argue or even ask questions about their orders.

The military isn't all bad. You have to have some fun even in the military. I remember one fellow on guard duty up near the General's headquarters. One night the General, his wife, and little dog were out taking exercise. They got near this Sentry and the Sentry hollered, "Halt! Who goes there?" "General 'so and so'," was the reply. The Sentry said, "Advance and be recognized; Wife and Dog, mark time!"

Parris Island wasn't large enough for us to take long hikes—just round and round the parade grounds. We did a lot of "double time" and "close order drill." We had ski training. After about two weeks we went to the rifle range to train. I came out of training as a Sharp Shooter. I would have made Expert but the day of that test the wind was blowing and the target was 500 yards away. In a standing position you were lucky to hit the target at all. When you completely missed the target they would raise a red flag "Maggie's Drawers" they called it.

While stationed at New River, I also spent about six weeks at the Marine base in Quantico, Virginia. I was assigned to an artillery unit. From New River we went to Camp Pendleton, California, for about five months, then on to San Diego to board our ship. We had no idea where we were going.

I won't ever forget that ship. It was called an LST, had a flat bottom, and you felt every little ripple on the water. They said it was the only ship in the world that would go in five different directions at one time. I got seasick and so did everybody else. We zigzagged across the Pacific to avoid subs—from San Diego all the way to the Marshal Islands.

We entered combat and took some of the Marshal Islands, including Roi-Namur. After the Marshal Islands were secure, we boarded ship and went back to the Island of Maui in Hawaii.

That was our home base. We got back to Maui so quickly that our camp wasn't ready for us. We had taken the Marshal Islands in about five days and they expected it to take two or three weeks. It was the rainy season when we got to Maui and they had set up tents for us in a pineapple field. You can imagine how much mud we had. There was no place even to put the materials they had shipped us. Finally they got some warehouses together and we had to transport the materials back to the warehouses. We stayed on Maui about three months awaiting and training the replacements for the casualties we had from the Marshal Islands.

From Maui we went to the Mariana Islands and Saipan was our first mission. It was a hard island to take—many, many casualties. We landed two Marine divisions simultaneously. After two or three days the fighting was so rough we had to call in a reserve division. It happened to be an Army division. They came in and formed a line between the two Marine divisions. It took us a month to secure Saipan, then we rested for a few days.

Across the bay from Saipan was another island, Tinian. We set up our artillery there along the coast of Saipan—there must have been a mile of artillery pieces set up to fire over on Tinian. I don't see how anything could have lived through that bombardment, but they did. They were well dug in. Still, Tinian was an easier island to take than Saipan. On both places there were a lot of civilians. That was hard to get used to. We didn't want to hurt or kill them, but sometimes you have no other choice.

After Tinian we went back to Maui. We stayed there until the next January. We had a lot of replacements come in.

Our next operation began at Pearl Harbor where we joined a convoy. We had Destroyers going along to protect us. We went all the way to Iwo Jima. We had heard that it would be a rough island to take but nobody thought it would take as long as it did. Some of the men got up a pool to guess the number of days it would take to take that island. There were guesses from three to thirty days. We were all wrong. It took something like six weeks. The Japanese had boasted that the island was impregnable. They didn't think anyone could possibly take it. Before it was over, we began to think the same thing ourselves.

There were miles and miles of underground tunnels. Their hospital, their food, their water, their ammunition, all were underground. All the bombing and shelling that we did before we landed on Iwo did hardly any damage at all. The island is volcanic ash and tanks would just mire down in the ash. We landed two Divisions on Iwo. The Japanese waited until a wave or two of Marines landed before they started their bombardment. They figured they would wipe out the whole bunch at one time. We were beaten up so badly by the second or third day that we had to call in a third Division (they always have one in reserve).

When I was wounded, the Corpsman came and dressed the wound and told me I was eligible for the Purple Heart. I said, "No. Forget it." The reason was there were so many people there so badly injured, so many killed, mutilated in every way imaginable. We had a pile of dead bodies there three or four feet high and 50 to 75 yards long. We couldn't bury them until we took enough of the island so that it was safe to bury them. If we had tried to bury them earlier we would have had a lot more casualties. All we could do was stack them up until we got far enough inland to bury them.

The famous picture of the Marines raising the American flag was at a place I could see without difficulty, although I wasn't close to it when it happened. The flag was raised long, long before the island was secure. We cut the island in half and took Surbachi and then raised the flag. It took several more weeks to secure the other half of the island.

You may wonder why we fought so hard to take such a small island. There were three main reasons. First, when we flew our B-29's from Tinian and Saipan to Japan, the Japanese on Iwo Jima would radio Tokyo that we were coming for another raid. Second, they could send up fighters from Iwo to intercept our B-29's. And third, whenever the B-29's would get shot up pretty bad they would not be able to make it all the way back to Tinian and Saipan, so they would stop on Iwo. In fact, the first plane made an emergency stop there before we had the island secured. I understand that enough airmen's lives were saved by those stops on Iwo that it offset the number of Marines killed in taking the island.

By the time VE-Day was proclaimed in Europe (May, 1945), we were back in Maui. We were still there when VJ-Day was announced in August, 1945.

I believe that dropping the atomic bomb on Japan ended the war. Had we not done that we would have lost thousands and thousands and thousands of casualties before the Japanese were defeated. They had their *kamikaze* planes that they flew over the Philippines and Okinawa. They also had thousands of what I call "PT Boats" stored away. They were going to use women and children to drive them into our ships to try and sink them. We would have had so many more casualties had we had to land in Japan.

I was discharged in November, 1945. I had met my first wife, Mildred, when I was stationed at New River. She was going to college in Greenville, North Carolina. We hit it off pretty good and she was still waiting for me when I came home. I was working for the W.P. Stephens Lumber Company when I went into the Service and took up where I left off when I got back home.

I have a few mementoes from my war experience. I picked up this shell, a 40 mm Japanese anti-tank shell, on Iwo Jima. When you first land on an island everything is so rough you aren't thinking about souvenirs. But when things quiet down you start looking for souvenirs. By that time they are gone because everybody else had the same idea. I have battle stars for the four invasions I was in. Then there are Presidential Unit Citations to the Division for Saipan and Iwo Jima.

Several years ago, I visited Pearl Harbor with my sons and their wives. While at the Arizona Memorial we met a man who was a bugler at the Memorial. He had been on the battleship *West Virginia.* When the Japanese attacked Pearl Harbor the *West Virginia* was hit by several torpedoes and eventually sank. One armor-piercing bomb went through the first floor and didn't explode; it went through the second floor and didn't explode, and it stopped on the third deck. Had it gone through the third deck where the ammunition and gasoline was stored they would have been blown sky high. This man was badly wounded but he swam out from the ship to Ford Island and was picked up there and taken to the hospital. He recuperated and they put him in a Marine outfit and he wound up on Iwo Jima.

When this same man got back to civilian life, he decided to contact the Japanese man who had dropped that bomb. He called Tokyo, and because the attack on Pearl Harbor had been so carefully planned, everything was recorded. He got the name and address of that Japanese pilot and talked to him several times on phone. Then he flew over to Japan and met the man, and they became great friends. The Japanese man gave him 1300 Yen and asked him to put a rose on the Arizona Memorial when he did his programs there.

This man told us he was doing one of his programs and invited me to come out and see it. When we got there he told me I was on the program. He got up and made his speech; I mumbled a few words (I am not a great speaker and I didn't know what to say). Afterwards he blew "Taps" and we went back to the docks. We were standing there talking about our experiences on Iwo Jima—just the two of us. By the time we got through, there was a crowd of at least 50 people listening and not a dry eye amongst them, including myself. My sons were so moved that they went into the store there and bought me a U.S. flag which had flown over the Arizona. I'm very proud of this flag.

For a while after the war, we used to have a Battery reunion but there are few of us left now. I do still hear from some of my buddies. I believe the Division has reunions but those are so big, I might only know two or three people.

Fifty-six years after being wounded, I applied for the Purple Heart. Our government has passed a law that a veteran with a Purple Heart will have medical care if he needs it. I don't know when I might need it but I'd like to have it available if I do need it. I will be awarded my Purple Heart at Dobbins Air Force Base on September 6th, 2001.

I feel like I was one of the lucky ones. There are a lot of things wrong in the U.S. but when you get right down to it, it is still the best!

—Interviewed by Ernest Wester, August, 2001

Kenneth Bramlett

WILLIAM CLYDE BRAMLETT
And
Marian Bramlett

I had graduated from Marietta High School in 1937 and attended Georgia Evening College in Atlanta. In 1938, I got a Civil Service job with the War Department, and was working in the Hurt Building in Atlanta. In fact, that's where I met Marian.

The first Draft registration was in 1941. I was 21 years old and single. I was just what they wanted so I was included in the first group for the Draft in Cobb County—before Pearl Harbor. When I reported for duty at Fort McPherson, they turned me down and classified me 1-B. It seems they didn't like my dental work. I had a partial dental plate due to getting hit in the mouth while playing baseball. At Fort "Mac" they said they would take me if I got a permanent bridge. Well, I didn't want to go into the Service anyway so I went back to work. A week after Pearl Harbor the Army forgot about my teeth and reclassified me 1-A. Since I had to go, I started trying to get into the Air Force Cadet Program and eventually succeeded.

I was sworn in on September 1, 1942, and sent to Miami, Florida, for thirty days of basic training. After testing, six hundred of us were sent to the first college training detachment at the University of Tennessee. We went to school from 7:30 AM to 5:30 PM, studying history, trigonometry, meteorology, and a lot of military things. It was a struggle and many nights I would study in bed, after lights out, using a flashlight under the bed covers. There were about five of us in each room. One of my roommates was a senior at M.I.T. so I had night time instruction.

Next, I spent three weeks at a classification center in Nashville, Tennessee; then on to Maxwell Field, Alabama, for pre-flight pilot training. I took flight training at three different places. First, in July and August, 1943, I was at Librook School of Aeronautics (a private school) near Lakeland, Florida. I did my primary training there on an old PT Steerman dual wing cockpit type plane. It was a nice airplane. If you got into trouble with it, you just turned it loose and it would straighten itself out. I soloed after five hours. A hot shot pilot, H.P. Howell, said that I was the only one out of his five students who flew the plane. He said most cadets sit there and just herd the thing.

For my next training, I went to Cochran Field at Macon, Georgia, and trained with a BT-13 ("Cadet Killer," we called it). You could do all kinds of maneuvers with that plane—chandelles, immelman turns, snap rolls, slow rolls—but it was hard to get it straightened up. We had six cadets killed at Cochran, four flying with instructors. We had two run together right over the field one night. They came down on top of one another. The guy on top bailed out and the guy on the bottom came on in and landed. At Cochran they divided us for Fighter training or Bomber training. You had a choice and I asked for Bombers all the way through. I wanted all the engines I could get.

My final training was at Moody Field in Valdosta, Georgia. We flew a twin-engine AT-10, strictly a trainer, built out of plywood, but it was good. It would just run off and leave the single engine T-6's. We would get in dog fights with the pilots from Dothan, Alabama. Not only could we outrun them, we could throttle back to about 40 miles an hour and stay in the air, which they couldn't do. I graduated from there and got my Wings and 2nd Lieutenant's bars on February 7, 1944. Marian came down and pinned on my Wings.

I left Valdosta in winter, headed for Chanute Field in Illinois. I think it snowed the whole time we were there. We flew B-17's. Before you ever soloed in a B-17 you had to get 30 hours just sitting in the cockpit going through all the procedures. They blindfold you and make you feather an engine and turn off all the engines in the right sequence while blindfolded.

From Chanute we went to Lincoln, Nebraska, to make up our crew. Then we took a troop train to Dyersburg, Tennessee, and in July, 1944, we picked up a brand new airplane at Kearning, Nebraska, to take overseas. We landed our plane, first, at Manchester, New Hampshire; then Goosebay, Labrador; then Reykjavik, Iceland. Our destination was a base in Scotland but the weather was so bad they sent us to Nutts Corner near Belfast, Ireland. We had to leave our airplane there and take a boat across to England. I ended up with the 95th Bomber Group, 334th Squadron, 8th Air Force at Horham (90 miles north of London). We had four squadrons of twenty crews each assigned to that base. All Bombers.

In that area of England, the air bases were so close together that we'd take off in the morning on a mission and circle and climb. If you got too far over you'd get into someone else's traffic pattern. The weather would be so bad that you couldn't see. One morning we were just climbing out and there was a B-17 so close that I could see the tail gunner flashing his warning lamp in our face. There were several mid-air collisions while I was there. One morning, as we climbed, we started picking up ice and slowly losing our rate of climb. The rate kept dropping and I figured we would soon be unable to fly. We finally broke out on top and the ice started coming off. You could hear it and say, "Whew!"

We arrived in England in July, 1944. Altogether I flew 35 missions but I must have flown at least 50 training missions also—all around the British Isles. The Eighth Air Force did a lot of training in formation flying. You got so you could sit right in there and stick your wing right in the next plane's window.

We flew just as tight a formation as we could. On my last twenty missions I flew as deputy squadron leader and I always flew on the lead ship's right wing. I would stay in so close that I could feel the wash off the lead ship. It kept trying to drive your wing down. The waist gunner on the lead ship didn't like my flying on his wing because he thought I was going to put my wing right in on him. But you had to get as close as possible when the weather was bad because you didn't want to lose sight of him.

One day as we were flying, I was looking at the lead ship and just happened to turn and look ahead. Just as I did, a squadron came out of the clouds right in our face. I pulled back on the stick just as hard as I could. I couldn't push down because there were three other ships underneath us. I don't know how our lead, Hal, missed me. I wasn't thinking about him, I was just trying to get out of the way of that squadron. Five ships collided. We lost #2 and #3. You could hear them exploding. We continued on with the mission but we never did get the squadron back together. We found another group with some planes missing and we just latched on to them. The Germans had somehow gotten some B-17's and were flying them. We had orders that if a B-17 came up and joined our squadron, and then started to pull out when we got to the target, we were to shoot him down because he was probably a German. So we stayed with that squadron on their bomb run and dropped our bombs. When they turned back to England, we lost them in the soup. That was one of the times when our navigator gave me all the right headings to avoid flack areas and big cities.

Our navigator was so good, you couldn't lose him. He

would tell me when we hit the coast of England and give me a heading. He'd say, "Start circling." I would circle, drop down through the soup and be right over the base. If we were flying a mission and the lead ship (which had radar and two or three navigators) got a little off course, he would get on the radio and tell them, "You are off course." On one mission, he said, "There's heavy flack over there and we're heading right into it!" He kept telling me, and I didn't tell the lead. I said, "Oh, they know what they are doing." But they didn't. He finally got on the radio and told them to get "off the air." But they kept the same heading, and as a result we lost three airplanes. The flack was awful.

On most missions you would get hit, usually with flack. We didn't have too much trouble from German Fighters because we had fighter escorts. If you flew a long mission you didn't have the same fighter escort the whole way. They flew so much faster than we did, they would have to zig-zag through our formation. They would escort us just so far then run out of fuel and have to go home. Except for the P-51's, which could go a long way, the Fighters would pick us up when we hit the coast. Then we'd have another group of Fighters pick us up to escort us to our target and part way back home. And a third group would escort you home.

The Fighters were almost always on time, but one day they weren't. The Germans engaged them on the coast and they were down there having dog fights while we were approaching our target area and wondering where our escorts were. They never did show up. Sometimes those bomb runs would be 50 miles long and you couldn't do anything but hold it straight and steady for the bombardier. The Germans picked us up and escorted us down the bomb run. We started that run with twelve airplanes and when we came off the target we had five still in formation. Two of those who were still with us got home.

On that mission, we got a hole right through the wing, just outboard of the #1 engine. In the movie, "Schindler's List," it describes how they made shells that wouldn't work. We must have gotten one of those shells without a firing pin. It came through the wing but didn't explode, and made a big hole. The wing was waving a little bit. I was scared that thing would fold up and come off, but it didn't! When we got out over the North Sea, the five of us that were still together started letting down. We stayed at 20,000 feet. I told them, "We'd better stay here because that wing may come off and we want plenty of time to get out of the airplane." We got over England and my copilot, John, and I decided we were going to take it in and land it. We would go over the base and let the crew bail out if they wanted to. But they didn't. It was our 20th mission and we had been together a long time. We were awarded the DFC (Distinguished Flying Cross) for getting that plane home—more than 400 miles, mostly over water.

Basically, our mission was bombing runs over Germany. I flew my first mission, to Sindelfingen, Germany, on August 13, 1944. It was a "milk run."

My second mission was to Warsaw, Poland, to drop canisters of arms, ammunition, and medical supplies for the Poles. We made the drop and flew on into Poltavia, Russia (halfway between Karkov and Kiev). In the process we lost an engine over Warsaw and had to stay several weeks while they brought in a new engine. The Russians put us in tents on the opposite side of the base and we were not allowed to go to the Russian side. No fraternizing at all.

Twice, we went to Berlin. The second time was to drive down the Germans' morale so that they would force Hitler to quit. There were three squadrons in my group. The first carried twelve 500 pound bombs to explode on contact. The second came in with bombs that had two-hour delayed action fuses on them. The third squadron's bombs had six-hour delays on them. The theory was that people would go to the air raid shelters when the first bombs were exploding. About the time they would think it was over and start coming out of the shelters, the two-hour bombs would start exploding. When they went into the shelters the second time, they would stay longer and the six-hour bombs would catch them when they came out. They said we killed about 35,000 people on that one mission. I always felt that there were people down there who, just like me, didn't want to get killed.

We were fortunate enough to get two or three day passes every two weeks and could go into London. Once they sent us to a big resort hotel at Bournemouth for "Flack Leave."

A lot of our men had problems. Some were grounded. One of the guys would fly a mission, then come back and cry like a baby. He'd say, "I'm not going out there again." But the next time he was scheduled to fly he'd be there. Sometimes, in the winter, we couldn't fly because of bad weather. Sometimes we'd fly two or three days in a row. When you get close to the end of your tour, they fly you every day and don't give you a chance to think. At the end of my tour, we flew four consecutive days. They get you up sometimes as early as 3 AM for the briefing. You fly the mission, come home, eat, and go to sleep. First thing you know they're waking you to go again.

On March 9, 1945, Marian got the cable that I was coming home. We came by troop transport and had to wait out in the Atlantic Ocean for a convoy to be made up. It took us until April 19 to actually get home. Our ship came into New York Harbor, right past the Statue of Liberty. We took a troop train to Camp Kilmer, New Jersey, and another train to Atlanta. In the meantime, I had proposed by V-mail and Marian had accepted.

We were married at Fort McPherson a week after I got to Atlanta. We had a week's honeymoon in New Orleans. Then we went on to Florida, where I served as a flight instructor at Hendricks Field in Sebring, until November, 1945. I was actually in Marietta on VE-Day. I still had two brothers-in-law in the Service—one in Europe and the other in the Pacific. We went down to the Marietta First Baptist Church that afternoon for a celebration service.

I was discharged at Maxwell Field with the rank of 1st Lieutenant. Besides the DFC, I received three Battle Stars to go on the European Theater of Operations Ribbon; four Air Medals with Oak Leaf Cluster; and the Victory Medal. Our unit was the only group that got three Presidential Unit Citations. In 1992, we went to Poland, where they had a big ceremony and presented us with the Polish Air Force Cross. When Russia had its 50th anniversary they awarded a medal to everybody who had taken part in the shuttle runs into Russia. To get your medal you had to send them four dollars for postage, so I did.

I keep up with my Group. We have a reunion every year.

Following the War, I worked briefly with a paper company but most of my years were at Lockheed, in Engineering Flight Test. I stayed there 25 years.

—Interviewed by Charles Miller, August, 2001

The Bramlett's wedding.

ROBERT BRAWNER

Although I was born in Spartanburg, South Carolina, I grew up in Rome, Georgia. I graduated from high school there in 1939. I wanted to join the Marine Corps but I was underage and my parents wouldn't sign for me, so I got a job at McClellan's Five and Ten Cent Store as a stock boy.

McClellan's soon transferred me to Laurel, Mississippi, where I was sort of a combination stockman and assistant manager. From there, I went to Columbus, Mississippi and that's where I met my late wife, Ruby. That's also where I was drafted in 1942. The people at McLellan's promised that I could have my job back after I came out of service.

I processed into the Army Air Corps at Camp Shelby, Hattiesburg, Mississippi. We were issued blue denim fatigues. I was then sent to Miami Beach to live in a hotel. Soon after we arrived, they had us fall out to do some work and we from Camp Shelby came out in our blue denims. The other guys came out with their nice twill coveralls. They asked where we had gotten those fatigues and we said Camp Shelby. The man in charge said, "Well, you can't wear them here. That's the uniform we put on prisoners of war. Go back to your rooms and stay there and don't come out unless you're in Class A uniform." Eventually they did issue new fatigues to us, but the day they were issued, I shipped out. I never did get a chance to work there.

From Miami Beach, I went to Chicago and lived in the

Congress Hotel. They had made me platoon leader so I had to take my platoon out to the park across the street and do a little drill every once in a while. The food at the Congress Hotel was wonderful. We didn't have to do any KP duty because the hotel chefs stayed on and worked for the government. I was in Chicago eight or nine months, taking courses in radio operation and radio mechanics.

I was then sent to Truax Field in Madison, Wisconsin. I arrived to three feet of snow all around. We lived in barracks which housed about 50 people each. At each end of the barracks we had a pot belly stove. Someone would have the chore of keeping those things full of coal all the time. At this point, I still had not gone through any basic training. We were learning to build radios. I got mine built first and was able to get WSB or some other station. They offered me an instructor post but I got to thinking about that cold weather and said, "No, I think I'll take my chances on whatever comes up next." They were just beginning to develop radar, and I was selected to go to electronics school in Boca Raton, Florida.

It was cold when we left Truax Field. I had on my uniform and overcoat and carried a barracks bag. When I arrived in Boca Raton, it was a long walk from the train to my barracks. It was so hot I didn't think I would make it. I finally threw my barracks bag in a ditch and went on. Later I went back and got my bag.

After I finished airborne electronics school, I stayed on as an instructor. We sent several hundred people through that school. I feel that I was doing as much for the war effort as anyone by training others on how to maintain their equipment.

I finally got my basic training there in Boca Raton. We learned to shoot rifles, Tommy Guns, and all that. We waded belly deep in water in the everglades and camped out overnight. We took swimming training at the officers' club pool and played volleyball for calisthenics. Whichever team won the volleyball game during the week didn't have to stand inspection on Saturday.

When I got my first furlough, I went first to Rome to visit my parents, and then to Columbus, Mississippi, where I proposed to Ruby. She said, "OK," so I went back to Florida and bought a set of rings, which I mailed to her.

Before very long, I got a wire from Ruby saying, "Meet my train in Del Ray Beach. I'm coming down to get married." We were married on January 16, 1944, at the West Palm Beach courthouse.

We rented an apartment for 35 dollars a month. We washed our clothes out in the back yard in an old wash pot, and wrung them out by hand, and hung them on the line. We had a kerosene stove with an oven on top of it. The stove was prone to catch on fire so we kept a bucket of sand to throw on the fires when they started. I think the Army gave us a housing allowance of eight dollars a month. My pay amounted to 66 dollars a month. Ruby got a job as a grocery store check-out clerk and made more money than I did. After I had been instructing for a while, I made Sergeant and got a raise.

When VE-Day and VJ-Day occurred, we went into town and celebrated along with everyone else. We were then sent to Pratt, Kansas, and later to Greensboro, North Carolina. Greensboro was a shipping point to send you overseas. When we got there, a man asked us how many points we had. We told him 36. He said, "Well you're not going anywhere. You're going to stay right here." We stayed there a little while and then I was sent to Maxwell Field, Montgomery, Alabama, to be discharged. That was in the spring of 1946.

We went back to Columbus, Mississippi, and I went back to work for McClellan's. I stayed with them, but moved from one location to another, until Lockheed opened in Marietta. I got a job in Electronics Quality Control at $1.75 per hour. I eventually joined the field service and we have lived in a variety of places: California; Tripoli, Libya; Oklahoma; Charleston, South Carolina (three different times). They wanted me to go to Chad but said I couldn't take my family so I refused to go. As a result, I had to go back to being an electronics inspector on the flight line. I retired from Lockheed in 1983, after 32 years.

I think my War experience was a good one. I don't know that I would want to go through it all again, but I think it was good for me. I never shot anybody, nobody ever shot me.

—Interviewed by Charles Miller, February, 2002

George Brown

GEORGE W. BROWN
With
Reid Brown

My late brother, George (G.W.) was the eldest of seven children. He was actually born in Athens, Georgia, but because of our father's work in the insurance business he also lived in several other cities. G.W. graduated from Elberton High School in 1938. At that time high schools usually had only eleven grades. Elberton High School offered an additional year of training in commercial skills—typing, shorthand, etc. So G.W. took the additional year and finished in 1939. Then he started working in the insurance business.

G.W. met his wife, Frances Campbell in Rome, Georgia. They married in 1940 and their son, George, Jr., was born in 1941. G.W. knew that even though he had a wife and child he would be drafted so he decided to enlist in the Army Air Corps. It was February of 1943, and G.W. was twenty-three years old. A few months later our brother, Horace, also enlisted in the Army Air Corps.

G.W. took his early training at various colleges. I recall our family visiting him while he was at Maryville College in Tennessee. Later, he received training at Nashville, Tennessee, and Omaha, Nebraska. He graduated from pilot training as a 2nd Lieutenant, at Stuttgart Army Air Field,

Arkansas, and then received additional training in Tucson, Arizona. G.W.'s wife, Frances, opted to go with him to his various duty stations and George, Jr. lived with all of us who were still at home with our parents.

In late August, 1944, G.W. was sent to Italy as copilot on a B-24. He only made two missions. On his second mission, September 10, 1944, they had dropped their bombs over Vienna, Austria, and were heading back to their base in Italy when they were shot down. Only three or four crew members survived. G.W. said that he didn't really know how he got out of the plane—whether he was blown out or what. The impact knocked him unconscious. He remembered floating through the air, his parachute open, his copilot seat still strapped to him. When he got down, he immediately disposed of his pistol so that he wouldn't be branded a spy. He was in the process of trying to hide his parachute when he heard whistles and some of "Hitler's Youth" reported him and he was captured.

I recall our family's receiving a telegram on September 21 (he had been shot down on the tenth), informing us that he was missing in action over Austria. I was ten years old and out on my newspaper route when my daddy came and told me he needed me to come home. On October 25, word came from the government that the International Red Cross had reported G.W. as a prisoner of war. Then a letter came, which told us how we could write and send things to him.

All seven children in our family were taught to have faith and trust in God. The Brown family filled the second row pew of Crestview Baptist Church every Sunday. Immediately, when word came that G.W. had been shot down, we were surrounded with love and care from the people of our church. Our faith and trust in God never wavered. We prayed for G.W. faithfully. I recall hearing my mother pray, "Not our will but yours be done." My mother prayed for each of her children. On many occasions, I heard her praying for G.W. and for Horace, that they would be brought safely home. I attribute both of them being spared to the prayers of my parents. It was a day of jubilation when we received that telegram. Even though he was a prisoner of war, we knew that he was alive, and we would see him again this side of eternity.

When his plane was shot down, G.W. was wounded, with shrapnel in his legs, but he was able to walk. After interrogation they took him to a series of different camps, including one called Stalag, Camp 3. While he was there he met a fellow Mariettan, Harry Livingston, who was also in the insurance business.

During the time G.W. was in the prison camp, he never received any correspondence from home, even though his wife, Frances, and my parents wrote to him daily. Frances did receive several postcards and letters from him. Food was scarce, not only in the prison camp but all over Germany. G.W. said that if it were not for Red Cross parcels, he probably would not have survived. On Christmas Day, 1944, GW wrote in a letter, "We had the Red Cross parcels with cake, turkey, nuts, and candy in them. We had saved up some stuff, so we ate very well. We had a Christmas Fair, last night, that lasted until 1:30 AM. We all sang carols. The Poles sang some of their Christmas songs—altogether different from ours. The trumpeter played 'Silent Night' at taps. Today there was an ice hockey game and ice skating with music. There are many people from all the allied nations here: British, Poles, French, Russians, Danes, Norwegians, Americans. This is an officers' camp altogether." So that was his Christmas in Germany.

While G.W. was in the prison camp, I believe he was looking up. His letters tell of praying and thanking God that he was alive. He writes, "We have a British Chaplain, Church of England minister. I went to church this morning and several times he mentioned praying and thanking God." He tells his wife that he is praying for her daily, as he knows she is for him. Even though he had shrapnel in his legs, most of his letters are upbeat, and talk about his plans for when he gets out of prison.

As the War drew to a close, G.W. mentions that he could hear the bombing. Finally, in April, 1945, Patton's Third Army, and the Russians, closed in on Germany and Patton's Army liberated the prison camp. G.W. writes of the joy of seeing the Allied solders advancing and the Germans retreating. In a letter dated May 6, 1945, he writes, "Here it is Sunday again, one week and a day since we were liberated and there's still no news as to when we leave . . . I have been listening to the radio all morning telling of the surrender of the German Army . . . I guess you all are at church this morning. Sure do wish I were there with you . . . God has certainly been with me or I wouldn't be alive today, for I didn't have a chance of getting out of the plane when it was hit and caught fire."

Finally, in June, 1945, G.W. came home. All eleven of us went to Union Station in Atlanta to meet him. We were all there when he stepped off the train. There were tears, and hugs, and kisses, on that day of rejoicing in our household. G.W. held the rank of 1st Lieutenant when he got out of the service. He was awarded the Purple Heart. He had other decorations, too, but I'm not sure what they were.

G.W. went back into the insurance business after the War. He and his family lived in several different towns. In 1960, he was transferred back to Marietta, where he lived until his death on December 11, 1971. At the time of his death, G.W. was serving as Chairman of the Deacons at Marietta First Baptist Church.

George W. Brown was a very patriotic person. Our family has a background of military service. Both of our grandfathers were Civil War veterans. Our dad served in World War I, having fought in France and Germany. G.W. was dedicated to his Country and to the principles of democracy. God and Country: I think those were what he stood for in his life.

—Interviewed by Marcus McLeroy, November, 2001

HORACE ELWOOD BROWN
And
Dorothy Brown

Horace Brown

I was born in Clarke County, Georgia, the second of seven children. My father was in the insurance business so we moved around a bit. I graduated from high school in Elberton, Georgia, in 1939 and went to work in the insurance company my father was with. I was working in La Grange, Georgia, in 1942, when they changed the draft age to twenty. Since I was twenty, and I wanted to go into the Air Force, I didn't wait to be drafted. I enlisted and entered the Army Air Corps, September 29, 1942.

I took my basic training at Miami Beach. Then I went to Nashville Classification Center and was sent to an aircraft mechanics school in Amarillo, Texas. From there, I went to a Long Beach factory school on four-engine B-17 bombers, then on to Salt Lake City, Utah. Mechanics wasn't really my cup of tea so I requested reassignment as an aviation cadet and was classified as a navigation student. After navigator training at Selman Field, Louisiana, I was commissioned 2nd Lieutenant. Then came gunnery school because on every bomber the navigator had a flexible 50-caliber machine gun on his station. When that training was completed, we went to

Camp Park in Tampa, Florida, to be assigned to a flight crew. Normal crew for B-17s and B-24s was ten. When our crew was assembled we began flying training missions out over the Gulf of Mexico, down toward Cuba, and over the Atlantic. We then went to Hunter Field in Savannah, Georgia, to be assigned the plane we would fly overseas.

We flew from Savannah to Bangor, Maine, and from there to Reykjavik, Iceland, where we were grounded for a few days by bad weather. When the weather cleared, we flew to England, overnighted there, and flew on to join the Fifteenth Air Force Base in Foggia, Italy. During that trip, I had my first navigation experience with a combat crew. We used celestial navigation. We could have had radio assistance but they wanted us to keep up to date on our celestial navigation. Once we arrived in Italy, our combat missions were delayed by bad weather.

My first combat mission was to some military manufacturing installation in Ruhrland, Germany. We encountered a lot of flack, which did some damage to the plane, but we were able to make it back to our base.

Two days later, March 24, 1945, we were to bomb a target in Berlin. In our briefing we learned that the Germans were using jet fighters in that area. It was to be the longest mission the Fifteenth had ever flown and it was too long a haul for the Fighters, whose range wasn't as great as ours, to go along with us. We were supposed to rendezvous with Fighters flying in from bases in France to support us. For some reason the Fighters didn't show up and we did encounter heavy, heavy canon fire from German jet fighters—ME262.

As a navigator, I was supposed to record the planes (with the plane number) that we saw go down. I saw several. Then the tail gunner called that a German jet fighter was coming at his position, and almost immediately I felt the plane jar as it was hit. Apparently it severed some of the control cables and the pilot wasn't able to bring our plane out of the spin we went into. He gave the order to "abandon ship." We didn't have any other choice. We were going down and unless we got out of the plane, we were going to the ground with it. In emergencies like this, the navigator, the bombardier, the pilot and copilot were to leave the plane from the front escape hatch, which was nearest their position. So the four us were there struggling and kicking at that door, trying to get it open but it wouldn't open because of the force of and type of the spin. We still had our ten or twelve 500 pound bombs when we were hit. I don't know if they blew up or not.

The next thing I remember, I was floating down, chute open. I don't recall opening the chute. The Lord was there and saw that that happened. I was in a state of shock for a while and events are not clear in my mind. As I was floating down, I saw pieces of the plane floating down around me like leaves. So I guess the plane blew up and I was blown out. I hit the ground fairly hard. I was injured—some from the explosion and some from hitting the ground. Of the four of us trying to get out that front escape hatch, I was the only one who survived. I learned later that four of our ten-man crew got out and lived to tell about it. They were taken to a regular POW camp until the War was over. I learned from the Veterans Administration that two of the four are now deceased. John Kitchens, who lives in Columbus, Mississippi, and I are the only two still living.

The Germans had the Home Guard—people too old or disabled to fight actual combat. They would spot where the parachutes landed, pick up the flyers, and take them in for interrogation. One of them came running to capture me and I was marched into town to some military facility. The German questioning me spoke perfect English. He said he had grown up in Brooklyn and had gone back to the homeland just before the War. He wanted to know all about our mission. I told him I was only allowed to give him my name, rank, and serial number. When it became apparent that I had no information to give, and that I was injured, they sent me to a hospital in the town of Torgau, south of Berlin, on the Elbe River.

I was kept in the hospital, locked up with some German Army prisoners. They examined me. I had internal chest injuries, a damaged lung, broken ribs, broken shoulder and clavicle. They put a wad or bag of cotton under my arm to extend the bone out and then strapped my arm to my chest. I'm sure the medical supplies were limited at this point.

While I was at Torgau, a person in an American uniform came to see me. He told me his name was Dean Van Dusen, and that he was First Sergeant with an infantry unit that was captured on D-Day. He was a POW, and what the Germans called "An American Man of Confidence." He was allowed to visit prison camps locally and be of any assistance he could to American POWs. I was a little suspicious at first when he told me his reason for being there. You hear stories where the enemy would pretend to be somebody else in order to get information. It turned out he was there for the right reasons. When he first saw me in the hospital I had a sock over one of my eyes. He just insisted to the German in charge that they do something about that.

It was apparent to all that the War was winding down. The Russians were advancing from one side and the Americans from the other. When the Germans determined that I was able to make the trip, they sent me, with one German guard, to the German air force base at Altenberg. I don't know how far it was. We walked, and we caught rides on trucks that would stop for German soldiers who were escorting prisoners. We marched through one town that had been heavily hit by American bombers and the citizens weren't real cordial. In fact they were kind of rude.

I arrived at the air base at Altenberg and was detained there for a week or two. At one point, an American pilot strafed the airfield at the runway, trying to knock out some fighters there. I was the only American there. I received no medical treatment. The Germans were more concerned about which way they could run for safety. I recall that the officers were flitting here and there and putting on civilian clothes. Apparently they were trying to escape both incoming armies that way.

I was rescued by General George Patton's Third Army. They came in jeeps and tanks and there I was. I feel kind of insignificant when I think of some people who served five years overseas. Some of them were prisoners for three or four years. All of mine was over quickly.

You might be interested to know that my older brother, George, was also in the Air Force. He went through aviation cadet school and trained as a pilot. He served overseas as copilot on a B-24 Liberator. He was with the Fifteenth Air Force also. George was shot down over Vienna, Austria. He, too, was blown out of the plane with his seat still attached with the belt. He was one of four that survived from his plane. He was helped and released and got back home. It was quite an amazing coincidence. Our mother was a praying lady. She prayed for all her children. She had a real prayer load with us.

After the War, I went back to the insurance business. In 1976, I had heart surgery and went on long-term disability.

I'm thankful that I was able to serve. I hope that I did some of the things that contributed to the War effort. I don't have any regrets. Somebody had to do it.

Dorothy Brown

Horace and I met at a YWCA party out at Ft. McPherson in 1942. When he would come home we would date, but nothing serious. I was working as a bookkeeper for McKinney (behind the Firestone Store). I remember Horace's mother coming in and telling me that he was a POW. The first time I saw him after he got out of the Service, he was in a neck brace.

I first came to Marietta in 1944. My sister persuaded me to quit my job in Atlanta and work with her. I remember the shortages and rationing during the War—shoes and gas . . . . Horace and I were married at Marietta First Baptist

Church, where I was a member, in 1946. We have one daughter who now lives in Durham, North Carolina. She works as a rehab counselor for the State. In 1974, I worked as a volunteer at Kennestone Hospital. They wanted me to become an employee so I did part time and then full time. I was there 18 years until I retired in 1998.

Horace has been quiet about his War experiences. I learned a lot of it from his friends, Van Duesen, and John Kitchens. The members of the POW organization talking about their experiences has brought him out.

—Interviewed by George Beggs, April, 2001

Horace Brown

J.W. BURNS

I was nineteen years old when I joined the Georgia National Guard in November of 1939. Three brothers from my family were directly involved in the War—two in the Army and one in the Marines. I was a member of the 214th Coast Artillery and Anti-Aircraft Battery H of Calhoun, Georgia.

At that time, war was not a reality to me. Many of my friends and relatives (including a cousin, an uncle, and a brother-in-law) were members of this same company. We all joined together. It was the patriotic thing to do. My Company also included nine separate sets of brothers. We were all close—it was as if we had all joined the same club and were going on a long camping trip. Although we were training for a possible attack by the Japanese, our perception of war was still far removed.

Almost a year after I joined the National Guard, our company was mobilized and sent to Camp Stewart in Hinesville, Georgia, to help develop the camp there. We literally hewed that camp out of farmland. We slept in steel roll-away beds, in five-man tents which were heated by wood-burning stoves. We were paid $30 a month, and we were still on our camping trip, unaware of the seriousness of the situation. Today, Camp Stewart is Fort Stewart, home to the Desert Storm 24th Armored Tank Division.

Our training at Camp Stewart consisted of learning to read maps and compasses, shooting guns, and marching.

We did calisthenics to increase our physical endurance. Our one year of training was extended to eighteen months and it became apparent that the Japanese were on a war path. On December 7, 1941, the Japanese attacked Pearl Harbor.

I will never forget that day. It was a cold wintery Sunday and I was visiting my family in Calhoun for the weekend. We had to be back at Camp Stewart by 5PM. Five of us rode the 350 miles back to Savannah in silence, listening in disbelief to the car radio. Our "camping trip" was over.

Battery H was split up. Half of the men went to Ascension Island in the southeast Atlantic to protect the shipping lanes in Europe and North Africa. The rest of us stayed at Camp Stewart to train incoming recruits. A few weeks before we were to travel to California, three of my friends were killed in a car accident. Two of them were cooks in our Company. Since I had helped out with kitchen duties and could cook, I was assigned to the kitchen. By the time the War was over, I would be a Master Sergeant in charge of the Officers' Mess of the 5th Command.

When the new recruits were trained and the Company was at full strength, we were put on a train to the west coast to help protect against the threat of Japanese bombings. About a mile out of Valdosta, Georgia, after stopping to take on coal and water, our second locomotive's fire box blew up. The large steam boiler blew into the woods and the wheels of the train jammed into the track bed. The fireman and two engineers were killed. The explosion blew off everything they were wearing except their shoes. These were the first dead men I had ever seen. All of us on the train thought it was sabotage. The incident was never in the news and our families never knew about it.

On arriving in Sacramento, California, we were assigned as anti aircraft defense at Mare Island Naval Base. We were there from May to September, 1942, and then we shipped out to Auckland, New Zealand, aboard the *U.S.S.*

Mount Vernon, a luxury liner. This was quite an experience for a country boy who had never been in anything but a fishing boat. Nine thousand of us slept on cots and bathed in salt water, which left you sticky. We played cards, had cigarettes, and drank beer. There were no movies or radios, nothing that the Japanese might intercept.

We trained for about six weeks in New Zealand and then went to New Caledonia to join up with other forces. Late in December, 1942, the convoy left New Caledonia, with a naval escort to go to Guadalcanal.

The night before we landed at Guadalcanal, our naval escort left our convoy to decoy the Japanese navy. We didn't have any communication between the two ships so we thought they had abandoned us. Later that night we saw what we thought was an electrical storm about 60 miles away. The next day, we learned that it was our naval escort engaged in battle with the Japanese. Many naval escort ships were sunk.

We disembarked our ships at Guadalcanal on January 12, 1943. Pistol Pete, the Japanese artillery piece, fired at us as we unloaded into small landing craft to go ashore. We were out of the firing range but nevertheless I was very frightened. Once ashore, a noncommissioned officer ordered us to march away from the beach. We marched right into a marked mine field. After we had gone about 30 feet into the field, he realized where we were and we backed out. Luckily nobody was hurt.

Our mission at Guadalcanal (my home for the next 32 months) was anti aircraft defense for Henderson Field. We were ordered to dig small foxholes for ourselves and to pitch our tents. Later that evening the Japanese bombers came in. Unbeknownst to us, the 3rd Marine Anti Aircraft Batteries were surrounding us and they began firing their 90 millimeter artillery at the bombers. With all the commotion, we thought we were being bombed. The next day, we dug our foxholes wider and deeper.

While on Guadalcanal, I went through five naval bombardments, three earthquakes (while in my fox hole) and 187 air raids. One of the largest bombardments occurred when the Japanese tried to leave the Island. They sent out a large naval force to decoy the U.S. Navy away from the beach from which they planned to evacuate; however, our Navy intercepted the Japanese messages and learned of their plans. The U.S. destroyed those Japanese ships. There was nothing left but burned remains.

The Japanese continued to raid us by air for many months. We gradually pushed them to the north and things began to settle down. We got visits and entertainment from celebrities. We had open air theaters with current films, bands, and supervised dances with the Red Cross girls. Food and supplies improved. Many of us enjoyed fishing despite the sharks that circled in the water, often eating our catch before we could reel it in.

During that time, my brother had joined the Marines but I didn't know where he was stationed. One day he called me to say he was on the Island, just 40 miles away. Because I was the Mess Master Sergeant, I always had a good jeep. So I picked him up and brought him back to my area. I had one of the best equipped mess halls and my living area had good tents and good food. I let my brother stay in my tent and I fed him well. We would go fishing, at night, for red snapper. He was on the Island a month before he was shipped to Saipan.

I stayed at Guadalcanal until September, 1945. The atomic bomb was dropped on Hiroshima, and then Nagasaki, and the Japanese surrendered. I was sent to Fort McPherson, Georgia, to be discharged. On our way home we stopped in Kansas City, where I got a shampoo, shave, and a haircut—my first visit to a barber shop in years.

I was 25 years old when the War was over. I rode the bus home from Atlanta to Rome. My youngest brother, Cliff, came to pick me up at the bus station. When I had left home, Cliff was just eleven years old, and at fifteen, I didn't recognize him. Finally, he recognized me and drove me home in my car, which I had left for my family to use. After the War I had the opportunity to get "52-20"—$20 a week for 52 weeks. I enjoyed being back with my family and fishing with my brothers.

—Information taken from an account written by J.W. Burns' granddaugter, Kimberly Smith Campbell on March 4, 1993. J.W. Burns is the brother of Cliff Burns. Two other brothers, James Malcolm Burns and Buren Burns, along with a brother-in-law, Adair Ables, also served in the military during World War II.

LORAN BUTLER
with
Ann Butler

I was born October 20, 1922, in Haiti, Missouri. My parents, and some of my grandparents were born there, as well as my two sisters and two brothers. At times we lived in St. Louis and in Michigan but Haiti was home and that's where I graduated from high school. In 1943, my parents moved to Florida for my daddy's health. I was fortunate to get a job with the only bank in Coco, Florida.

Loran, my husband was born September 11, 1919, in Chumfey, Georgia, near Eastman. I don't think the town even exists anymore. His family moved to Florida and from about the age of seven onward, Loran lived in Merritt Island, Florida. He attended Coco High School.

Loran entered the U.S. Navy in July, 1940. I'm not sure where he took his basic training, possibly at Jacksonville. I think he also spent some time at Great Lakes Naval Base and at Norfolk.

I was working in the bank with Loran's sister-in-law when he came home on leave and came into the bank to visit. I look back on our meeting and our romance and I know it was meant to be. I was dating another boy and we went to a church ice cream social. Loran drove—he was the only one in the crowd who had a car. That night, in May of 1944, Loran left to go back to Baltimore, where he was stationed. I was very attracted to him but I thought I wouldn't see him again.

When Loran got to Baltimore, the new ship on which he was to sail was not finished. He was given a thirty-day leave. So he came home, and we just fell in love. We were married in August of 1944. We really didn't know each other. I knew his family background and he went to church with me, but was not a church member. Loran accepted Christ while he was aboard ship with his chaplain, and I heard from his chaplain. He was baptized later when he came home from the service.

I remember the day that I got word that Loran was coming home and we could have a church wedding. We had thought I would go to Baltimore and we would be married there. Mother had been making my wedding gown. I walked through where we had a full length mirror, and it seemed like I was shining—not just my face. I had never had that feeling before or since. I think it was sheer happiness. My gown was made of net (you couldn't get satin) and mother literally sewed me into it. Mother and one of the neighbors did the wedding. I even had a shower. We were married in Coco First Baptist Church. I was so thankful that we did have our church wedding. Loran was on delayed orders between Baltimore and Ft. Pierce. We had a very short honeymoon in Ft. Pierce, which is more than a lot of couples had during the War.

I didn't go to Baltimore with Loran because they were supposed to ship out for amphibious training. He served in the North Atlantic. The weather was horrible. They would be out all week and only have a couple of days in port. I can't even remember now where home port was. We did meet for three days in New York City that Christmas. We went to Radio City Music Hall and did a few other things.

Loran moved up through the Navy ranks and became Chief Warrant Carpenter. That was the highest noncommissioned rank and he had all the privileges of a commissioned officer. He had amphibious training, as well as training in welding, damage control, interior preservation, and quarter mastering. He also taught some of these subjects. His friends used to say that if there was a hole in the ship Loran had to nail something over it so the ship wouldn't sink. They did have little pegs that they used to pound into any underwater holes in the ship.

The first ship on which Loran served was the *U.S.S. Dallas*, a destroyer. They were in the Atlantic Ocean, as far north as Iceland. During that time we had German submarines coming right down the Atlantic coast. People who lived in Coco were in brown-outs for many years. All the street lights were painted black on one side, the ocean side, of each lamp.

Loran's second ship was the *U.S.S. Dauphin*, a T-97 transport ship, and he served on it in the South Pacific. While he was there, he ran across his brother, Vic, a Navy lieutenant. Vic was very sick and needed to come home and Loran helped arrange that. He literally brought his brother home.

We kept in touch by mail. I wrote to Loran every night and he wrote quite often but our letters came in bunches. I was able to visit with him several times while he was in port. Because of his rank, I was able to go on board the ship and eat dinner (on fine china and crystal) in the officers' ward room mess. I remember one night in San Francisco a storm came up while we were on the his ship and they had to get us back to shore quickly. In those days ladies didn't wear slacks, we wore dresses and high-heeled shoes. So, here I was coming down a rope ladder in my high heels.

I was able to join Loran in Philadelphia once. My brother was a Lieutenant in the Navy and he happened to have some duty there too. I was out on the town every night with these two good-looking Navy officers. But we never forgot there was a war on.

Loran earned a number of awards and decorations. He had the Good Conduct Medal. He also received the American Defense Service Medal with Fleet; American Campaign Medal; Asia Pacific Campaign Medal; World War II Victory

Medal; Navy Occupation Service Medal; and Presidential Unit Commendation. He was proudest of that one because they actually took their ship down a very narrow place between enemy lines. And he had the Philippine Liberation Medal too. Loran never talked much about the details.

When Loran's ship was in the Pacific, they were out for ten months. He used to say that he had more than his share of food because he never got seasick. He said that he could lie down under the big guns and sleep. He learned to sleep through anything. Sometimes they had gone three days and three nights without sleep, so they would just pass out on the deck right under those guns.

Meanwhile, back at home, I can't say that we really suffered. Things were rationed and it may have been a nuisance but we were able to borrow and trade. The bank where I worked had to create a whole new department to track the ration coupons. They were counted and treated just like checks. Since we lived in a Navy town, my mother fixed Sunday dinner for extra boys every week because my brother was in the Navy, too. On any given Sunday there would be two or three boys from the base. They would bring things like sugar and soap powder that they got at the Base and didn't use.

After I got word from Loran that his ship was coming in, I flew to California. I stayed there, living with several other navy wives, until his ship was decommissioned in 1946. He had to help bring the ship through the Panama Canal, back to the east coast. Bobbie Longworth, another navy wife (and my dearest friend) and I returned to Norfolk by train—a trip of several days.

I was home alone on VJ- Day so I didn't have anybody to celebrate with. Like everyone else, I'm sure I cried and thanked God.

After the war, we lived in Coco, Florida. Loran worked as a firefighter at the Banana River Naval Air Station. Then he became a successful builder. We raised four children: Beth Butler, Ruth Sinclair, Jo (our youngest daughter), and

David Butler. We were all active members of Coco First Baptist Church. Loran worked in the church nursery for 40 years, helping to raise about three generations of children.

Loran died on September 17, 1995. Many of the children he had cared for in the church nursery (and their children) sang "Jesus Loves Me" at his funeral service. Loran was that kind of person, very masculine and yet able to care for little children. I don't know how I was so fortunate . . . .

I now make my home with our daughter, Ruth Sinclair, in Marietta, Georgia.

—Interviewed by Ruth Miller, August, 2001

The Butler's wedding.

SHERMAN CLINTON "S.C." CAGLE

Realizing that he and his brother, Billy, would probably be in action during the War, S.C. Cagle wrote a code in the front of a world atlas. He made a copy for Billy and one for himself. When they would write home they would use this code to tell the family where they were. Some of the code words were: I saw my girl—Pearl Harbor; Oak Tree—Okinawa; Hello Folks—Action; Japan—Yellow Jacket.

When S.C. learned the news that his younger brother, Billy, had been assigned to the *U.S.S. Kimberly*, he wrote, "I know he will make it O.K. and come out on top. He has what it takes and that's what counts. I always pray for him and for the Lord to keep him and you all in good health and watch over all of us if it is his will. I read the Bible most every day. Some of the boys kid me and call me the flying chaplain."

S.C. Cagle was born, October 29, 1920, in Maryville, Tennessee. When he was four years old, his family moved to Talking Rock, Georgia, where he attended school. He graduated from Jasper High School in May, 1937, at age 16. S.C. then enrolled in Southeastern Engineering Schools, Inc., in Atlanta, Georgia, and was there two years. In 1940, he began working for LeTourneau in Toccoa, Georgia, and worked there until he enlisted in the Navy on November 3, 1941—34 days before the Japanese bombed Pearl Harbor.

S.C. entered the Navy in March, 1942, at Norfolk, Virginia. In December, 1942, he was appointed Aviation

Cadet and sent to Navy pre-flight school, St. Mary's College, California. He graduated with honors, from pre-flight school on March 8, 1943, and was sent to Los Alamitos, California, for flight training. He soloed on March 28, 1943.

After additional flight training at US Naval Air Station, Corpus Christi, Texas, on September 16, 1943, S.C. was commissioned an Ensign. He served as Assistant Maintenance and Engineering Officer with the VP-202 Patrol Squadron, Norfolk Naval Air Station and Key West Naval Air Station until he was assigned to the Pacific area.

On January 1, 1944, S.C. departed for the Central Pacific (Patrol Search), where he flew a PBM (patrol bomber). His squadron covered the Pacific area from Tarawa to the Philippines, and participated in the Mariana and Caroline Islands campaigns.

S.C. had not seen his brother, Billy, since S.C.'s enlistment in 1941. When he heard that the *U.S.S. Kimberly* had left the Aleutian Islands, Alaska, for Pearl Harbor, S.C. managed to surprise Billy with a visit aboard the *Kimberly*. They spent several hours together, during which time S.C. gave Billy a silver dollar dated 1923 (the year Billy was born), and Billy gave S.C. some Cat Eye shells from the Pacific. They did not see each other again until after the War. Billy still carries that silver dollar in his wallet.

After a three-month assignment (and promotion to Lieutenant J.G.) at Banana River, Florida, S.C. returned to the Pacific as Patrol Plane Commander of a Combat Crew, Patrol Bombing Squadron 25. He was there from April, 1945, to December, 1945. Following World War II, S.C. was an instructor at various Naval Air flight and ground schools. He was promoted to Lieutenant on January 1, 1949.

S.C. returned to Marietta in December, 1949, and on January 14, 1950, married Hilda Jo Colquitt. S.C. continued his career with the Navy and was promoted to Lt. Commander, July 1, 1954. He served as Command Duty Officer and CIC Officer aboard the aircraft carrier *U.S.S. Intrepid* beginning March 29, 1957. He was promoted to

Commander in October, 1958. S.C. Cagle was killed, January 27, 1959, at the age of 38, in the crash of a P5M Patrol Bomber near Norfolk, Virginia. He is buried in Kennesaw Memorial Cemetery, Marietta, Georgia.

During his Naval career, S.C. Cagle was awarded the Distinguished Fly Cross; Air Medal with three Gold Stars; World War II Victory Medal; American Defense Medal with clasp; American Campaign Medal; Asiatic Pacific Campaign Medal; European-African-Middle Eastern Campaign Medal; National Defense Service Medal; Philippine Liberation Medal; and the Philippine Unit Citation.

S.C. and Hilda Cagle had four children: Robert Clinton Cagle; James Colquitt Cagle; Patricia Lynn Cagle; and Mary Elizabeth Cagle.

S.C. Cagle was the brother of Elizabeth Cagle Gentry.

—Information furnished by Mary Lou Cagle, December, 2001

S. C. Cagle

WILLIAM HOWARD "BILL" CAGLE

I was just nineteen when I joined the Navy in April, 1943. Although I was born in Knoxville, Tennessee, I grew up and graduated from high school in Talking Rock, Georgia. At that time, everyone I knew, who was physically able, was entering the military service. Both Daddy and my uncle had been in the Navy; and my brother, Sherman ("S.C.") was in the Navy. So it just seemed right for me to go into the Navy too.

We had our basic training at Bainbridge Naval Station in Maryland. They kept us just long enough to get our shots (six or seven weeks), then they put us on a train to Portland, Maine. The day we arrived, they put us aboard the *U.S.S. Kimberly* and I didn't leave that ship until the War was over.

We entered combat in November, at Tarawa, Gilbert Islands. We were with the group that landed at Makin Island. There was just a little resistance. We shelled down on them and received a little flak but it wasn't too bad. One morning, as I was looking out, I saw an aircraft carrier hit by a Japanese torpedo. It blew up, killing about 1,000 soldiers.

From Makin Island, we went on down to Tarawa and shelled a little. It was quieting down there. That's where I saw dead Marines just floating like logs. When they had tried to land, they hit roots in the water and the Japs just mowed them down. That island was all shot to pieces. You wouldn't think that anybody could live there. Three or four thousand marines landed there and more than 1,000 were killed.

Normally, our ships would shell an island before the Marines or the Army made their landing. We also had radar and could pick up Japanese planes so that our fighter planes could shoot them down.

At one point, our ship hit a reef and messed up one of our propellers. We took all the ships that had been shot up back to Pearl Harbor. We could only travel as fast as the slowest ship and we had eighteen or twenty of them. It took us six weeks to go from down on the equator back to Pearl Harbor. We just about ran out of food. We arrived on Christmas Eve day and the first thing I did was find something to eat.

We went from Pearl Harbor back to San Francisco to get our heaters working and then went to the Aleutian Islands. The Kurile Islands were under Japanese control. The weather was terrible. Cold and windy, and not much daylight in winter. We would shell those islands, I guess to keep some of the Japanese fleet and airplanes up there. We would go down the coast of Siberia and just before we got to the islands we would go out to sea a little bit. Then, going as fast as we could, we would shell the beaches before they could pick us up. One time they sent out torpedo boats and it was like something out of the wild west. It was dark, and we'd shoot this way and that way. I don't know whether we ever hit anything or not. They never hit us.

One cold and windy night I was standing watch. We were anchored but because of the wind, the ship was jumping up and down and could drag its anchor. Somebody had to stay up front, two hours at a time, to make sure the ship didn't start toward the beaches. I was out there freezing when the Captain came up and asked me if I was cold. I said, "Yes, Sir!" He said, "Go back inside. I'll make it all right." His name was Smith and he was a wonderful person who really knew the Navy.

After about nine months in the Aleutians, we went back to Pearl Harbor. That was in July or August, 1944, and that's when I met my brother, S.C. Cagle. I hadn't seen him for a year. He was an officer and could get information. He found out we were in port so he came over and we spent a couple of hours together. That same afternoon, our ship left for the Admiralty Islands near New Guinea. We picked up troops and went to the Philippines. That's where we learned about *kamikaze* pilots.

It was while we were at Okinawa that a *kamikaze* hit us. When we first began firing at him with our five inch guns, they turned him upside down and he almost ran into the ocean. Then he straightened up and he would change up and down. We kept shooting at him. He was on fire all the way from the cockpit on back. You could see the pilot. He was wearing a helmet and goggles and had a white scarf around his neck. He flew right in and hit us mid ship, killing a lot of people. He had a bomb and I guess some of our ammunition blew up too, so it was pretty explosive, a lot of fire. I was firing a 20 millimeter gun and I just kept moving it so I had a little bit of protection in front of me. That's probably what saved me because I didn't get hurt. My clothing was burned a little though.

When the *kamikaze* hit us, being a Destroyer, we had depth charges on the port and starboard sides and on the back. The ones on the back were thousand pounders. The explosion had cut some of them loose and the power was running. They were all tangled up. A man named "Barky" said to me, "We've got to do something with this." I said, "If you cut them loose they will blow up on you." He said, "No, I'll keep water on you." So I had to lay down to get under those depth charges and we cut them off one at a time. I don't know how many were damaged but they didn't explode because they hadn't had the charge put in them yet.

The Japanese were still in control of the Philippines at that time. After the initial landing at Leyte Gulf, the Americans made another landing at Mindora in order to establish an airfield for invading the main island. The Japanese still held a lot of our people prisoners up there. Our ships fired all along there until we got the troops landed. We just about wore out our guns. We lost several ships. One LST was hit and we took off all the men we could. It was two days of pure hell.

Then we went back to Leyte. That's where MacArthur landed. The troops landed then turned and went back down to Manila where the prisoners were. In two or three days they got to them and rescued the ones who were still alive. The Japanese were very inhumane in their treatment of prisoners. I used to pray that I'd be killed rather than taken prisoner.

On VE-Day, I was home in Marietta on a 22-day leave—almost the first leave I had had since I went into the Navy. Our ship had been pretty badly torn up so we brought it back to California to get put back together again.

We were in Yokohama when the Japanese surrendered. After that, I stayed in the Navy a little longer than I needed to because I was helping decommission our ship. We brought people back from Japan who were going to be discharged. We did escort the Missouri from Tokyo to New York.

I left the Navy on February 6, 1946, with the rank of Carpenter Mate Second Class. I helped keep the ship running and in good repair. I got my Battle Stars and other awards but I never did get the Good Conduct Medal. That's because soon after I got into the Navy, I was late getting back to base one night due to the train stopping on the track for about four hours. Everybody else was lying about why they were late. I could have told the Captain I had been in jail, or drunk, or something. Instead, I told the truth because that's what I was raised to do and the Captain got angry. That kept me from getting the Good Conduct Medal.

I stayed in the Reserve after I left active duty, mainly because I needed the money. I was trying to go to school and to work. I almost got sent to Korea. They sent me my discharge about three weeks before the Korean War started. I married Helen Withrow on January 4, 1958. We have one son, William David Cagle, and one daughter, Carole Ann Cagle. We have five grandsons.

I have spent my civilian career in the mechanical contracting industry, working as a pipe-fitter. I have worked on some of the famous John Portman projects in Atlanta: the Peachtree Plaza Hotel, the Regency Hotel, the Atlanta Gas Light Tower, as well as many other buildings around the country. I retired in 1988.

I am glad I was in the Navy during World War II. I wouldn't want to go back, but I was young then. We had some rough times and some good times. I think a lot of this Country. As you travel, there is a world of people who want to come here. That's a pretty good indication that this is not too bad a place to live.

Bill Cagle is the brother of Elizabeth Gentry.

—Interviewed by Harland Armitage, November, 2001

Bill Cagle

BRANTLY CALLAWAY

I usually say that I won the War single-handedly. I was inducted into the Army on September 9, 1943, and that same day Italy surrendered. Then I went to Germany, and after I was in combat just a month, Germany surrendered. The Army then cut my orders to go to Japan. While I was at Camp Lucky Strike awaiting transfer, the Japanese surrendered. That's why I say I won the War.

I graduated from Boys High School in Atlanta, Georgia, in February, 1943. I turned eighteen on June 25, 1943, and a month later I was drafted. I went to Greensboro, North Carolina, as a Pre-Aviation Cadet but I only weighed 113 pounds, which wasn't enough. So I hung around Greensboro, eating bananas and drinking lots of milk. Eventually I got my weight up and they transferred me to an Air Corps base at Charleston, South Carolina, where I became a mail clerk.

Another boy, Frank Capotian, and I were guilt ridden about not being more involved in the war effort. The only thing that was available to us was to volunteer for infantry OCS. Well, we didn't want to do that because Infantry OCS was tantamount to suicide. Six months later, we were able to volunteer for aviation mechanics school and were sent to Keesler Field, Biloxi, Mississippi.

At Keesler, I was operated on for a hernia. I spent 30 days in the hospital and another 30 days on limited service. Keesler had doctors and surgeons who liked to do hernia surgery. Every third man at Keesler Field had a hernia. In the course of my recovery, the Army decided I was needed in the Infantry so I was transferred to Camp Hauser, Denton, Texas. That was in December and it was cold and windy. The barracks were tied down with cables to keep them from blowing away. We heated the barracks with pot bellied stoves.

I didn't go to the Infantry willingly. I resisted going. I used some of the worst language I have ever used in talking to the Colonel. I was trying to get a court martial. The Colonel just sat there and smiled and I stayed in the Infantry. Then when I went from Atlanta to Fort Meade, Maryland, I was AWOL because I missed the train. I thought I was being innovative but a lot of other people were AWOL too.

From Fort Mead, we went up to Camp Miles Standish and got on a boat headed for Europe. At the time, there were still U-boats so we went in a convoy. After sixteen days on the water, we landed at LeHavre, France. Then it took us about five days to go by train across France. It seemed like they had to lay the track in front of our train as we traveled. At Worms, we got on a truck and went down to southern Germany to join my unit, D Company, 157th Armored Infantry Battalion, 10th Armored Division, Seventh Army.

It was night when I arrived. I was in Platoon Headquarters Squad. I went in and there were blankets over all the windows and a Schnapps bottle with a candle in it. You couldn't ask for anything more picturesque. I set down my pack, spoke to the Lieutenant, and sat down in a corner. They were all just sitting around a table. All of a sudden a fellow named "Makin Smart" came down the stairs, drunk, and starts hitting the 1st Lieutenant. They dragged him off and it didn't seem to bother the platoon leader very much. I guess he was used to it. The man was probably shell-shocked.

We were in combat every day but most of it was pretty easy because the Germans were in full retreat. The opposition was spasmodic. The last action we saw was at Oberamergau. The Germans had put up a road block and our men got out of their half-track to look around and were ambushed. We lost eight men. I lay in a ditch four hours waiting for our artillery to come in and clean out that little German nest.

Most of our casualties were due to carelessness or exuberance. At Schaungau, our Company Commander was riding in a tank through a town that he thought we had taken. The top of his turret was open and somebody at the side of the road shot right through him with a bazooka and killed him.

I never had to dig a foxhole out in combat. We slept, mostly, in houses. You would go into a house, pull out your bayonet, and tell the inhabitants of the house to "Get down to the cellar." We would also ask them for food. We would appropriate whatever we wanted. We just helped ourselves to money or jewelry. That's the way you fought in a war. Once a little old lady came up to me and said, "Somebody has taken all our money!" Well I knew I had taken money so I got out a handful of marks and gave them to her.

I never did have the heart to kill anybody. Often, when I spotted a German, I would take aim and then move my rifle a little bit. I wanted him to retreat. One beautiful shiny spring day we were going down the road when a little airplane came over the horizon. He started down at the end of our column and we all looked up. I said to myself, "That's a German plane! Why hasn't somebody shot him?" It turned out to be an artillery reconnaissance plane, flying about 50 feet above us. I raised my M-1 rifle and shot one round. When the Lieutenant heard my shot, he raised his fifty caliber and shot two rounds off. That little plane just went "whirrrr" and landed. The pilot got out of the plane.

By that time every gun was trained right on him. The plane burst into flames and he died.

I can still remember coming into a town and seeing the people carrying a little child's casket up to the top of a hill to bury a child. I can still see a tall, bald-headed, distinguished looking man in a black suit, with a single bullet hole in his suit, lying dead in the street. Sometimes I had to eat lunch right within sight of dead bodies.

I also know the feeling of rage that can come over you, causing you to react thoughtlessly. I didn't do very much of that but I did hit a prisoner with a rifle. The Germans had ambushed us and we lost some people. A little time later the Germans had surrendered and this gentleman officer, with one of those high German hats, was so arrogant that somebody started hitting him and I joined in.

The War ended when we pulled into Garmisch Partenkirchen, site of the 1936 Olympics. It is beautiful country. I ended up living there, at Walgau, for two or three months. We were then transferred to Mainz, and then to Camp Pall Mall, near Paris. While we were there, Japan surrendered. We came back to the States in September, 1945. I was sent to Camp Swift, Texas, and finally mustered out, as a Private First Class, in January or February of 1946. I was awarded the Good Conduct Ribbon, and the Battle Stars of the theater of operations. The Combat Infantryman's Badge was the most valuable one because it gave you an extra ten dollars a month. I never did anything exemplary.

Serving in the military was something that I resisted with all my heart, but once I had that sort of experience I wouldn't take anything for it. It was a very significant part of my life.

In the Fall of 1946, I started at Georgia Tech on the GI Bill. I graduated in 1950 with a degree in Chemistry. I worked for a small company in Decatur then came out to work for North Chemical in Marietta. I worked there for 42 years.

I met my wife, Farrice, in September, 1951, at Druid Hills Church. We began to date and were married eight months later.

—Interviewed by Charles Miller, September, 2001

Brantly Callaway

WALTER CAMP
And
Virginia Camp

Walter Camp

I graduated from Marietta High School and was drafted into the Army. My basic training was at Camp Fanning, Texas. I was there six months and the war ended. I was discharged and came back to Marietta.

I have worked at the Bell Bomber plant (now Lockheed). Then I worked at the Marietta Hospital (it was on Cherokee Street then) as their accountant and was there until Kennestone Hospital opened in 1951. After that, I worked for a while at Brumby Press. Eventually, I decided to open my own accounting and tax business.

Virginia and I both still work in my business but we have cut back to just tax work. I would say we do about 25 per cent of what we used to do. I also opened Walter Camp Realty and founded WEC Enterprises, Inc., a home building business. We have built several hundred homes in Cobb, Cherokee, and Paulding Counties.

Virginia Camp

I remember the Sunday afternoon when Pearl Harbor

was attacked. I was playing a card game with my sister and my cousin. I was fourteen years old. It was a terrible time for Americans for several years.

I had two sisters. One of them was married just two years when her husband was killed in France. The husband of my other sister spent three solid years in the Air Force, stationed in England without ever getting to come home.

We dealt with rationing and other inconveniences. I think people were very patriotic. They dug in and did what they had to do. Women went to work and did men's work, like at the Bomber plant. I finished high school at age sixteen and went to work for Southern Bell Telephone company in Atlanta. I worked there for a total of ten years.

Walter and I married in 1947. He had been a member of Marietta First Baptist Church since 1936 so of course I joined there. Eventually, I got my real estate license and joined Walter in his accounting and tax business. We have worked many long, hard hours and days but we have cut back quite a bit now. We have three sons, Barry, Jimmy, and Stanley.

—Interviewed by George Beggs, January. 2002

Walter Camp

GRIFFIN CHALFANT

My family was living in St. Louis, Missouri, and I was working as a bookkeeper at the Pulitzer Publishing Company when World War II broke out. I had graduated from high school about five years before that and was serving in the Home Guard. We did M-1 practice, Manual of Arms, the whole bit. I had to get a release from the Home Guard in order to enlist in the Army.

I enlisted one day in February, 1942, and the next day I was sent to Jefferson Barracks. From there, I went to Shepherd Air Force Base in Texas. I was assigned to the Air Corps right away, which made me very happy. I think I was there about two months and then went to Lowry Field, Denver, Colorado, to learn to be a Gunner. They needed radio operators and since I had some experience with that through the Boy Scouts, I started studying radio operation and wound up being a radio operator and tail gunner.

I went on to McDill Air Force Base, where we finally got in some flights in the B-26. They used to call that plane the "flying prostitute"—no visible means of support. Short wing and powerful engine. We then went on to Lakeland, Florida, for combat staging. We began to fly as a crew but there was trouble with the aircraft. We had an expression, "One a day in Tampa Bay." We lost two of our own crews because of a carburetor problem. Some of the representatives from Martin, the manufacturer, came down and got it squared away.

We went on, by train, to Baer Air Force Base, Fort Wayne, Indiana. In a month or two, we were all organized with a crew and new planes. We were to fly our own planes overseas so we flew first to Morrison Air Force Base in Florida. Then we went to Puerto Rico, British Guyana, and after a few more stops we landed on Ascension Island. From there, we flew on up to North Africa—Accra and Marakesh.

We were right behind the invasion and stopped at the Kasserine Pass. We were doing practice flying because they said we weren't ready for combat. In early 1943, we got into the rainy season and that was a miserable time.

Finally, as the Eleventh Army moved toward Tunis, we came up to Phillipsville, where we did bombing runs on Sardinia shipping. We lost one plane there. That's when we learned how the Messerschmits fought. They had all their armor on the bottom of the plane, and had reinforced the steel bottoms. They would fly in upside down, right at our head plane, and take that one out. I don't think they were ME-109's, but they had a yellow nose, one of Goerings special group.

In April of 1943, we were pushing Rommel's army toward Tunis for their evacuation. On our second mission, we were the lead ship, with a pilot named Brewer on our right wing, and someone else on our left. Something happened and I felt us reduce power. It sounded like somebody was throwing gravel at the plane. I looked out and saw those little black dots coming at us. We got hit in the right engine and in our electrical system. We left the formation and headed down over Tunis. Brewer stayed with us. We went down the coast on one engine and started getting flack from the side. A Folkewolfe Fighter (FW) came in from behind us and started shooting.

I had been sitting behind the pilot in the radio operator's position. I went back to my gunnery position in the tail to see what I could do with the 50's against the FW. But I didn't have a position. It had been shot away. Then the turret gunner and I disarmed a 250 pound bomb that was hung up in the bomb bay.

Brewer, our right wing man took a lot of blows. One caught the plexiglass nose cone, where the bombardier was sitting. I could see him bleeding from the bits of plexiglass. Still, Brewer rode on in with us. That pilot was a story in himself. He later became a Colonel.

Our pilot saw a field and he set the plane down. The bomb bay doors collapsed and started acting like a scoop. I was sitting in the radio position, locked in with my head down. It was scary. When the plane came to a stop everybody jumped out. The doors opened out over the copilot's head and the hatch opened. The waist gunner, who was sitting right behind the copilot, stepped on the copilot's back and was out of there. That was the only injury we had.

We had landed about a quarter mile from where they were fighting. They were bombing and artillery fire was coming in right over our heads. We removed the bomb site from the airplane and took it with us. We were picked up by an ambulance crew from New Zealand and spent the night in one of their hospital tents. Then, bit by bit, we worked our way back toward our base.

After that, we did a lot of bombing runs to Italy. We didn't have oxygen on the planes so we flew mostly at 10,000. Occasionally we had to go to 14,000 feet to get over the mountains. We would have blue fingernails and all that, but we weren't up there that long. We took out a lot of bridges and then, when we went back, we would see that they had rebuilt them.

On one mission we went to bomb an oil collection point near Naples. At the briefing, they mapped out our route and said, "As near as we can tell, you will get the least amount of flack this way." The least amount of flack? I've never seen anything like it! I saw planes falling apart, engines falling off and going down like helicopters. It was pitiful. As we pulled out over Naples Bay, a big ship started shooting at us. We really caught it there.

On Christmas Day, 1943, we bombed Rome. We did Pisa on New Year's Day

Soon after that, I developed acute yellow jaundice and had to come home on a "sick" ship. That ship listed three degrees to port. Since we didn't have any escort, we zigzagged a lot. I recuperated in the hospital at Jefferson Barracks in St. Louis. Interestingly, Father Joseph Walker (former rector at St. James Episcopal Church in Marietta) was on that ship. I was in the hospital for a month and then decided that I wanted to put in for pilot training. I wanted the front end of the plane. I was too lonesome and scared in the back. I was a Tech Sergeant at the time and had completed 46 missions. They sent me, first, to Miami Beach for R&R, and then on to Greenville, Mississippi.

I made it into pilot training and while I was at OCS in Greenville, I met a young lady on a Greyhound bus. She was engaged to somebody else but said she would get dates for my buddies and me. Well, she was able to get dates for everybody but me, so she decided to go with me. We went to the USO. That was August, 1944. The young lady's name was Kay and she was a telephone operator in Leland, Mississippi.

I shipped out to Telleri, California. Kay came out to Telleri in May of 1945, and we were married in the little Methodist Church there. We were to be married on Saturday afternoon and that morning, I had soloed. My whole squadron was there for the wedding.

We went from Telleri to Bakersfield, by bus, with all our wedding gifts in two footlockers. We rented rooms in Bakersfield and we were there on VE-Day, May 8 of 1945. I've never seen the whole world as happy as they were that day.

We had a choice to make then. We decided to stay in the military and make it a career. In February, 1946, I finally got my pilot's wings, having trained in a Steerman, then a T-6, twin-engine B-25's, and C-47's. At that time, I was commissioned as a 2nd Lieutenant.

We spent the next 17 years moving from place to place with the Air Force. We were at Williams, Arizona, for five years. Our first child, Chet, was born there. By the time the Korean War started we had two children—Steve was our second. We were sent to Bryan, Texas, to help open the base there.

In 1952, we were sent to Casablanca, a beautiful place. Our youngest son, Philip ("Flip") was born there. In 1956, we came back to Stewart Air Force Base in Newburgh, New York. Kay had to learn to drive in the snow. She says it was worse than driving in Casablanca, under armed guard, when the Arabs and the French were fighting.

Then, in about 1959, we came to Dobbins Air Force Base, here in Marietta. I was in charge of the radar station on Windy Hill Road. At Christmas, we put a Santa Claus, with his arms waving up and down, on top of that big radome. I stayed there until I retired in 1963. At that time, I held the rank of Major. I had been awarded the Air Medal with eight Oak Leaf Clusters. I also had some campaign ribbons. I'm proud to have served in the Air Force. It was a great life. What helped so much was having Kay so supportive. If I had it to do over I would do it again as long as she went with me.

Following my retirement from the Air Force, I worked for about five years at W.P. Stephens Lumber Company. I then went across Church Street and worked as director of maintenance at Marietta First Baptist Church for thirteen years. When I turned 65, I retired again.

—Interviewed by Charles Miller, April, 2001

Grif Chalfant

FORREST LEON CLARK, JR.
With
Sarah Clark Goff

I was just eleven years old when my brother, Leon, went away to the War. He had graduated from Marietta High School, gotten married, graduated from Draughn's School of Commerce, and become a father twice-over, when he enlisted in the Army. Although he hated to leave his family, he loved his country and felt like it was something everyone had to do. He was twenty-one years old when he entered the Service.

When Leon came home from basic training, he was tan and fit. He said the food in the Army was good. I don't know a lot about Leon's wartime experiences because I was so young. I remember feeling special when he would write letters to me. One time, he sent me a pack of needles from Germany. I still have them.

I know that Leon was in Germany when the War ended. He had attained the rank of Master Sergeant by that time. He told his son, David, that he was always good to the men who were under him because you could never really tell where their bullets were going to go. Apparently there had been cases where American bullets had killed American sergeants.

When the news came that the War was over, we at home

were all ecstatic. There were shouts of praise and shouts of "Thank you, Lord." It was a great feeling.

I remember the day Leon came home from the War. He was discharged at Fort McPherson and, I guess, took a taxi to Marietta. Leon's son, Mike, tells how our aunt, Annie Ledford, who lived next door, saw Leon get out of the taxi. She started shouting, "Leon's home. Lord have mercy, Leon's home. Thank you, Jesus!" Aunt Annie was crippled, only had one leg, but she somehow got herself off the porch and over to our yard where Leon was paying the taxi driver.

After the War, Leon worked as an accountant for Marietta Lumber Company. At one point, he was elected City Clerk of Marietta, but he didn't stay in that position long. He was asked to compromise his integrity so he quit and went back to Marietta Lumber Company. He was working there when he died, January 14, 1962, at age 42.

Leon and his wife, Evelyn, were childhood sweethearts and married when they were both eighteen. They had four children. Two, Mike and Tommy, were born before the War. After the War, they had David and Debra.

—Interviewed by Marcus McLeroy, April, 2002

Leon Clark

RUFUS CLOPTON

I enlisted in the Army on February 12, 1941, to serve in the Philippine Islands. I received my basic training on Corregidor and served there until December 2, five days before the War broke out on December 7th. I was then sent to Bataan with my company and served there until the Japanese broke through our last line of defense on April 9, 1942.

Our company commander ordered us to evacuate to Corregidor. Corregidor covered our retreat with big guns. It seemed as if the fire almost hit the tip of our ship. We reached Corregidor about daybreak and I could see the dust from the Japanese trucks on Bataan where I had just left.

Corregidor was worse than Bataan. After Bataan fell the Japanese were able to move their big guns up to within three miles of Corregidor. We were continually shelled and bombed until Corregidor fell, after approximately one month. The Japanese finally made a landing and, after heavy fighting, we were ordered to surrender.

We were marched to an area of about four acres, surrounded on three sides by steep hills, and on the fourth side was the bay. As soon as we were settled, we were given a speech, in English, by the Japanese high command. He told us what we must and must not do. He said that the lowest Japanese private outranked the highest American General and we would be treated accordingly.

We were allowed only the clothes we were wearing. There was no organized method to feed us. What food we were given was confiscated American food. Anything that had to be cooked had to be cooked in the cans or on open fire on the beach. The water was contaminated and just enough to live on. We stayed there for about two weeks, sleeping on the ground with no shelter.

They then took us from Corregidor to Manila by ship. There were no docks, so the ships had to anchor some distance from shore. They loaded us into landing barges, which could have landed, but they made us get off in waist-deep water and wade ashore.

They marched us through Manila to make a big show for the benefit of the Filipinos. They took us to Bilibid Prison, which had been a Filipino prison in peacetime. The Japanese used it as a distribution center. During the three weeks I was there, we were fed absolutely no food except rice, which was cooked in big iron pots set in cement fireplaces. Twice a day we each received about one-half to three-fourths of a canteen of rice.

The Japanese asked for volunteers for a detail of electrical and telephone linemen. I had worked as a telephone lineman before I came into the service. I knew I would have to work regardless of my physical condition so I volunteered. We thought we had volunteered as linemen but it turned out they used us as stevedores.

They took us to a camp called Bouti. I understand that conditions there were better than in many camps. We were in the city and had a shower. We had plenty of good clean water for bathing and drinking. We seldom had soap. Other camps didn't have enough drinking water.

We were never given enough to eat but I became quite proficient at stealing when the cargo we were unloading was food. Despite being raised in a good Christian home, I soon learned not to feel bad about stealing to stay alive. The Japanese searched us after each work detail. We learned an ingenious method to get food past the guards. The Japanese socks were like tubes, with no heel. We would fill these socks with loot, tie a string around the top of the sock, and tie it to another string which we had tied around the waist. The sock would hang down in back like a tail. Then, reaching between the legs, we would tie the other end of the sock to the front of the waist. The Japanese never caught on. If they happened to feel the loot, they just thought we were swollen from Berri Berri (a form of malnutrition).

We all worked unless our physical condition prevented us from walking. The Japanese knew we would work better for our own officers so an American officer was in charge of each detail. The Japanese soldiers were there strictly to guard us. They knew we could turn out about three times as much work as the same size Japanese detail so they didn't bother us too much on the job.

On night details, when we were not too well guarded, we took every opportunity to drop guns, ammunition, even airplane motors, into the water. Often a 100-man detail had one guard who would go to sleep, having instructed one of the Americans to watch for him. It would have been impossible to overpower the guard and escape because the Japanese had the city occupied. If we had escaped we couldn't have gotten very far and each man attempting to escape would jeopardize the lives of nine other men.

A friend who had transferred into our camp told me that at his previous camp, nineteen men were executed to pay for two who had tried to escape. My friend witnessed these executions.

The worst thing that ever happened to me was when a Japanese captain, with no provocation, stomped on my bare foot with a hobnail boot. We were waiting to unload a ship and were told to rest. I sat down on the pier and took off my shoes because my feet hurt so badly from Berri

Berri. The Japanese captain, not part of our guard, came by and hollered, "She-go-to" (go to work). The others jumped up and grabbed a winch line. I hurriedly tried to put on my shoes. One foot was still bare when he came up to me and hollered, "She-go-to." Without looking up I said, "Scoce Motti motti" and "bucke," (wait a little, sick), pointing to my bare foot. He replied, "Bucaru, boke nic," and stomped my bare foot. I had to be carried back to camp and lost about ten days of work.

During the time I was laid up I received about sixteen letters and one cablegram from home. That is all I received during my whole 40 months as a POW. I estimate that my share of the Red Cross supplies that got through without being stolen was about 47 pounds. Friends at home had contributed items and my brother had packed the boxes. In one box there was a deck of cards and in another a pair of dice. I knew those boxes had not been packed by my family because those two items were never allowed in our home.

My mother had died, at the age of 72, on April 10, 1942—the same day I escaped from Bataan to Corregidor. My family agreed not tell me about her death. Of course there were no letters from my mother and somehow I knew she was dead. But she never knew I had been captured. Shortly after my capture, they notified my father that I was missing in action. Eighteen months later they let him know that I had been captured.

From time to time the Japanese allowed us to send preprinted post cards to our families. You were supposed to block out any part of the message you didn't want to send. We were allowed to sign the cards but not to write anything else. The message didn't mean much because you knew if you didn't block it out to suit the Japanese that your family would never see it anyway. I thought my family would know I was still alive if they saw my signature. They did receive a few of those cards.

As the War got closer to Japan and American planes were over Manila, the Japanese realized that they would lose the Philippines. They decided to take the healthiest POW's to Japan to work. On July 17, 1944, I, along with 1500 other POW's, was loaded onto the *Nisha Maru*, one of seven ships (six freighters and one tanker) in the convoy. The ships bore no markings to show that POW's were aboard. Eventually the tanker was sunk. We thought our time had come. I don't know why the whole convoy wasn't sunk, unless our boys had some way of knowing POW's were on board.

Of the 1500 loaded onto the *Nisha Maru*, 900 were crowded, like cattle, into one cargo hold, and 600 others were herded into a smaller hold. The Japanese ordered us to leave everything we owned, including our shoes, in a pile on the ship. Except for the shoes, we never saw these things again. We were allowed the clothes we were wearing, a canteen, a canteen cup and a spoon. We were aboard for nineteen days. We laid out in the China Sea for seven days while the Japanese were making up their convoy. I don't know why they didn't let us stay ashore until they were ready to go, unless they just wanted to be mean.

On this trip we had nothing to eat but barley. I managed to get as much of this as I could eat because so many of my friends were too sick to eat at all. We were allowed one canteen of water per day and the temperature in the hold never got below 103 degrees, even at night. I would get a little extra water when one of my friends would die.

Everybody was sick. Most had diarrhea. The toilet was two five-gallon cans. When the cans got full two men were assigned to pull them up on deck and dump them over the side. Everyone wanted that detail because otherwise no one was allowed on deck.

When we arrived in Japan, all of our shoes were in a pile on the pier. A Japanese guard stood with fixed bayonet. We each had to grab two shoes with no time to check for size or match. Luckily, I got two shoes tied together and only one size too big. That night, while we stayed in a big building, we tried swapping shoes. I wasn't able to do any better than the shoes I already had. Later, I marched eight miles in those shoes. They made blisters but at least I didn't have to march barefoot. Lots of men did.

The next morning, we were loaded on a train bound for Kameoka, in northern Honchu. We spent two days on the train and were fed one time. Finally, ordered off the train, we were put on small flat cars, six men to a car, and pulled by a speeder for about 40 miles. We walked the last eight miles to Kameoka. There were already 400 POW's there in the camp. Another 200 of us came from the 1500 on the ship.

Kameoka was a lead mining camp. Now I was really destined for trouble. We had almost no opportunity to steal food. Our blood was thin from having just left the tropics and where we were now had snow from September to May. Our quarters were flimsy wooden structures with rooms about sixteen feet square, sixteen men to a room. Each room had two platforms on each side of the room, one about ten inches above the floor and another about three feet higher. Four men slept on each platform. In each room there was a little box lined with tin and filled with sand. That was for heat. We were given a half gallon of charcoal each day and if we saved it we could have a little fire on our day off, which was every seven or eight days. Another room, ten-feet square, had a 50 gallon drum made into a stove. We could keep a fire in there any time we could get scraps of wood for fuel, but not many men could fit in that room.

We worked three shifts around the clock, eight hours on and sixteen hours off. Of the 200 men who arrived at the camp with me, seventeen died and one committed suicide. Twice I swelled up in the groin area as big as your head and spent three months in the hospital each time.

The happiest day of my life was the day they told me the War was over. I could not have made it through another winter. I weighed 90 pounds when we were released from prison. I gained 47 pounds back during the first six weeks we were back in American hands.

They flew me from Yokohama to Manila—a twelve hour flight—quite a different trip from my 19 days in the hold of a Japanese ship. I came by ship from Manila to San Francisco, and by hospital train from San Francisco to Oliver General Hospital in Augusta, Georgia—ninety miles from my home in Eatonton, Georgia. I stayed in the hospital ten days and was allowed to go home. I spent the next three months between hospital and home. The doctors all said I could do as well at home because all I needed was good food to treat the Pellagra and malnutrition.

My church held a welcome home celebration in my honor. From October 11, 1945 to the end of December, 1946, I was stationed at Warner Robins, near my home. That's where I met my wife. We have two wonderful children, a son and a daughter.

I hold no malice. Some of the Japanese I came in contact with were following orders in time of war. Others took advantage of the situation to be mean. History has shown that war brings out the bad in some people. I do not hate anyone. I have no desire to be reassigned to Japan; however, I would not ask to be relieved if I were. Through all my experiences the comfort of God is mostly what kept me going. Then, too, I always felt sure the Americans would win.

—Rufus Clopton was the great uncle of Greg DeLoach. Our information was taken from the transcript of a taped speech he gave in 1956. A family member remembers that Rufus Clopton still liked to eat rice. "It's what kept me alive," he would say.

WILLIAM E. COLLINS
And
Marjorie Collins

William Collins

I was born on a small farm in Dunville, Kentucky, in March, 1927. I went to high school in Kentucky and then on to Berea College. I was then enrolled in the University of South Carolina.

My first recollection of the War is listening to news on the radio. Some of the good news reporters were saying that the situation was serious and something was going to break out. Sure enough, it did. By the time I was fifteen, I began thinking seriously about volunteering for military service. Two weeks after my seventeenth birthday, I entered the Navy and stayed five and a half years. I loved the Navy and still do.

When I enlisted, I thought I was going to Great Lakes to boot camp but then I had countermanding orders to go to the University of South Carolina, to go into the V-12 Naval ROTC program. So I went there and finished my degree in Naval Science. I was commissioned and went out to Coronado, California, for amphibious training. We trained in landing ships on a beach, off-loading troops and tanks and vehicles, and how to do it in harmony with others so as to avoid causing confusion. I also had signal corps and navigation training. Radar was new at that time and we had intensive radar training.

I then got orders to go find my ship, the *U.S.LSN 468*, in whatever port it might be. It turned out to be in Shanghai but I didn't know it at the time. I rode the train to San Francisco, and caught a plane to Honolulu, only to find out the ship wasn't there. It was heading for Guam. So I went to Guam and they told me, "No, it's in the Philippines." In Manila, they told me to go to Shanghai and when I got there they said, "Guess what. That ship ran aground over in Okinawa and they took it back to Honolulu." Because it was badly damaged, that ship was sent back to the U.S. and decommissioned.

Then they put me on another ship, the *432* and we went to the South Pacific, down to Pelilu, Manus, and other islands. I wound up in Australia and New Zealand. Although I was all around the action, I was never shot at, and I never shot at anybody. Because I liked to navigate, I was considered to be the Deck Officer. While we were on our way to Guam, the Japanese surrendered. So we were sent to La Coska.

There was a huge naval base at La Coska. Many of the Japanese ships were being brought there in order to turn them over to the Americans. We did a lot of debriefing. I got to take the train to Tokyo pretty often. We always stayed at the Imperial Hotel, MacArthur's headquarters.

My heart really cried out going in and out of Tokyo. They were going through picking up dead bodies that were lying around. I don't know how they died. Malnutrition, discord, suicide? The people would come into that area during the night and die. The next day, someone would come and move out the bodies. I could never get over the fact that there wasn't somebody to take care of a dying person.

From Japan, I went to Guam. Then I joined the new Admiral's operations intelligence staff(AFA Leadership).

They sent us to Subic Bay in the Philippines to protect our military assets there. The area was surrounded by some dissident Filipino troops. They were called "Huks," and they were trying to steal Army equipment, ships and everything else for the Chinese communists.

I was awarded seven or eight area ribbons. I think they were for the eastern area, the American Theater, the Pacific campaign, the South Pacific, Southeast Asia, Occupation of Japan, and something about military government in the Philippines.

I came out of the Navy in October, 1946. I could have gotten out in October of 1945, but stayed another year because I was considering making the Navy my career. I changed my mind about that but I did stay in the Navy Reserves. Altogether, I was credited with 22 years of military service. During my Reserve service, I was in strategic intelligence and Russian studies. I trained at various places including the Pentagon and the CIA. But I went back to operational intelligence.

When the Korean War came along, I was not asked to go—partly because I had already spent an extra year in the Navy, and partly because of the intelligence work I was doing in the Reserve. During the Cuban Missile Crisis, I had verbal orders to prepare to relieve the District Director of Intelligence if war broke out. By that time, I was married and had two baby boys so I wasn't all that eager to go back to being a Navy cadet. Fortunately, the Russians backed down and I didn't have to go.

Marjorie and I were married in 1953. We have four sons. Most of my civilian career has been in human resources, personnel and labor relations, and behavioral sciences. We came to Georgia in 1965 and I retired in 1985.

Marjorie Collins

I'm from a small farming town in West Virginia. I remember Pearl Harbor Day. I was helping my father in his restaurant when people came in to tell us about the bombing. My father worked with the Rationing Board, issuing the stamps. He wasn't eligible for the Service so he took a job at a train Round House service unit in Kaiser, West Virginia.

After the War, men came back and went to college using the GI Bill. It had a great impact on the colleges. A lot of government money went to the colleges for this purpose.

None of our four sons has had to be in the military. They haven't experienced anything like that.

(William and Marjorie Collins' son and daughter-in-law, Jim and Kay Collins, are members of Marietta First Baptist Church.)

—Interviewed by George Beggs, Marcy, 2001

William Collins

Jimmy Colquitt

JAMES A. COLQUITT
And
Betty Medford Colquitt
James Colquitt

Because of my age I qualified for my military commission long before I got it. I was born in Thomaston, Georgia, on December 3, 1918. I graduated from Robert E. Lee Institute, then took a post graduate course at Georgia Military Academy. From there, I attended the University of Georgia, majoring in Business Administration (Class of 1940). I was finally commissioned a 2nd Lieutenant in the Army on November 8, 1941, and was called to active duty on January 3, 1942.

I was the greenest 2nd Lieutenant in the entire Army. The first thing I did was to make friends with my 1st Sergeant, who had served many years. I told him that I was putting myself in his care. He really looked after me.

When I attended the Company Commanders' School at Fort Benning, Georgia, I was interviewed by some officers in the Airborne, who wanted me to come with them. I was so impressed with them that I joined the 88th Airborne Infantry. I was sent to Fort Bragg, North Carolina, and on July 3, I was promoted to 1st Lieutentant.

From Fort Bragg, I was transferred to Fort Mead, South

Dakota. It took us four days and five nights on a troop train. I thought I should have gotten immunization shots because we were surely outside the U.S. We arrived in February, 1943, one o'clock in the morning, 35 degrees below zero. The amazing thing was that the temperature climbed to twenty above zero, a swing of 55 degrees. I stayed in South Dakota about eight months and then transferred to Camp McCall, North Carolina.

Next, I went to Battalion Commanders School at Fort Benning. On July 1, 1944, before I had finished the School, I was ordered overseas. I was a Captain by then and became a member of the First Airborne Task Force.

We went, first, to North Africa. From there, we went to Sicily, Corsica, Sardinia, and Rome Delito (Rome Beach, a short distance out of Rome). It was Mussolini's old headquarters. They were planning the invasion of southern France and I was to jump as part of that. On a Sunday afternoon, Major General Robert T. Frederick called me into his office and said, "Jimmy, we're going to assign you to the Sixth Corps of the Seventh Army as Liaison Officer." I asked, "What happened to the Liaison Officer we had?" "He got killed," was the answer. To which I replied, "Oh, Hell!"

I was sent to Naples. They had me on a ship and were trying to teach me how to come down a rope ladder for the southern France invasion. I told them, "Just get me on the beach and I'll know what to do next." We landed in a Landing Craft Infantry (LCI) and I went across that beach in record time, I can assure you of that! I was really anxious to get back to my own outfit because I was resented in the Sixth Corps. All of them had sleeping bags and cots. I just rolled up in my parachute and slept out on the fields, or trenches, or wood yards, or gardens—wherever I could find to sleep.

Finally, I was ordered back to my outfit. I rode with a Sergeant, in an open air Jeep, through a little town called Demure, France. He couldn't find his way and there were snipers shooting at us from both sides of the main street down which we were driving. Then I was ordered to join the Eighteenth Airborne Corps under General Matthew Ridgeway. Soon they transferred me to the First Airborne Army under Lt. General Louie Burriton. His love was the officers' clubs so he put me in charge of those. I stayed there at Mazzona Beach, France. Our rear was in Ascot, England. I ended up going back and forth from Ascot to Mazzona Beach.

By the time VE-Day came, I was in Berlin. I was still there on VJ-Day. Sometimes I thought I never would get home. My commanding officer was General Lucius D. Clay from Marietta. I remember all the staff but I guess the one who impressed me the most was Secretary of State Byrnes. I also remember Secretary of War Stimson. Of all the generals I ever knew, the most outstanding was General George C. Marshall. He stood head and shoulders above the rest. He was supposed to lead the invasion in Europe but President Roosevelt wouldn't let him go because he was too valuable.

General Harry Vaughn was the number one military aide to President Truman. I was his assistant. When President Truman came back to the States, I was left behind in Berlin. They wanted me to go with them but orders were not issued at the time. Eventually, I came back, first to Camp Miles Standish, near Boston, and then to Fort McPherson. The next day, I was supposed to be a civilian. Instead of that, as I was standing in front of the Henry Grady Hotel in Atlanta, a Captain came up to me and asked, "Are you Major Colquitt?' I told him I was. He said, "We have orders to deliver you back to Fort McPherson." I said, "I don't want to go." To which he replied, "Do you see those two MP's sitting in the back of that jeep? You're going." When I got back to Fort McPherson I learned that there were orders for me to report to Washington to join Mr. Truman and his entourage.

Betty and I had been corresponding throughout the War. She had sent me a photo of herself where she had dressed up as Daisy Mae from the comic strip, "Li'l Abner", for a USO costume party. I had shown that photo to Mr. Truman during the time of the Pottsdam Conference. After that, every time he would see me, Mr. Truman would ask, "How is Daisy Mae?"

When I got to Washington I walked right into the White House. I knew all the secret service men on a first name basis. I walked into the room where Mr. Truman was holding a press conference. I am six foot three so I stood in the back. When the conference was finished, I saluted and Mr. Truman said, "Hello, Major. How is Daisy Mae?"

After serving President Truman a short time, I went in and said, 'Mr. President, I'm going to have to resign this position." When he asked, "Why?" I replied, "Daisy Mae has said yes, and we're going to get married." I admired Mr. Truman greatly. I thought he was one of the finest men I have ever known, but it was not a job for a married man. It required too many duties away from home.

Betty and I were married March 13, 1946, in the Chapel of Marietta First Baptist Church. I stayed at the Pentagon until the first of August and then came to Marietta. Mr. Truman promoted me to Lt. Colonel, which I have always appreciated. Betty always said she would never leave Marietta, so I worked for her father, Earl Medford, in his insurance agency. Eventually, I bought the Agency and in January, 1963, Wilson Owen came to work with me. He has since bought the Agency from me.

Because we loved Marietta and intended to make it our home, we both have become involved in many community organizations. I have served in many positions, from being director of several banks, to the Red Cross, to the Georgian Club, to Kiwanis. The things of which I am most proud, though, are being on the Board of the Georgia Military Academy (now Woodward Academy) and being a Trustee of the University of Georgia.

Betty Colquitt

Marietta was a wonderful place before the War. We could take the streetcar to Atlanta to shop and visit relatives. I remember once my aunt, who lived in College Park, let me dress up in her shoes and hat and jewelry and we took the streetcar from College Park to Atlanta to have lunch at the Frances Virginia Tea Room. My parents, Earl and Samye Medford, were both very active at Marietta First Baptist Church. Mother was a soprano soloist and Daddy was always willing to do whatever needed to be done.

I graduated from Marietta High School in 1939 at age sixteen. Shuler Antley was our principal. He would stand out there in the halls with his arms crossed and you could hear a pin drop. I am still very interested in Marietta High School and am involved with the Marietta High School Foundation. Following high school, I attended Sullins College in Crystal, Virginia.

During World War II lots of things were rationed, but the thing that hurt the worst was losing close friends with whom we had grown up. I would write to some soldiers and the letter would be returned with the message that the addressees had been killed. Marietta only had about 8,000 residents at that time.

Jimmy and I were married in Marietta First Baptist Church Chapel, in 1946, by Dr. George F. Brown. Jimmy says that Dr. Brown sure did tie a hard knot. In March, we will be married 56 years. We have two daughters, Ginger and Cathy, and two granddaughters.

—Interviewed by George Beggs, November, 2001

DENVER CORN
With
Ann Corn

Denver and I met after the end of World War II so I don't know a whole lot about his military service. I know that he was born on August 29, 1921, and that he was in the first class to graduate from Osborne High School, Cobb County, Georgia, in 1934.

Because he knew he would be drafted, Denver enlisted so that he could get into the Army Air Corps. He entered the service on May 30, 1942, and took his basic training at Keesler Field, Biloxi, Mississippi. He used to talk about how hot it was and how bad the mosquitoes were.

After Basic, Denver went to Eglin Air Force Base, Florida, and stayed there the rest of the time. He was on limited service because his eyes were so bad. That's why he didn't go overseas. He became an aircraft mechanic and held the rank of Sergeant.

Denver didn't tell many War stories. I know while they were out swimming he rescued a man who was drowning. He also told about having to go up in an airplane with a pilot and the plane didn't act right. The pilot told Denver to bail out and Denver said he would go down with the plane but he wasn't jumping out. They did land safely.

I met Denver in 1947 or 1948, when I was teaching at

Osborne High School. We married in 1949. Denver was involved in several business enterprises. He and his father were in the chicken and egg business. Eventually, he owned the distributorship for Quaker State Oil, for Georgia, Alabama, and Florida.

Denver and I had four children: two sons (Johnny and Robert), and two daughters (Lynn and Mary). Denver died on February 11, 1979.

—Interviewed by Marcus McLeroy, April, 2002

MERRILL CRISSEY

I have always been interested in airplanes. One of my first toys was a metal model of the Spirit of St. Louis (Lindbergh's plane). As I grew older, I built model airplanes and hung them from the ceiling of my bedroom. During high school I worked at Truman Fletcher's Photo Studio, earning enough money to take flying lessons. I would take the street car to Candler Field in Atlanta and fly a little yellow Piper J-3 Cub. Candler Field, which later became Atlanta International Airport, consisted of three or four metal hangars and one runway. There was no reliable weather information so you just looked at the sky and the wind sock, and phoned the traffic tower. They usually kept in contact with other towers around the country and could tell you the weather conditions in those areas. No one could predict the weather for more than an hour or two.

During World War II, the Army and the Navy sent teams of recruiters to high schools to talk with the senior boys. If you passed their test, you had the option of enlisting in the Navy or Army Air Corps Reserve.

I was called to active duty on March 27, 1945. We were issued uniforms at Fort McPherson in Atlanta and put on a train for Sheppard Field, Texas. What a train that was! Because of the severe transportation shortage every kind of vehicle was used. We were put into a car which must have come out of a museum—a beautiful little day car with red velvet curtains, oil lamps, and a potbelly stove in the middle of the floor. The tracks were single lane so trains would have to pull onto sidings to wait for oncoming trains to pass. With no food preparation facilities on the train, arrangements had been made with restaurants along the way to supply us with bag lunches—usually a sandwich, a piece of fruit, and a cookie. The train had to stop to pick up the lunches. Needless to say, it took us several days to get to Texas.

Except for the extreme Texas weather (cold enough in the morning to form ice on the fire buckets, and the thermometer reading in the 90's by noon), I didn't find basic training as strenuous as I had heard it would be. It only lasted a month.

One day we were to do a twenty-mile hike. We all put on our wool sweaters—regulations were that any sweaters we wore had to be worn under our fatigues. Our hiking path, a dusty road, went around a square wheat field, five miles to the side—no shade, and nothing to break the monotony. Then it got hot. We weren't allowed to take off our steamy hot sweaters so we just suffered. Such was the discipline at that time. Sometimes we found ourselves following really stupid orders.

Following basic training we took a battery of tests—scholastic, logic, spatial awareness, physical coordination, and an interview with a psychiatrist. The tests went on eight hours a day for three and a half days. I passed and qualified as an aviation cadet. The War was progressing well and the government was beginning to close down flight schools, so I was sent to aircraft mechanics school at Keesler Field, Mississippi.

The train car in which we rode to Mississippi was the worst type the Army had. It was a wooden boxcar that had bunks made of two-by-fours nailed around the walls. There were no windows so we spent most of that trip sitting in the open door, watching the southwest roll by.

Aircraft mechanic school lasted five months. During

that time the war in Europe was won and the two Bombs were dropped on Japan, essentially ending the War.

While I was at Keesler Field some of us were marched out to the middle of the drill field one day. There, an officer told us that, because we had IQ's of 140 or higher, we had been selected to join the G2 (Army Intelligence Service). He also told us that the war was nearly over and that we would not be trained to fly. I felt that I had been betrayed. If I couldn't fly, I wanted to get out of the Service so that I could get on with my life. I didn't transfer to G2.

At the end of the war, the Army discharged 25,000 of us in one month. An officer advised us to join the Army Reserve or we could be drafted back into the Army within two weeks and sent anywhere they chose. I signed up for the Reserve, took my discharge on November 30, 1945, and returned to Marietta.

Soon afterwards I enrolled in the University of Georgia. There was a huge influx of veterans enrolling in colleges. The Army closed Hunter Field in Savannah and turned the hospital and some other buildings over to the University to operate as a branch college. So, once again, I found myself back at another Air Force facility.

—Information furnished to Harland Armitage by Merrill Crissey

JACK PERCY CUMBAA
With
Lillian Cumbaa

My late husband, Jack, went into the Marine Corps, July 21, 1942. He was eighteen years old. He went first to Parris Island, South Carolina, then to Miami, and then to Camp Le Jeune, North Carolina. From December, 1943, through January, 1947, he was overseas. He was part of First Battalion, Company B, Sixth Marine Division.

Jack told me that while he was based in Miami, they guarded President Roosevelt's entourage when it was on its way to Casablanca. It was one of the best kept secrets of the War. They removed everyone from the base and then the Marines took over.

Once he was overseas, Jack participated in battles at Saipan, Tinnian, and the Marianna Islands. He also took part in the battles at Okinawa and Reyeuku Islands. Then he was part of the occupation of Japan from September 23, 1945, to December 10, 1945. You had to be young to go through what he went through and I think there were a lot of things he wanted to forget.

I have a copy of the base newspaper telling about Jack. It says, "How many of you know that Cuumba's middle name is Percy? He does not live up to that name. He is a real tough salty Marine that got his boot training in P.I.

(Parris Island). He is twenty-one years of age, six feet tall, brown hair and eyes and comes from Georgia. He likes to dress up in his blues and strut over on the beach. While treading down the street the other day a soldier on guard came to, 'Present Arms!' thinking Cumbaa was an officer. Cumbaa stopped and asked him what the seventh general order was. He got the soldier all excited and he couldn't answer. Private Cumbaa just told him to go on and walk his post."

I also have this little booklet entitled "Going Home," written by Harold Stassen. It reads, "While you're looking for a job and taking part in a veterans' group you should not forget the church on the corner. It could be your church. The only way we can be sure that justice and brotherhood are included in our national life is to see that the church is strengthened."

Although Jack's and my families knew each other when I was growing up, I don't remember knowing Jack until he came home from the War. We dated and then were married on Thanksgiving Day, November 23, 1950. We had two children: Jackie, our son, was killed in an auto accident in 1972; and our daughter, Lynn, was also killed in an auto accident in 1976.

Jack worked in several different businesses and finally, in 1953, took a job with Lockheed. He worked there until he retired on February 28, 1986. I started attending Marietta First Baptist Church when we came to Marietta.

Jack died of lung cancer, July 23, 1993.

—Interviewed by Ruth Miller, October, 2001

Jack Cumbaa

WILLIAM RALPH DAVIS
with
Ruth Richardson Davis

My late husband, Ralph Davis, was born in Phoenix City, Alabama, on December 13, 1924. He grew up on his grandfather's peanut farm near there.

Ralph entered the Navy, May 22, 1942. He was 17 years old and his mother had to sign for him. He never did talk much about his war experiences but he did write it down. This is what he wrote:

"Upon graduation from Aircraft Radio Operator and Gunnery school at Millington, Tennessee, I was transferred to CAPFA, CASU#1, Ford Island Hawaii. My duties were as follows: Receiving coded and plain language messages on continuous circuit at a speed of 18 to 20 words per minute and Transmitting by hand key. Our station had six teletype machines in operation at all times. During my stay there we stood a four section watch—six hours on duty and eighteen hours off. I stood for and passed the examination for Radio Operator Second Class.

"I was transferred to the *U.S.S. Kitkun Bay* (Baby Aircraft Carrier) in March, 1944. We typed into our log sheets everything that was said on the two-way communications between the ship and our aircraft. I was on the Admiral's staff, Commander Carrier Division Six.

Due to a shortage of operators, we had to stand two section watches—four hours on duty, four hours off. Late in 1944, we (the Admiral's staff) were transferred to the *U.S.S. Enterprise* (Aircraft Carrier). After three or four months, we transferred to the *U.S.S. Hornet* (Aircraft Carrier). Two weeks later, we were transferred to the *U.S.S. Wasp* (Aircraft Carrier). At that time I passed the examination and was rated Radio Operator First Class.

"From the *Wasp*, we transferred to the *U.S.S. Ticonderoga* (Aircraft Carrier) where I was appointed supervisor over a group of about fifteen men in 'Radio One,' the main communications department of the ship. In January, 1945, the *Ticonderoga* was hit by two suicide planes. We were transferred at sea to the *U.S.S. Yorktown* as the *Ticonderoga* started back to the U.S. for repairs. During the first few months aboard the *Yorktown*, I was appointed supervisor but due to a shortage of men I was placed on a regular operating position. I served aboard this ship until I was discharged in December of 1945."

Ralph told me about being transferred from one ship to another at sea. They would bring the ships together and run a sling from one to the other. They would put the men in this sling and hopefully the two ships wouldn't roll at the same time. He said he got dunked a couple of times. He said that's why they want young men in the service.

Ralph enjoyed his time in the Service, except when they were under fire or when someone got killed. He told how one morning his best buddy tried to get him to wake up and go upstairs for breakfast. Ralph was so exhausted (they never got enough sleep because of four hours on and four hours off) that he decided not to go eat. His buddy went and just as he got on deck the bombing started. The buddy was killed. It grieved Ralph really badly.

The *Yorktown* was Ralph's favorite ship. It was the flagship under Rear Admiral Arthur W. Bradford. Admiral Bradford used to spend time in the communications room watching the messages come in. The *Yorktown* was in Tokyo Bay when the Japanese surrendered. Ralph and a friend walked around Tokyo. No one bothered them at the time, but later he realized how foolish that was. There was a big celebration on board the *Yorktown*.

Ralph had seven awards, five of them for major battles. He was proud of his service but ready to come home. Fifty miles out from San Francisco they saw the Golden Gate Bridge. He said it was the most beautiful sight in the world. He was discharged at Ford Island and traveled part way home by Service plane, and the rest of the way by train. He worked as an Engineer at Lockheed for 35 years, and retired in 1986.

I was born in Cedartown, Georgia, but we moved to Marietta when I was very young. I graduated from Marietta High School in 1945. My sister was working at Bell Bomber Plant (Lockheed) and kept telling about this "nice young man." Later, when I went to work there, too, she introduced us. Ralph and I were married May 18, 1947, by a Justice of the Peace at the courthouse. We wanted to be married at Marietta First Baptist Church but Ralph was not a member and the church, at that time, had a rule against non-members being married there. So, we just took ourselves to the courthouse.

We attended First Baptist Church all those years. In 1965, when our son was 16, he and Ralph were baptized at the same time. Ralph truly loved being involved with his Sunday school class, the Love Class, and served as class secretary and treasurer until his death. Ralph also served as cashier for the church Wednesday night suppers. He also liked to help out during Vacation Bible School. He and Barney Hagood would help do the refreshments.

Ralph and I had one child, our son, William Ralph ("Rick") Davis, Jr.

Ralph died suddenly on June 27, 2000.

—Interviewed by Ruth Miller, July, 2001

Ralph Davis

THOMAS J. "JACK" DAWS

I realized when the War started, that it was going to be the biggest event in my life. I followed it very closely on the radio and in the newspapers and in August, 1942, when I was eighteen, I joined the Navy. I was born and grew up on a farm near Monroe, Georgia, and had graduated from high school earlier in 1942.

From Macon, I was sent to the Great Lakes Naval Training Station in Illinois. They needed men so badly to fill the ships they were building that our basic training was only about four weeks—just long enough for them to give us a series of inoculations and see if we had any deficiencies. At the end of that time we were given a series of tests and I was fortunate enough to be selected to have another sixteen weeks training in gunnery school. There, we learned not only how to fire the guns, but how to keep them in good firing order. With that training, I felt better prepared and understood more of what was expected of me.

After Great Lakes, I went to Boston, Massachusetts, to the receiving station. I was assigned to a new Destroyer, the *U.S.S. Thatcher*, VD Destroyer #514, just being built up at Bath, Maine. It was part of the Destroyer Squadron 23, under the command of Ollie Burton. (He went on to greater things after that, eventually becoming an Admiral. They named a class of Destroyers the Ollie Burt Class after him.) We brought the ship to Boston Harbor, put it into commission there, and then took it to Casco Bay, Maine, for a shake down cruise.

Our first duty was to follow a convoy to Liverpool, England. Due to the zig-zagging we did to avoid submarines, the crossing took many days. We then came back to New York Harbor and made another trip, this time to Casablanca in North Africa, where Rommel had just been defeated. Then it was back to New York again, down through the Panama Canal, up the west coast to San Francisco, and from there to Pearl Harbor. We didn't stay long at Pearl Harbor but went all the way to Tulaghi Harbor at Guadalcanal, arriving in April, 1943. The Japanese had already quit the Canal itself in February, 1943, so there was no resistance at the Canal. However, the Japanese controlled everything from there to Tokyo Bay.

Soon after we arrived, another man and I were sent ashore to pick up the mail. A young soldier gave us directions and asked if we had any cigarettes. I gave him the pack I had. When we went back the next time, I took him a carton of cigarettes, and I asked him if there were any downed Japanese planes where we could get a souvenir. He said that the planes had all been stripped but that he knew where there was an abandoned Japanese command post. He got a jeep and took us to this bamboo hut—no door, no glass in the windows. I could see through the window a table with Japanese cigarettes, caps and helmets on it. I decided to go inside but the soldier said, "You can't go in. If you go in, it's booby trapped and will probably kill you." We finally wound up with the soldier and my friend holding me up by the legs while I reached through the window and got a Japanese folding fan and a porcelain *sake* container.

That soldier's name was Leo Diamond. He asked if we had ever heard of Al Schmid. I said we hadn't. Leo said, "Well, you will. He was from Philadelphia, Pennsylvania. Twelve hundred Japanese tried to cross the Tenaru River.

Al was the machine gunner and I was his loader. He killed over two hundred Japanese as they tried to cross that river. He was almost blinded by a grenade that they threw at us when they got close. When he could no longer see, he continued firing as I told him where to aim." After the War, they made a movie of Al Schmid's life. It was entitled, "The Pride of the Marines," and starred John Garfield. I never met Al Schmid, but I met his loader, and without his loader that never could have taken place.

We would go on bombardments through the islands there, taking barges of troops up, and then we would go looking for the Japanese. They came down almost every night in what they called "The Tokyo Express." They came looking for the same thing we were—trouble.

One night, we followed our transports up to Bougainville. The next morning we bombarded an airfield on a little island called Buka. Then the Japanese sent their task force, which was about the same size as ours (four cruisers and eight destroyers) to attack the transports that were unloading all the Marines for the invasion of Bougainville. We engaged them that night. It was pitch black dark when we encountered them and, unable to see, we collided with one of our own ships, the *U.S.S. Spence*. The officers on the bridges of both ships saw each other about the same time and tried to miss each other but we collided and smacked the sides of the ships. Both ships kept running despite being badly damaged.

The *U.S.S. Foote* had been torpedoed right in the stern and was dead in the water. Our ship was moving slowly because of our damage so we were ordered to tow the *U.S.S. Foote*. About the time we got underway with that, about ninety Japanese planes attacked us. We had to cut loose from the *Foote* in order not to be sitting ducks. I was in one of the gun turrets. I think we shot down about fifteen Japanese bombers. I was nineteen years old and frightened. Not scared, because when you're scared you get petrified and can't do the things you are supposed to do. What you have to do is try not to concentrate on your own self. You more react than think, because there is no time to think. If you're properly trained you do exactly what you are trained to do.

After the battle, we got back to port but were badly damaged so we went down to Noumea, Caledonia, where they had a dry dock. One of the shafts that go back to the twin screws was bent and couldn't be repaired there so we had to come back to the States. We went into Pearl Harbor and then on to San Francisco. That's where I got off the Destroyer. I really didn't want to leave that ship. I had been on there almost a year, I knew everybody, and I knew the job I was doing. But it's not what you want to do. It's what they tell you to do....

They were building ships hand over fist and needed people who had been to sea and had combat experience. I was promised 30 days leave if I would transfer. My 30 days turned out to be twenty, but I got to come home during that time. When I went back, it was to Seattle and the new Carrier, the *U.S.S. Petrof Bay*. I spent the rest of the War on that Carrier.

Our ship was part of the formation that accompanied General Douglas MacArthur back to invade the Philippines. Remember, he said, "I shall return." On about October 20, 1944, our pilots began dropping leaflets telling the Filipino people to rise up and fight the enemy, that MacArthur had returned. That's when the Japanese started using their planes as suicide weapons, the *kamikaze*. In fact, I saw them before I ever knew what they were and what they were up to.

About the 25th of August, the Japanese began to attack all the ships but went mainly after the carriers because they were bigger and made easier targets. At first they did vertical dives straight down, then they quit that because all of the ships in the formation could fire at them. Instead, they would drop down to about eight or ten feet off the water and come in at us. Once they got inside the formation, we couldn't fire at them because we might hit another ship. One *kamikaze* got into the formation. He had two 500-pound bombs under each wing. We were firing at him as he came in and we cut one of those bombs loose. It exploded about 50 yards from where I was manning a five-inch gun on the fantail of the ship. The explosion knocked me off the gun seat and wounded several of our crew. I couldn't hear anything. I could see peoples' mouths moving but I couldn't hear a word. The *kamikaze* pilot skimmed the flight deck and as he went across somebody was pouring ammunition into him. He exploded about 500 yards after he went over us. A number of the gun crew were badly wounded but the gun captain rounded up some more people and we got the gun back in operation.

That wasn't the end of the attack. They kept coming at us and we kept the gun in operation, and shot a lot of them. We put up enough flak to get them out of the way. But they came back day, after day, after day.

While we were preparing for the invasion of the Philippines, I went out onto the dock with a working party. We were to receive some boxes. Along came two jeeps followed by a truck. One of the jeeps stopped, this officer got out, and I saw the stars on his collar. Then I saw that famous corncob pipe in his mouth and I realized that it was General MacArthur. I saluted and he saluted me back. He said, "How are you, sailor?" I said, "I'm just fine, General. I've been sent here to get material off this truck." He said, "Yeah, it's in those boxes." Later, I learned the boxes contained the leaflets that our pilots were to drop on the Philippines.

We were in the States on VE-Day, having just spent 70 days in Okinawa. That was the last island they planned to take before the invasion of Japan. We had come home for two reasons: First our guns had fired so much they were no longer accurate, so we had to get the barrels changed. Second, the Captain knew (but we didn't) that we were scheduled to be part of the invasion of Japan. He wanted everybody to go home one more time because if we invaded Japan many of us would not come home again.

It was while I was at home, that time, that I met Ruth (whom I later married). Then I got back on the Carrier and we started back to Pearl Harbor. We were en route to Manila when they announced, on August 14, that the Japanese had quit. We had never heard of the atomic bomb and could hardly believe that atomic power had destroyed two cities.

President Truman issued an order that the men with the five highest decorations would be the first to get out of the Service. I had the Silver Star Medal and that's how I got out. I also received the European African Middle Eastern Campaign Medal, the Asiatic Pacific Campaign Medal, and the Philippine Liberation Medal. In addition, both ships on which I served were awarded the Presidential Unit Citation.

I really didn't know what I was going to do after I got out of the Service but after I met Ruth I realized that the first thing I was going to do was see if I could get her to marry me. The ship I was on went on to the formal surrender in Tokyo Bay but I wanted to get home. We flew out of the Philippines back to Pearl Harbor. Then I rode another Destroyer back to the U.S. I went by train across the Country to Jacksonville, Florida. That's were I was discharged with the rank of Seaman First Class.

I went back to school for a short time but soon realized that I really didn't need more education to do what I wanted to do. I wanted to be a salesman and I spent 39 years at it—ten years with General Foods Corporation and 29 years with Kimberly Clark Corporation. I have been blessed. I married the girl that I wanted to marry, and we raised a family.

I feel very proud of my War service. I did what was asked of me. I was fortunate to return in good shape, considering what we went through. Many of my friends came home missing limbs and some didn't come home at all. Others came home with their minds messed up and could never get the scenes out of their minds. I was happy to do what was asked of me.

—Interviewed by Marcus McLeroy, February, 2002

Jack Daws receiving the Silver Star.

ROBERT DELOACH
With
Greg DeLoach

My uncle, Robert DeLoach, was the only one of the DeLoach family that went to the War. The rest of the DeLoaches stayed on their farms and were generally exempted from the draft, as were most farmers at that time. But, Robert DeLoach, after attending a one-room school, the old Rockville Academy in Putnam County, Georgia, went to Atlanta to pursue a career outside farming. It was there in Atlanta that he received his invitation (draft notice) to the War. My father was two years old at the time.

Robert DeLoach, became a Corporal in the Infantry, in the 78th Lightning Division, and fought in northern Europe. There isn't much family lore about him but we do have some of his V-mail letters.

One letter to my grandparents and my father begins with the title, "At Sea." He goes on to write, "As you no doubt know before now I've taken off on a free trip to see the world with the same destination that I've had for the last two years, that being 'unknown'." We assume from that that he had been in training stateside for two years.

Most of my uncle's letters were just a pleasant exchange of "How are you doing?" He wrote, "Little did I dream a few years ago that I'd be in the position that I am now that I would just love to see an old cow." At one point he wrote about being in a barn, and how delighted he was to actually be in a barn because it was a warm, dry place. He jokingly wrote about being back with the cows.

In December, 1944, my uncle did send my father a Christmas card. In the card he wrote, "How's the big boy? Was Ol' Santa Claus good to you this time, or were you a bad boy and he forgot you? Listen, if he brought you any toy guns, tanks, or anything pertaining to war, just box it up and send it back to him . . . Hoping to be back with you before next year at this time. Love, Bob."

I don't think my Uncle was by any means a flaming liberal in his day; he was just like any other good soldier—he had had enough of people shooting at him, and his having to shoot at others.

Robert DeLoach was killed in action. His body was brought back to Madison and given a military escort for the twenty mile journey to Eatonton. There were sentries posted, and a flag-draped coffin. He was buried in the city cemetery with full honors. Eatonton, being a small farming community, the merchants all closed down at noon out of respect. My father, almost three at the time, has a faint memory of hearing taps being bugled, and the 21 gun salute.

Robert DeLoach was the uncle of Rev. Greg DeLoach.

—Interviewed by Marcus McLeroy, August, 2001

KELLER H. DORMAN, JR.
With
Virginia Dorman

Keller Dorman and I lived next door to each other during our teenage years. His father was a conductor on the railroad and they were transferred to my little hometown of Smithfield, Georgia, (about nine miles below Plains, Georgia) when Keller was age 13. We graduated from high school together then got married on September 7, 1939.

Keller worked in the defense industry and I went to beauty college in Americus, Georgia. We had one child, a little girl, when Keller joined the Navy about 1944. He was stationed at the Great Lakes Naval Station. I remember going up there to see him before he was sent overseas. His ship was the *U.S.S. Ticonderoga*, a supply ship. They sailed from island to island dropping off supplies. Their ship had no guns but was escorted by Destroyers. They had some very close calls with Japanese submarines.

My husband didn't talk much about his war experience. He entered the Navy at Mather Field and was then transferred to Shelby Field, Hattiesburg, Mississippi. At one point, he was wiring guns on the Destroyers. I know that he went to Australia for R & R and thought it was a beautiful country.

After Keller left the Navy in the Fall of 1945, he studied electrical engineering for a while but eventually he became an accountant. He worked for thirty-two years for the same company.

Toward the end of his career, Keller began to develop the symptoms of Alzheimer's Disease. When his illness got worse I could no longer take care of him. Keller was admitted to the Georgia Veterans' Home in Augusta on January 9, 1989. I try to visit him several times a week because I believe he still knows my voice.

—Interviewed by Ruth Miller, February, 2002

Virginia and Keller Dorman

Bill Douglas

WILLIAM "BILL" DOUGLAS

I was a senior in high school at Griffin, Georgia, when Pearl Harbor came about. Within a week, all the National Guard young men in our county had been mobilized. We watched all the trucks going north on Highway 41, to Fort McPherson. After a very short training period, it seemed like only a month, some of them were on battlefields.

I was born in Griffin, September 11, 1925. When I was seventeen I wanted to join the Navy but my parents wouldn't allow it. Then a special group was being formed to be stationed at the Naval Air Station in Atlanta. My parents thought I would be safer in Atlanta, so they relented, and I spent my two-month boot camp at the old Naval Air Station in Chamblee, Georgia. Since I had been in the grocery business, I was put in the supply department.

After serving three to six months in Supply, as I watched the airplanes taking off and landing, I wanted to be on every flight. I mustered my courage, made an appointment with our Base Commander, and told him that I wanted to be on one of those airplanes. By three o'clock that afternoon, I was on a DC-3 heading to Jacksonville, Florida, to attend radio operation and gunnery school.

Following my training, we moved to the Banana River (now, Cape Canaveral) for crew indoctrination. Then we flew to the Panama Canal Zone and were stationed at Colon. We were in a PBM (Patrol Bomber Mariner) group. I was assigned to Squadron BPB 304. We were treated well by the Panamanian people. They were always glad to see us but that all changed after the Third Army Engineers came through going from Europe to the Pacific. Those fellows had been in battle over in Europe for many months and were disappointed about having to go to Japan without going home first. They came off the ships in Colon, put their 45's under their blouses, got all liquored up, and didn't act like gentlemen when they went into town. They created a lot of hard feelings among the natives.

Many of the fellows in the Caribbean area were flying PBY's. These were smaller planes used for patrol, not for fighting. A lot of them got into combat with German submarines and were shot down. Our PBM's, on the other hand, had a nose turret, a tail turret, a top turret in the middle of the aircraft and two side guns. It had a lot of firepower and a lot of big gas tanks. Later, I learned they had called our airplane "The Flying Bomb" because of the big gas tanks.

The closest I ever got to actual combat was when we thought our radar had spotted a submarine. I went back to man the side waist gun while my other radioman took over the radio and reported our position. I opened my hatch and locked my guns into place. The pilot neglected to tell us we were ready to go. He nosed the airplane down very quickly. I had neglected to put on my safety belt and found I was floating in the air. The only thing I had to grab onto was the handles of the machine gun. I think my fingerprints are still in the stock of that machine gun. When the pilot pulled out of that dive my feet hit the floor again, and I held on a long time to make sure I didn't go anywhere.

A week or two before my discharge from the Navy, I went out on a night flight with our new Squadron Commander. He had just finished flight school and knew exactly how to make that PBM act. He was doing "touch and go" landings, where you come in and kill one engine, and land with the second engine. Then you get your speed up, cut in your other engine, and take off with two engines. Well, he missed a step and instead of cutting in the other engine, he killed the remaining engine. We went blossoming all over that place, dug an outboard pontoon into the water, and did a cartwheel on the ocean. I decided right then and there that I would not be a twenty-year man.

I came home at Christmas time in 1945. We just about froze to death when we arrived, without proper clothing, in New Orleans. We caught a train to Jacksonville, Florida, to be discharged, then shared a ride to Atlanta. When I got home, I went around to the back of our house where my mother was on the porch. I said, "Mama, have you got any food for an old fellow?" And she screamed. My brother came in about a week later from Europe. He went to the University of Georgia, and after about three months I went to Georgia Tech, where I got a degree in textile engineering.

I worked for several years in the textile industry. In 1954, I came to Lockheed, where I was an industrial engineer. I worked on just about every project out there: the B-17, the B-29; the C-130; the C-5. I retired from Lockheed on June 30, 1990.

I feel that my time in the Military was very educational because I was young enough to absorb and learn from what I was seeing. It opened me up and broadened my horizons. I learned that we don't all have the same values. I have compassion for people in foreign lands who come here. They're just trying to make a living. I just thank the Lord that I don't have to go to foreign lands to make a living. I have been very blessed to be back here in Cobb County.

—Interviewed by Marcus McLeroy, February, 2002

CECIL DUDLEY
With
Elizabeth Dudley

I met my late husband, Cecil Dudley, at the military hospital in Savannah, Georgia, where I was working as a nurse. He had come to the hospital to visit his mother, who was a patient there. Cecil's father was an officer in the Coast Guard, which entitled Cecil's mother to have medical care at the military hospital.

Cecil was born, July 6, 1923, in Ocala, Florida, but grew up and finished high school in Fort Knox, Kentucky. He was drafted into the Army (the paper I have reads, "A-303rd") in 1943, and served until October 3, 1945. Cecil was known as a "Bazooka Man." He carried a bazooka on his shoulders. He used to say that he walked all over Germany and wore out two pair of boots. He didn't like to talk much about his military experiences. He served because he thought it was his duty to fight for his country. Cecil was a great dancer and when he would get his passes he would always go to the USO and dance. He was honorably discharged in 1945.

At the time Cecil and I met, I had finished my nursing training at Southern Baptist Hospital in New Orleans, Louisiana, and spent a year at the University of Georgia. At the hospital in Savannah, I was a Lieutenant but we didn't use that rank much. It was a wartime appointment, just on paper. I worked there until our wedding.

We married on July 1, 1946, at the home of Dr. Leroy Cleverdon, pastor of First Baptist Church, Savannah. Then we moved to Gainesville, Florida, so that Cecil could attend the University of Florida. After graduation he worked briefly for Pittsburgh Plate Glass but came to Lockheed when it opened in Marietta. He worked in design control. He retired in 1986.

When we came to Marietta, I started working at what was then the "new" Kennestone Hospital. I was an Operating Room Supervisor and worked there for fourteen years.

Cecil and I had one son, Bryan Franklin Dudley. We joined Marietta First Baptist Church in 1950. Cecil died on February 7, 1996.

—Interviewed by Ruth Miller, November, 2001

VERNON DUNCAN
with
Ann Duncan

My late husband, Vernon Duncan, was born on a small farm near Shadee, Alabama, during the Depression. His father died when Vernon was quite young. Vernon's older brother was drafted so Vernon had to quit school in the eighth grade to help support his mother. Then he came to Marietta and worked as a coach for some athletic association here. He was drafted into the Army in February, 1943, at the age of twenty and was inducted at Fort McPherson, Atlanta, Georgia.

Vernon started in the army as a cook. He then attended Ordinance Technical School in Nebraska, and ASF Technical School at Ft. Sheraton, Illinois. He became an expert in rifles and carbines so he ended up as Acting Drill Sergeant on the firing line. One day during training, when Vernon wasn't looking, one of the soldiers accidentally shot him through the calf of the leg (but he was all right). As Acting Drill Sergeant, he helped train McGuader's Raiders. That's how he lost his hearing—no ear protection at that time. He did receive a Marksman medal. Vernon was also awarded the Good Conduct Medal, the American Service Medal, and the World War II Victory Medal.

Vernon never did go overseas during World War II. He

was on a ship to go overseas and they came and pulled him off the ship. They had discovered that he was his mother's sole support. (His older brother was in the Pacific). That was a result of the Sullivan Act, which said something to the effect that they couldn't send the last child in a family overseas if he was the sole supporter of the family.

Vernon came out of the Army in February of 1946, and the first thing he did was get his GED (General Education Diploma—equivalent to a high school diploma). He started attending a business college in Atlanta (riding the trolley from Marietta). He said he ate "White Castle" hamburgers because they were the cheapest thing he could find. While taking a course in business law, he got so interested that he read the whole text book in one night. That's when he decided to study law. He got a job as a bookkeeper and went to Woodrow Wilson Law School at night until he got his degree. It was about that time that he married his first wife, Betty.

Vernon stayed in the Army Reserves, and got called back in to the Korean conflict. He entered as a Master Sergeant at Ft. Rucker, Alabama, and took Quartermaster training in North Carolina. On graduation he was commissioned as a 2nd Lieutenant and did legal work for the Adjutant General's office. He was stationed at Ft. Lee, Virginia, and Pine Camp, New York., where he ran the Officers' Club. Vernon was discharged (the second time) in 1955. He also got himself discharged from the Reserves at that point. He said, "That's the end of that."

Vernon went back to practicing law. At one point he became a trial lawyer. One fellow he was defending was guilty and Vernon couldn't get him to tell the truth. After that he said he would never take another criminal case as long as he practiced law. And he didn't. He served one term in the State Legislature in the 1960's. Then he ran for Probate Judge (they called it "Ordinary" at that time) and served until 1985. He practiced law, then, (mostly doing wills and other probate matters for people) until he retired in 1995 or 1996. He was an honest attorney, an honest man, who wouldn't do anything he didn't believe in. And he did love his church!

I grew up in a little bitty town in Alabama. I wanted to go away to college, so I went to Washington College, University of Virginia. I was so homesick I could hardly stand it so I transferred to the University of Alabama. I majored in speech and radio. I wanted to be an actress. I got my teacher's certificate from Auburn, then taught in Alabama and then in Moultrie, Georgia. I was teaching with my cousin and we decided to go someplace glamorous. We wrote to Alaska, and Aruba, and other places we thought might accept our teaching certificates. We wound up in Colorado Springs (because Colorado would accept our teaching certificate).

I lived in Colorado twelve years. I married the first time there. Then we came back to Georgia. My first husband died while we were living in Canton, Georgia. I was teaching in Canton, and met Vernon on a blind date arranged by Liz and Lamar Haley.

I love teaching. I preferred the seventh and eighth grades. I have directed plays. One time I even had to direct the Glee Club because I could play the piano and they didn't have anybody else to do it. I have no regrets where and what I've taught, or where I've lived. The Lord took me all over the United States and brought me back to North Georgia so I could meet Vernon. We were married on October 6, 1977.

Vernon Duncan died June 22, 1998.

—Interviewed by George Beggs, September, 2001

Vernon Duncan

LEON DURHAM
With
Joyce Durham Barber

My brother, Leon Durham, was born September 14, 1926, in Athens, Georgia. He moved to Marietta in 1939 and went through the Marietta school system. Leon and Daddy would take part in soap box derbies. I remember watching he and Daddy build and race their cars. He had a paper route and worked as a soda jerk at Atherton's Drugstore for a while. He joined the Navy in 1944 after graduating from Marietta High School. He was seventeen years old.

Leon took his basic training at Camp Perry, Virginia. He always wanted to see action, but he spent most of his tour of duty at Camp Perry. He was a Stores Keeper. I believe the rank was Yeoman. He didn't talk much about his service. I believe he also served the European Theater.

My brother was a very peaceful, accepting person. He didn't complain. He just did his work and did his time and came home. I think the military service was an adventure for him. Back then we didn't have opportunities to travel much. This was a chance for him to have some new experiences, meet new people, and to serve his country at the same time.

When Leon was discharged from the Navy in 1946, I

went up on the train to Williamsburg, Virginia, and came home with him the next day. He married in 1948 or 1949. Leon worked as a mechanic for a while. He also worked for my husband, Bill, at the Veterans Administration. He began working at Lockheed in 1954.

Leon died December 24, 1988. He was just a sweet man. We were very very close

—Interviewed by Marcus McLeroy, August, 2001

Leon & Joyce Durham 1944

Leon Durham and sister Joyce

WILLIAM EDWARD "ED" EADS
With
Dale Eads

My Dad, Ed Eads, was born on July 29, 1923, in Corbin, Kentucky. His father was a railroad man and the family was transferred to Harlan, Kentucky, where Dad grew up and went to high school. That's also where he learned to box. Harlan was a rough town, with a town bully. In order for Dad to learn to defend himself, my grandfather got him involved in boxing at the local YMCA. The bully soon learned not to mess with my Dad. Eventually Dad and the bully wound up being good friends and actually did some Golden Gloves boxing together.

Dad began to get into a lot of mischief so when he was seventeen, my grandfather packed him off to join the Navy, little knowing what was just around the corner. Following basic training at Great Lakes Training Station, Dad was assigned to the Destroyer, *U.S.S. Dale*. I was actually named for that ship because Dad said I was like the *Dale*. I was a fighter and my bottom was always wet.

When he got time to come home on leave, Dad would hitchhike. It was easy for a military person to hitch a ride because people actually had respect for the military. On one of his trips home, he met and married my mother. She was sixteen and Dad took her across the state line into Tennessee where they could get legally married.

The *Dale* was at Pearl Harbor when the Japanese bombed the port. Prior to that morning, the men on the ships had been doing a lot of drilling. That Sunday morning, when they saw all the explosions at Ford Island, their first reaction was, "Gosh, they really make this look realistic." They thought it was a drill. Very few of the ships had live ammunition available to use because it was in storage. Dad watched as the *U.S.S. Arizona* exploded. The *Dale* was the second ship to leave the Harbor that day and it seemed like it took forever to get out of there.

When Dad would get together with his Navy buddies at reunions, they seldom talked about the battles. They mostly talked about furloughs and shore leave. They enjoyed being together. Dad used to say, "It's not what you do; it's who you do it with that matters."

The Battle of Midway was one that Dad did talk about and you could tell that it just shook him to his soul. He was one of the youngest men on the ship. The morning of the battle, while it was still dark outside, the Captain came on the loudspeaker and said they were going into a great battle. He said, "Gentlemen, we are going to go into a great battle that will have long lasting consequences on this War. We are significantly outnumbered, outgunned, and outmanned. I think it is time we all don our life jackets." Then they had a prayer and went to breakfast—steak and eggs. Dad told me that the napkin he was holding while he ate became soaked from the perspiration running off his hands. I believe that was the longest sea battle in the history of the world.

In one of the battles, Dad got a lot of shrapnel and they transferred him to the hospital. There, they called him the "Pin-Up Boy of Ward 13" because he had so many pins stuck in him. Following his recovery, he was transferred to another Destroyer, the *U.S.S. Farragut*. It seems that once you were trained for Destroyers that you stayed with that class of ship. It was almost like a fraternity of Destroyer seamen. When Dad left the Navy he held the rank of Yeoman First Class.

After the War, Dad came home and we moved to Florida where he took any job he could find. Jobs were hard to come by and for a while he drove a "Tom's Peanuts" truck. He often said that's about what we lived on for the next year. Eventually he got into the grocery business—wholesale and then retail. Later, Dad opened his own advertising agency and handled the advertising for the Republican political campaigns in Florida.

Dad also wrote a book entitled *The Bloody Harlanite.* It was an interesting account of a young man from Harlan, Kentucky, who was a Golden Gloves boxer. It told about the man's World War II adventures in the Navy. The book ended with the bombing of Pearl Harbor. Dad was in the process of writing a sequel when he died. The last time I checked, Barnes and Noble still carried the book.

My father was very active in the Pearl Harbor Survivors Association. In fact he founded the Georgia chapter. He would give talks at various high schools because he wanted people to remember Pearl Harbor—not so much for the people who died there but because our nation needs to be prepared to never let it happen again. When he was in the hospital with his last illness (he had non-Hodgkins Lymphoma) his former shipmates and other Pearl Harbor survivors were lined up outside his room. He wasn't getting any rest but he said he was going to be resting in eternity, and he told the family, "Let me see my buddies." They had such a bond. I have never seen anything so phenomenal.

My wife, Linda, has written the following about my father: "Ed Eads was a unique man with a lot of accomplishments during his life, but he felt his greatest feat was surviving Pearl Harbor. He had a life long bond with all the men who fought beside him on the *U.S.S. Dale* and he attended the crew's annual reunions until he died. It really upset him when he talked with school age kids and teens and realized they didn't know about Pearl Harbor. He was a substitute teacher in his later years, and I'm sure that gave him an opportunity to pass on his first hand knowledge of Pearl Harbor. Even today he would want all Americans to remember what happened at Pearl Harbor."

Ed Eads died on May 6, 1996.

—Interviewed by Marcus MeLeroy, February, 2003

Ed Eads on the left

HENRY ELDRIDGE

I was born in Hapeville, Georgia, in 1924. I attended North Avenue grammar school. Then our family moved to Mableton, so I graduated from Mableton High School. I was drafted into the Army when I was eighteen years old.

I entered service at Ft. McPherson and was sent to Abilene, Texas, for basic training. It took us six days on a coal burning train to get there. It was cold in Abilene and the wind would blow right through you. The dust was everywhere. When we got off the train they said, "We were not expecting you until tomorrow." So they fed us cream of wheat, and I haven't eaten it since then.

We did the usual things you do in basic training—obstacle courses, 25 mile hikes with backpack. I was training to go into the medics so we didn't learn to fire rifles. I was there sixteen weeks and then they sent us, by train, to Pennsylvania. We got off the train in Pennsylvania in knee deep snow and still it was warmer than it had been in Texas. From there, half of the boys were sent to Europe and our half went to California where we boarded a ship to Guadalcanal.

I don't remember how many days it took us to get to Guadalcanal, but it was a lot of sick days. It seemed like forever. I was assigned to the Medical Supply Depot where we shipped out medical supplies. I don't remember any shortages of supplies except alcohol. Some of the guys who had been there a long time would sneak it out and drink it.

We lived in tents. The food was pretty good. I learned to eat hot peppers, which grew wild there. The first morning at breakfast I saw a Mexican eating hot peppers, toast, and black coffee. We never had much Malaria and I think because we ate those peppers the mosquitoes would bite us and run.

We stayed on Guadalcanal several months. They cut back on the unit and sent us to a replacement depot on New Caledonia. Then we joined the 147th Chicago Infantry outfit—a national guard outfit—we called them the Old Happy Shooters. By then I was in the Infantry and I learned pretty quickly how to shoot a gun. We went to Tinian, then Okinawa, then Saipan, then on to Iwo Jima.

On Iwo, the marines had gone across the island and said it was secure. We moved in and started fighting the Japanese. Everything they had was underground in tunnels—hospitals, living quarters, everything. They would come out at night and walk all over you. Steal your food. One night I went down to the latrine and noticed two guys sitting there. They turned out to be Japs. In the daytime they would go back into the tunnels.

The first Jap I saw ran behind a rock and I just couldn't shoot him. But I got over that. It was either him or me. We would throw Satchel charges or shoot white phosphorous into their caves. The white phosphorous is so fine it sticks to you like hot tar and just burns. They would come running out and we'd shoot them. It was really awful.

When we would go out to pull an ambush, we had to carry a blanket and a poncho. The island was just sulfur so if you dug a hole and sat in it about three hours the sulfur would just blister you. Thus the blanket. And sand everywhere. The landing craft made a noise just like the sound of somebody walking through the sand. It was scary, but after a while you could listen and tell the difference. When the Japanese bombers would come over, boy, you would head for the shelter.

One time, we were on night duty, sitting out in foxholes. We could look across and see the rest of the guys watching a movie. We were up on a little bank and I saw some movement. The person pulled off his shirt and we shot him. It was a suicide Jap. Next morning we learned that about thirty of them had walked within feet of us. I think we captured, altogether, about four thousand in the caves and tunnels.

When we went out on patrols, the Japs would tell us where to find other Japs who wanted to surrender. This one Jap was taking us over there, I was right behind him and he stopped me. There was a trip wire and I would have walked right into that booby trap. I know the good Lord was with me all the time.

Morale in our unit was good. We had a company commander who would go out on patrol with us at night because he hated sending us out there. He stepped on a mine and it blew his leg off. Just because he was going out there to be with us.

After Iwo Jima, they sent us to Okinawa to get ready for the invasion of Japan. Fortunately, the War ended and we didn't have to go. Then most of the 147th Infantry outfit went home. I had to stay because I still needed three points, so they put me in the Signal Corps. I didn't know anything about the Signal Corps, but they had to put us some place.

When I left the service, we came into Tacoma, Washington, by ship. Then, by train, we crossed the Canadian border and down into Chicago. I was assigned to cook. I didn't know anything about cooking but they said I'd get better meals if I'd cook. So I did. I got home at Christmas.

I left the Army with the rank of Private First Class. During my time in service, I was awarded the Combat Infantry Badge, The Good Conduct Medal, the Asian Pacific Service Medal with two bronze starts, and the WW II Victory Medal. I kind of enjoyed my World War II experience. There were parts of it I didn't enjoy, of course. Would I do it again? I'd have to think about it. The Army these days is a lot different from what it was then.

After coming home, I worked at several different jobs. In 1951, I came to Lockheed, where I worked for thirty years. The last twenty or so years I was down on the flight line as inspector in quality control.

I met Kathleen on a blind date after the War. She was a student at Georgia State College for Women in Milledgeville. We dated for a year and then got married. We have four children.

—Interviewed by Harland Armitage, July, 2001

Henry Eldredge

WILLIAM FOWLER
with
Ann Tillery and Kay Elliott

Our father, Bill Fowler, was born October 17, 1908, in Canton, Georgia. He grew up around Canton and entered the military service the first time at age 17. His mother signed for him, and he and his friend went into the Army (about 1925). He came out of the service and became a professional boxer.

Daddy boxed in and around Cobb County, Rome, and Atlanta. He boxed under the name "Jimmy Fowler" and was quite well known. He was a light weight boxer. One time he got a swelled head and decided to box a welterweight guy. Daddy said he had to eat soup for a week afterwards.

When Daddy re-entered the military, he was first in the Coast Guard. He went to radio school in New London, Connecticut. Then during WW II, he was on the *U.S.S. Hunter*. Daddy said he was on the flag ship for Admiral Alston, somewhere in the South Pacific. He was in charge of the radio room when he received the message, "Japanese have attacked Pearl Harbor. This is not a drill!" He also served in New Zealand and the North Atlantic.

Sometimes, the radio men would have to go ashore ahead of the Marines to run the communication lines.

Daddy had all this radio equipment to carry and his senior officer told him he had to carry a rifle too. Daddy said he couldn't handle all that and asked for a pistol. The officer refused so Daddy just talked to the commanding officer, who gave him a .45 to carry ashore instead of a rifle.

On one island, the Marines came up with two Japanese prisoners and saw Daddy standing there. They just walked off, leaving Daddy with the prisoners. He said he wasn't going to be responsible for prisoners, so he walked off too. The prisoners couldn't really go anywhere because there were Marines all over the place. Another time, he came across some Marines having coffee and he asked for some. The Marines were willing to share but they didn't have another cup. Daddy found a rusty tin can, took it down to the beach, cleaned it with sand and ocean water, came back and had himself a cup of coffee.

Meanwhile, while Daddy shipped out, Mother (Eleanor Evelyn Downey Bishop) coped. We lived in some kind of Navy housing in Mobile. It was a good ways from Grandma's, where Mother had to take our clothes to wash. She rode a bicycle with the laundry basket taped to the crossbar, and me (Ann) on the back with my legs sticking out. Our brother, Lee, was born in 1941, and Kay was born in 1945. Mother dealt with rationing, and shortages and sick children by herself. When Kay was born, Mother took a taxi to the hospital.

Mother became very independent, having to be in charge of everything. When the war was over, things didn't go back to the way they used to be. That made the relationship with Daddy more difficult. I think that happens a lot in war marriages. A lot of them didn't last.

Daddy had the rank of Chief Warrant Officer during the War. Afterwards they downgraded everybody and he was Chief Radio Operator. Daddy retired from the Navy in 1951.

After Daddy retired, he worked at Lockheed as an electronic technician. He had a strong work ethic and a strong sense of responsibility. He spent his later years being a grandfather to our children and to neighbor children.

Our mother died on December 15, 1994, and our father died April 28, 1996.

—Interviewed by Ruth Miller, August, 2001

William Fowler

EUGENE M. FUNDERBURK

I was born in Orangeburg, South Carolina, and attended schools there until the ninth grade. I graduated from high school in Elloree, South Carolina, and then spent a semester at Newberry College. I didn't really want to go to college. I wanted to join the Navy but I was only seventeen and my parents wouldn't sign for me to go, so I wasted that whole first semester.

When I turned eighteen, I joined the Navy for the duration of the War. That was in the latter part of 1945. I was sent to Norfolk, Virginia, for basic training. Boot camp was just regular barracks—double bunks lined down each side of the room. We had a few people who didn't like to wash very often but we just carried them outside and washed them down with salt water. We had southern squadrons and northern squadrons.

One day our squadron was coming back from drill and a group from the north was coming the opposite way down the street. Each group wanted to make a left turn. The Chief Petty Officer who was guiding us ordered us to go right through the middle of them. About four men went to the hospital that day. Our weapons weren't loaded of course but they got used in other ways.

Following basic training, I was assigned to the *U.S.S. Fitch*, a Destroyer Mine Sweeper. For the first two or three months we would take the new boot camp crews out on their shake-down cruise. Basically, we had to show the new sailors how things worked on a ship and then they would be assigned to a ship. After that I was assigned to the "Black Gang," working down in the engine room. I was in charge of the evaporators which distilled water for the ship. I held that job, on that ship, for the rest of my time in the Navy.

While our ship was anchored in the Bay at Norfolk, a big blizzard came up and we were ordered to get underway. We did, right into the teeth of that storm—sleet and snow, and the ship listing eighteen degrees to either side. By the time the storm had subsided and we got back to port the fresh water was depleted. I was in charge of running a barge, with two 1500 gallon tanks, back and forth to bring water to the ship. That barge was also the way we transported the men going on or coming back from liberty. Needless to say, quite a few were inebriated.

The morale was good. The War was about over so we didn't worry too much about having to go into combat. Our ship went to San Juan, Puerto Rico, and then to Guantanamo Bay, Cuba. One of my jobs, when we were in port was to hook up to the fresh water on dock and fill our tanks. If we were in port long enough we had to tear down the evaporators and clean out all the salt and grit. I never got to go on liberty in Havana, Cuba. The one time I was scheduled to go was canceled because a couple of sailors had shot up a few people the night before.

One thing we did was to pull targets on a float about 500 yards behind our ship for the *U.S.S. Missouri* to shoot at. One day when we were doing that, I had to serve on the fantail as a spotter, scoring whether the *Missouri* had a hit or a miss. One of those shells went over my head, live ammo, and sounded like a freight train—just barely missed the back of the ship. I radioed up to the bridge and told our ship's commander. He was only a Lt. Commander, but he left the mike open and he called the Admiral on the *U.S.S. Missouri* and cussed him out.

Our ship also served as a target for submarines to shoot dummy torpedoes at us. The torpedoes were set to pass thirty or forty feet below the ship and then they would come up yards past us. We would score whether they were on target or not. Then we would pick up those torpedoes and take them back to the submarines to do it all over again. I got to visit on two submarines. It was interesting because they got treated very well but I wouldn't want submarine duty for any amount of money—too confining.

At one point, our ship went part way into the Panama Canal. It was a big ship and we had about one inch clearance on either side. Half-way into the Canal it becomes fresh water so we were able to wash down the ship. Any officer that came on deck was fair game. One or two got washed overboard, but they didn't seem to mind.

Our ship was in dry dock in Boston, Massachusetts on VE–Day. The place went wild. Somehow, I ended up driving a jeep with about fifteen or twenty servicemen hanging on it. I couldn't even see to drive. They would tell me when to turn left or right. All of a sudden they all took off and I found myself sitting in the jeep in the lobby of a theater. I took off too. I think I was in Columbia, South Carolina, for VJ–Day. There was a parade but we weren't part of it.

After the War, I was offered a chance to go to Naval prep school and then to the Naval Academy if I would resign. I asked, "What if I flunk out?" They answered, "Then you spend the rest of your four years in the Navy." I said, "No, thanks, I'm going home."

I went back to Newberry College and finished there. I played football there. I had met Martha while I was on leave and we corresponded during my time in service. I actually roomed with her brother at Newberry. Martha and I married in 1951. I taught school in South Carolina for about four years. Then we came to Marietta, basically because the pay was better, and because of Mr. Shuler Antley, who was Superintendent of Marietta Schools. I have been in the teaching profession 45 years. I taught Georgia history and driver education for Marietta High School for seven years, then I took a teaching job in Fulton County. My last thirteen years with Fulton County I was a school social worker. I am back teaching driver's education at Marietta High.

Martha and I have two children: one son and one daughter.

—Interviewed by Harlan Armitage, August, 2001

E. M. Funderburk

ROBERT GARRISON
With
Lorene Garrison

I was born in Sycamore, Georgia, in 1917. My father was in the construction business and we moved around. I attended schools in Florida and Georgia, including A&M School, which is now McEachern High School. From there I went to work in Atlanta, where I met Bob, who was with Peabody (Arrow Shirt Company). We married in May, 1940, and lived in our own little house on Jefferson Avenue in East Point, Georgia, until the War broke out.

Bob and I talked about what he should do. We had no dependents and Bob felt that he should volunteer. He enlisted at Ft. McPherson on July 16, 1943, went from there to Miami, then to Newark, New Jersey, where he shipped out for England. He was among the first of the U.S. forces to reach England. Bob was a good typist so his job was to write up orders, insurance, and family information for the soldiers arriving in England. During that time, I worked at Bell Bomber (now Lockheed). When Bob came back from England, I gave up my job so that I could be with him. I followed along wherever I could.

Bob decided that he wasn't happy being a Private, so he applied and was accepted for Officer Candidate School (OCS). He was sent to Kathleen, Virginia. I was only with him about a week while he was at OCS because it was a very concentrated course. We called him a "Ninety-Day Wonder." I joined him when he went to Philadelphia. We had a small apartment there. But Bob wasn't really satisfied with what he was doing there so he went to Battle Creek, Michigan, as Supply Officer in the transportation office. Then he went to Washington, D.C., as a guard. I stayed with him while he was in Washington.

Eventually, Bob was sent to San Francisco, where he began to prepare supplies for the Pacific. It was in 1943 that his ship sailed. They had a rough trip-storms, and a crowded ship, lots of seasickness. You were lucky if you got a bed. He used to say, "I should have been in the Navy, not the Army. That way I would have had a bed in all of this."

They landed in the Philippines, where Bob was involved in the Battle of Manila, and the Battle of Luzon. He worked as a supply officer. He told about having to take a jeep from one place to another and the Filipinos would throw rocks at them. Our men got tired of that so one day they loaded their jeep with rocks and "returned fire." That scared the Filipinos and the men were able to take their jeep trips without rock throwing. Bob was a person who could get along with people. He worked hard and made many friends.

In 1944, Bob came back here and then went back to the South Pacific. I know he was there for Christmas of 1944. Part of his job was to supply food to the Japanese prisoners of war—very large numbers of people. They used to have riots. Something they were feeding the prisoners didn't agree with their stomachs. While he was still a Lieutenant, Bob helped establish the first Prisoner of War (POW) hospital, where surgeries of all types were performed on hundreds of POWs. Bob was later promoted to Captain.

Meanwhile, I lived with my parents in East Point. We dealt with rationing of food and gasoline. We were thrifty and made out OK. I would go to the movies to see the news of the War. I kept thinking it might be Bob. There was so much going on and it was very secretive. His letters were censored but he wrote a little something everyday. On our fifth wedding anniversary he had his dad plan a dinner for me with some friends at Herrens in Atlanta. Another anniversary he had roses sent. He was just always thinking....

A written history of the POW Camp records the following:

"As in any organization supplies are a vital segment or the backbone. Thru (sic) the birth, the infancy, and maturity of the camp this vital and important function was ably supervised and planned by Capt. Robert T. Garrison. The S-4 section was charged with drawing and distribution of all supplies used in the camp. Two ration dumps were set up (a POW dump and a GI dump) where rations for both military and prisoner rations were distributed. Since the military personnel at one time exceeded 3000 the supply problem became comparable to that of a permanent stateside post. Arrangements were made by Capt. Garrison for rail deliveries of supplies and a rail head was established near the camp."

The report goes on to describe the building of this camp from a fenced-in rice paddy, with no food facilities, and water trucked in, to a fully functioning camp where more than 81,000 prisoners and detainees were interred and processed. Prisoners included Filipino collaborators as well as Japanese, Korean, Formosan, and German soldiers.

After the war, Bob wanted to get back home. He felt like he had done his part to serve his country, but they kept delaying his return. Several ships came in with replacements but the replacements were sent back. The authorities told Bob, "We want you to stay because you know what you're doing and these guys don't." Eventually, Bob spoke to his commanding officer and told him, "If you don't have enough authority, I'll go to the next person who does have authority." Finally, they gave him a release. He came home on March 4, 1946. I met him at the gate at Ft. McPherson.

Bob went back to work for Cluett Peabody, in the shirt business. We built a house and, in 1947, adopted our daughter, Linda. Soon we were transferred to Minnesota. Two years later we were sent to Troy, New York, and from there to Scarsdale, New York. We attended the Baptist Church in Scarsdale.

In 1954, Bob and I came through Marietta on our way to Florida. We saw signs on Garrison Road that the house (now the 1848 House Restaurant) Bob's grandfather had lived in was for sale. Bob made an offer and we bought that place. My parents moved into the house to keep it open while we still lived in New York. In 1958, we decided to move into our Marietta home and Bob would commute to New York. By the time he retired, at age 55, he had helped establish shirt factories in England, Germany, and Central and South America.

Bob spent the rest of his life in community service, including helping to get Kennesaw State University established. He was also involved in Cobb General Hospital and the Red Cross. He was a good community citizen.

Robert Garrison died April 9, 1998. He was 88 years old.

—Interviewed by George Beggs, September, 2001

Lorene and Bob Garrison

EUGENE WESLEY HAGOOD
With
Ruth Hagood

My late husband, Eugene Hagood, was turned down for the Draft because of a congenital heart problem. So he enlisted and was accepted into the Army Air Corps in January, 1942. He was already in the Service when we met in September, 1942.

Eugene was born, February 23, 1915, in Marietta. His family moved to Atlanta when he was quite young. That's where he grew up and went to public school. I was born in Ellijay, Georgia, and grew up in Cherokee County. My family moved to Cobb County when I was thirteen.

I had gotten a job with Genuine Parts Company in Atlanta, in 1942. Eugene had worked there as a purchasing agent before entering the Service. While he was home on leave, one of his former coworkers said, "Hagood, we've got a new blond working up in the purchasing department. You better come up and meet her." He did, and we started dating. We married a year later in the chapel of First Baptist Church in Atlanta.

Following his induction at Fort McPherson, Eugene trained at Lakeland, Florida. He wanted to be a tail gunner but was soon grounded because of his breathing problems. From then on, he served mostly in a clerical capacity. I continued working in Atlanta. In November, 1943, Eugene was transferred to Sarasota, Florida, and I was able to join him for a month. He was about to go overseas and after a tearful good-bye, I came home and moved in with my parents.

On Christmas Day, with our family scattered, my mother and I made Christmas dinner for the three of us—my father, my mother, and myself. Just as we were ready to eat, someone drove up in the yard. It was Eugene. He had gotten a last minute leave. When it was time for him to return to duty, I went with him to the train station for another good-bye. I didn't see him again for two years.

Eugene went with the Headquarters Squadron, 57th Army Air Force Base Service Group to the South Pacific—Okinawa and Guam. At one point, he spent a few weeks in Honolulu, Hawaii, studying water purification. We used to laugh about that hard duty in Hawaii. Although he had a gun and had a marksmanship medal, Eugene was never in combat. His group was a support group that would go in after a battle and prepare airstrips.

Eugene didn't talk much about his war experiences. He mentioned *kamikaze* pilots but didn't say much else. The most unusual thing was when he and his three brothers, each in a different branch of the service, all met on one of the islands.

Meanwhile, I continued to work for Genuine Parts. In those days we worked a half-day on Saturday. The girls in my department would often then go to lunch at the Frances Virginia Tea Room. On the appointed Saturday morning we would all come to work wearing hats and gloves.

I don't remember that we had any problems with rationing. The hardest thing to get was hosiery. You couldn't get silk or nylon. A friend's sister worked at Davison's Department Store downtown and she would get us hosiery when they came in.

When the War was over, Eugene came by ship to

California. Then he flew to Georgia. After spending a week at a hotel, we found an apartment right off Peachtree Street. Eugene was separated from the Service at Fort McPherson, in January, 1946, with the rank of Sergeant. He went back to work at Genuine Parts. In 1947, he was transferred to Tennessee, and, in 1949, to Waynesboro, North Carolina, for three months. Then we came back to Marietta and joined Marietta First Baptist Church. Eugene began working for Lockheed in 1952 and was there for 21 years before he had to take a medical retirement.

We have two daughters, Claudia Breed and Ann Coker.

Eugene Hagood died of complications from heart surgery on August 20, 1979.

—Interviewed by Ruth Miller, July, 2001

Gene Hagood

GEORGE BARNETT "BARNEY" HAGOOD
With
Christine Bramlett Hagood

Barney Hagood and I were married on December 6, 1941, and as he liked to tell it, "The War started the next day." Dr. George Brown, pastor of Marietta First Baptist Church, performed our wedding ceremony at the pastorium. We had about seven weeks together before Barney was called into the Army (Combat Engineers), January 26, 1942.

Barney was born in a house on Waddell Street, just off the Marietta Square, but his family moved to Atlanta when he was six. He graduated from Hapeville High School. I was born near Blue Ridge, Georgia, and my family moved to Marietta when I was eight. I graduated from Marietta High School and then attended a small local business school.

Barney and I met on a blind date when I was a high school senior. My big sister, Louise, usually went along on our dates as a chaperone. At the time Barney was drafted, he was working for General Electric.

Following his basic training at Fort Belvoir, Virginia, Barney became part of the Eastern Coast Defense, They traveled up and down the coast for amphibious training. Then he was sent to the South Pacific as part of the Combat Engineers.

The Combat Engineers were attached to the 77th Infantry Division and took part in the invasion of Guam. He was also involved in battles on the Philippines, Okinawa, and Le Shima. Often the Combat Engineers would go in ahead of the Infantry in order to lay bridges and clear roads. They had some pretty rough service. There was a lot of hand to hand combat. At one point, Barney wrote to me and I had Dr. Brown write him a letter to assure him that he was doing the right thing.

They were in the jungle most of the time and the heat was terrible. At times, the famous war correspondent, Ernie Pyle, was with Barney's unit. They were all very appreciative of Pyle because he went right into battle with the men. He was later killed near Okinawa.

Barney and three of his brothers were able to meet while they were all in the South Pacific. His older brother, Hubert, was in World War I and World War II. He went into the Navy at the age of seventeen before Barney was even born. Then there were Cecil and Eugene. My brother, William Clyde Bramlett, was also in the Service as a bomber pilot in Europe.

While Barney was overseas, my sister, Louise, (whose husband, Arthur Poor, was also in the Service) and I moved back in with our parents. By pooling our resources and ration stamps we did pretty well. We rode the streetcar to our jobs in Atlanta every day.

After the War ended, Barney spent some time in Japan and then came back home by way of Seattle. He mustered out on December 3, 1945, with the rank of Private First Class. He had been awarded the Good Conduct Medal, the Rifle Marksman Medal, the Pacific Theater Medal, and the Philippines Liberation Medal. I still have the outfit I wore the day he came home.

Barney returned to his job at General Electric and later went to work for Bell Bomber (now Lockheed), where he worked for 33 years.

A lot of the men who were in the War didn't talk much

about their experiences. Later in their lives, when they were with other veterans they would tell their stories. Until he became unable to travel, Barney and I attended a number of the reunions of Barney's military outfit. He was the only southerner in his Company. Most of the men were from New Jersey and they liked to give him a hard time about being a Georgia Redneck but it didn't bother Barney.

On his first furlough home after entering the Service, Barney was baptized and became a member of Marietta First Baptist Church. When he came home from the Army he taught junior boys in Sunday school. He was a Life Deacon at First Baptist and he loved his KB Sunday school class.

We had two children, a daughter, Vickie, and a son, David (who later died of Cystic Fibrosis). Over the years, I have worked in various clerical positions, including secretary to the pastor at First Baptist Church.

Barney Hagood died on October 3, 2000.

—Interviewed by Ruth Miller, March, 2001

Barney Hagood

HARRY JACKSON HAMBY
With
Elizabeth Adair Hamby

I am a Cobb County girl. My family moved from the County into Marietta when I was ten. I remember walking all the way from where we lived, up near the hospital, to Waterman Street School. I would day dream along the way, pretending I lived in the beautiful homes along Church Street. Harry was a Smyrna boy, although he graduated from Marietta High School. We met at a family reunion. I went to the reunion with one of his cousins and came home with Harry. We married on March 19, 1938, in Smyrna, at the home of the preacher, Dr. Gresham.

We were sitting around the fireplace on Sunday afternoon, December 7, 1941, when the news came that the Japanese had bombed Pearl Harbor. Harry did not want to go into the Army, so he enlisted in the Navy. We lived in Gainesville, Georgia, for thirteen months while Harry attended radar school. Then Harry was sent, first, to Charleston, then on to San Diego, and finally to the South Pacific.

When we learned that Harry would be going to the Pacific, we decided to learn more about the area. We got a map and assigned a girl's name to every island as our own private code. He would write and maybe ask, "Have you seen Lucy lately?" I would look it up on the map and know just where he was. That's how I followed him across the Pacific. Once Harry left, I didn't see him again until the War was over.

We wrote to each other every day but of course he didn't get mail every day. One time, he received 52 letters all at once. Sometimes I would go for a week or more with no mail. If that mail came on the weekend, Carl Abbot, who worked at the Marietta Post Office, would bring the letters to me even if it was Saturday or Sunday. He would say, "I didn't think you'd want to wait until Monday to get these." That's how people were back then.

Harry was in charge of maintenance on board the *U.S.S. Daniel P. Griffin*, a Destroyer. His ship was in a number of battles, including Okinawa. Mostly, I remember the stories he wrote and told.

While he was in the Philippines, Harry wrote, "Our ship was only here for several days and on Sunday night some of the boys and I went to the little thatched roof church they had built. One of the native girls sang, 'God Will Take Care of You'." That hymn became one of Harry's favorites and I had them sing that song at Harry's funeral because it meant so much to him.

During one battle, Harry became so extremely sick that they thought he was going to die. They didn't know what was wrong with him and the Captain said, "Let's turn back. The hospital ship is just a short distance." They turned that ship around and got near enough to the hospital ship that they put Harry in one of those baskets and passed him across to the hospital ship. It turned out he had kidney stones. When he recovered, he went right back to his same ship.

Harry's favorite pie was lemon. One night, as he was going through the officers' mess, he saw a beautiful lemon pie on the table. He didn't really steal the pie, he just took it to the tool room, locked the door, and ate every bite of the lemon pie. The next morning, nobody knew what had happened to the pie. When we attended the 25-year reunion of his ship, they were all telling funny stories—officers and enlisted men. I urged Harry to tell about the lemon pie, but he never did.

Meanwhile, back in Marietta, I had a garden. There was a cannery up on Canton Road and they let us can all the food we wanted to send overseas. I sent Harry cornbread and a can of peas. He shared that food with all the boys.

Harry was a new Christian when we married. While on the ship, he wrote to Dr. Brown (the pastor of First Baptist) and said, "I want to teach a Sunday school class of boys when I get home." He had a good friend on the ship and they would study the Bible together. When Harry came back home, there was a class in the Junior Department for him to teach.

At one point, Harry's ship was caught in a typhoon. We found out later that Jack Shifflett's ship was in that same storm.

Harry's ship was in Tokyo Harbor, preparing for the invasion, when the War ended. He came home the same way he went over, on board the ship, and they ran out of food before they got home. Word had gotten out that the ship was out of food, so there were young ladies on the dock handing out milk and fresh tomatoes. Now Harry had never liked milk or tomatoes, but he ate them then and has eaten them ever since. And he drank so much milk that he got kidney stones a second time.

Harry left the Navy with the rank of Chief Petty Officer. After the landing at San Diego, he came by train back to Charleston. Then he flew to Atlanta. My brother took me to meet him at the airport. It was three or four o'clock in the morning.

Following the War, Harry worked in the automobile business until he retired. We had two children: a son who died at birth, and our daughter, Harriette Hamby Davis.

Harry Hamby died on April 21, 2000.

—Interviewed by Ruth Miller, March 2001

Harry Hamby

HARRY OWEN HAMES
With
Margaret Delk Hames

My late husband, Harry Hames, was not called for military service immediately because he was already married. He did join the Marietta National Guard. It was March, 1943, when he was inducted into the Army at Fort McPherson in Atlanta.

Harry and I practically grew up together in Marietta. I was born, May 19, 1918, in a little Victorian house on Atlanta Street. My sister, Ginny Ruth Delk Smith was born eighteen months later. Harry was born on West Dixie Avenue in Marietta. His father was a motorman on the street car line between Marietta and Atlanta. I knew Harry at church from the time he was in the Royal Ambassadors (R.A.'s) and Grady Eubanks was their leader. Harry and I dated for four or five years. After high school, I got a job at Stephens Lumber Company and he went to work for Anderson Motor Company.

We were married by Dr. George Brown, on August 14, 1940, at Marietta First Baptist Church. We bought a house on Henderson Street—where the YWCA now stands. Harry went to work operating heavy construction equipment for C.W. Matthews, helping to build the Bell Bomber facility. That's what he was doing when he was called up.

After just one or two weeks at Ft. McPherson, Harry was put on a train, and without knowing their destination, they rolled and rolled. They finally wound up at Camp Edwards, Cape Cod, Massachusetts. There was nothing there but sand dunes and cranberry bogs. He was to learn to drive half-tracks and it was a good place to do it. Six months later (October 26, 1943), he went to Greensboro, North Carolina, to anti-aircraft school. His next stop was a technical school in Ft. Logan, Colorado. Then it was on to Fresno, California. Finally, he wound up near Spokane, Washington. He stayed there until he was discharged.

Meanwhile, back in Marietta, I continued to work for Stephens Lumber Company. I converted our house into two apartments and rented them out. I moved in with a friend, just two blocks from Marietta, and we could walk or ride our bicycles to work.

In May, we decided that I should go to visit Harry in Massachusetts. His brother, Luther, was stationed in Cambridge and was to get me accommodations in Boston. Harry was to come in to Boston, from Cape Cod, to meet me. I had never been further north than Tennessee so I was rather apprehensive. Charles Watson (a friend from Marietta) had been stationed in New York and was to meet my train. But Charles got transferred to Louisiana. I was so frightened that when I arrived in New York City, I just went out one door of the station, around the building, and back through the same door. I didn't go anywhere. On the train from New York to Boston, I sat with a woman whose husband was meeting her. They kindly accompanied me on the subway to my hotel.

Unbeknownst to me, Luther and his wife, Katherine, had also been transferred and the hotel had no record of a reservation for me. This couple whom I had met on the train would not leave me at the hotel until I was given a room. Harry was not there. I went to my room, got into the bed, and cried and shook. Finally, Harry got through by telephone to say he couldn't get a pass. I would have to go out to the Camp.

The next morning, in the pouring rain, I caught a train and then a bus to the Camp. We had no reservations at the camp but a lady with whom I sat on the bus offered to let Harry and me have her room and she would stay with a friend. So that's what we did. Harry and I had two nights together. Then he headed back to camp and I headed back to Marietta. The next time he got a three-day pass, we decided to split our time between Washington and New York. We didn't see much of either city because there were blackouts while we were there.

I joined Harry in Spokane in May, 1944. I rode the train, sitting up, all the way from Atlanta to Spokane. The seats were the old straw kind because they had put any train that would run on that line. At one point, a serviceman took me under his wing and got me a better seat.

We were able to get a little efficiency apartment in Spokane and I got a Civil Service job. While we were there Harry had an emergency appendectomy and was in the hospital almost six weeks. Because the patients would sometimes try to leave the hospital, the nurses would take away their pajama trousers and just leave the patients wearing the tops. At one point, when Harry was not rational, he pulled the tube out of his nose and was halfway down the hall to the nurses' station when they caught him.

We came back to Georgia for Christmas in 1944, riding the train through North Dakota. The snow banks were higher than the tops of the railway cars. They heated the train cars with pot bellied stoves. We had to put on all the clothes we had in order to stay warm.

Soon after that trip, I found I was pregnant. Harry was afraid he would be sent overseas and I would be left in Spokane. He decided to buy a car and drive me back to Georgia. We didn't have much money left so we asked Mr. Earl Medford for a loan. He immediately sent us a check.

Unfortunately, it was a business check and since nobody in Spokane knew Earl Medford, they wouldn't cash his check. Finally, our landlord cashed it for us and we bought our car.

Luther and Katherine Hames were stationed in El Paso, Texas, by then. We decided to drive home via El Paso in order to bring Katherine and their baby home with us. Then Harry headed back to Washington and my sister, Ginny, was the one to drive me to the hospital at Fort McPherson for Peggy's birth. It was about six weeks before Harry got leave to come see us.

Harry was discharged February 23, 1946 in Washington, D.C. Following his discharge, Harry and his father operated a furniture store for several years. Then Harry went into the real estate business and that's what he did the rest of his life. Harry and I had three children: Peggy, Hank, and Buck.

Harry Hames died on May 8, 1996.

—Interviewed by Ruth Miller, April, 2001

Harry Hames

HOMER MCCOY HARRISON

There were eighteen in my graduating class at Acworth High School—nine girls and nine boys. I was born in Acworth and grew up there. After high school, I went to the University of Georgia and to Draughn's School of Commerce in Atlanta. Draughn's is where I met my wife.

At the time I joined the Navy, my wife was expecting our first child. I did my basic training in California then shipped out. I left on one Wednesday and the next Wednesday, I got a telegram from the doctor saying, "Mother and babies doing fine." We had twins, Betty Ann and McCoy Harrison. They were thirteen months old before I got to see them.

We went to Okinawa. We were the closest ground forces to the mainland of Japan. The *kamikaze* pilots were still active. One night I heard an airplane and told the commanding officer we needed to turn out the lights. He said, "I don't have the authority to do that." I said, "Authority or not, if you don't turn those lights out . . . ." Just then that plane hit about a hundred yards from the camp.

After the atomic bomb was dropped and the Japanese surrendered, the next thing was to get back home. They were flying us out and I was to be on the last flight and they forgot me. I was walking down the road and some Army guys in a jeep picked me up. They said not to worry, they would see that I got off the Island.

When I finally got back to Jacksonville, Florida, and was discharged, I rode the bus all the way to Marietta. I haven't been on a bus since, and I'm not going to get on one either. I got to Marietta and walked up the hill from Cherokee Street to 702 Church Street. When I got there, my little boy wouldn't have anything to do with me but my little girl came right to me.

I left the Navy with the rank of Chief Petty Officer. I was glad to serve my country but I was glad to get home.

I went into the banking business and worked 31 years at the Cobb Exchange Bank on the Marietta Square.

—Interviewed by Marcus McLeroy, November, 2001

JAMES DAVID "BLINK" HARTSFIELD, SR.
With
Millie Hartsfield and Jim Hartsfield, Jr.

According to a taped interview done by his oldest granddaughter, Shannon Holloway, Dave Hartsfield was drafted into the Army in June, 1943. He said, "I graduated from (West Fulton) high school on a Saturday night and was drafted the following Monday morning."

Dave was a very good baseball player. He had a baseball scholarship from the University of Georgia. Like most of the young men of that time, instead of taking a deferment to play baseball, he went into the military service.

Dave did his basic training at Fort McPherson, Atlanta, Georgia, and at Camp Wheeler, Macon, Georgia. He left Camp Wheeler in October, 1943, spent a month at Fort Mead, Baltimore, Maryland, then was shipped to Camp Miles Standish, POE (Point of Embarkation), Boston, Massachusetts. On December 27, 1943, Dave sailed for England. His ship, the *Kaiser Wilhelm*, was the largest ship in the German fleet and it had been taken over by the Allies at the beginning of World War II. The *Kaiser Wilhelm* was the flagship of the Convoy.

After a journey of seven days, the Convoy arrived at Birmingham, England. Dave's unit traveled by train to Badenhope, about 30 miles inland from Plymouth. He was part of the Ninth Infantry Division, Third Battalion, Company F, 47th Infantry Regiment, Third Army (Patton's Army). The Ninth Infantry Division had landed, originally, in North Africa and fought their way across North Africa and Sicily. Then they went back to England. They were not supposed to go to Normandy on D-Day because of their previous experience. They were to be kept as backup. But the First and the Ninth did go to Europe about four o'clock on the afternoon on June 6, 1944.

Dave said, "As far as we were concerned, the invasion of Europe actually took place on June 6. That's when I landed on Omaha Beach, in France. From France we went to Belgium, then on through Germany, through Cologne, Eupen, Zurin, and Eshwire, right up to the Elbe River before we finally stopped. I was at the Elbe River on VE-Day. The U.S. Army Command would not let us go any further. The Russians were coming in from the east, pushing into us. We had to stop and start taking German prisoners as they came across the River."

In describing their living conditions, Dave said, "After we got into Europe and started into combat we mainly ate K-Rations and C-Rations. The K-Ration was in a box like a Cracker Jack box. It would have cheese and crackers and canned meat. The C-Rations were canned beef stew and things like that. We also had a D-Ration. It was a solid chocolate bar. When you had that one candy bar it was so potent and so rich that was all you needed for the meal that day.

"If we were lucky, we would wind up in a house with the roof torn off but mainly we stayed out of town in the woods and slept on the ground. Or, we would dig us a foxhole and sleep in that hole that night. Usually, we dug a hole every night before we could go to bed, setting up a certain perimeter to keep people out in case they counterattacked."

Dave didn't talk much about the battles. He did tell how,

walking down a street in France with his buddy, one day, they were talking one minute and the next minute the other man's head was blown clean off his shoulders. The man was a walking corpse. Dave also told about being pinned down in a ravine for several hours after he had warned the officer in charge that they could be heading into a trap. When the officer said, "Hartsie, you'll have to find us a way to get out of here," Dave replied, "You got us into this mess. You lead us out." He was known for being feisty, with a colorful personality.

Mostly, Dave preferred to talk about the good things. How, when they liberated towns the villagers would come out and offer them a loaf of bread and a jug of wine, and hug them and say, "*Viva L'American!*"

He also told about digging a palace of a foxhole when they were at Bastogne. They dug so deep that they could actually stand up in the foxhole. They got some old timbers from farmhouses and put a roof across the foxhole. They put dirt on top of the roof and installed a smokestack, built a fire, and had a warm place to stay. Dave said they fought continuously. It wasn't an eight to five job. They often would go two days without eating and three or four days without washing. He also said there were no atheists in their foxholes. Everybody believed and everybody prayed.

Those experiences made a light sleeper out of Dave. His family says that you never dared touch him when he was sleeping because when he awakened he was alert and ready to fight. They learned to call his name to waken him.

Dave left Germany, by way of Munich, on September 19, 1945, and arrived back in Newport News, Virginia, on October 20. He traveled to Augusta, Georgia, and was discharged on October 22, with the rank of Private First Class. Dave Hartsfield was very proud of his military service. Freedom meant a lot to him.

Following his discharge, Dave worked for Atlanta Metallic Casket Company and then for Southern Railway.

At the same time, he played semiprofessional baseball. He would work all week for the railroad, earning $45 to $55 for the week. Then, on Saturday, he would pitch a baseball game and get paid $125 for one game. Dave also was active in the railroad union affairs, even traveling to Washington, D.C. to help make policy and to resolve disputes.

David Hartsfield died on March 2, 1994.

—Interviewed by Marcus McLeroy, February, 2002

Dave Hartsfield

FRANK HATCHER

I was born on February 16, 1924, in Griffin, Georgia. That's where I grew up. After graduating from high school in 1941, I spent one year at North Georgia College. I was there on December 7, 1941—Pearl Harbor Day.

In June of 1942, I had an opportunity to go to work in an aircraft defense plant in San Diego, California. My older brother was already working there and when I joined him we had a good time seeing that part of the country. I remember the hospitality extended to us by the First Congregational Church there. The Church had a "lunch and linger" program after the morning services. They served a good meal and afterwards everybody helped clean up. Then there would be some kind of outing or sight-seeing opportunity. There were a lot of military people in San Diego and the church met a real need for fellowship. It is a good memory for me.

I returned home in 1943 and went into the Air Force. After basic training at Keesler Field, Biloxi, Mississippi, I was accepted into the aviation cadet program. I spent some time at Mississippi State College and then went to aircraft mechanics school in Amarillo, Texas. Then it was on to B-17 orientation in Burbank, California, and Advanced Transition School—transitioning from two-engine to four-engine aircraft—in Hobbs, New Mexico.

By that time the focus of the War had shifted from Europe to the South Pacific. They were more interested in long range bombing with the B-29's so I was sent to mechanics school in Roopville, Illinois, for training on the B-29 engines. Then I went to a replacement depot in Greensboro, North Carolina.

While I was at Greensboro, the War ended. I remember that I was in Chicago on a weekend pass on VJ-Day. We had been invited to go swimming at a local country club and after supper they announced that Japan had surrendered. The party almost came to a dead stop. Everybody went into a kind of quiet deep thought of thankfulness that it was all over. Then the big push by Congress was to "bring the boys home." Those without enough points to get out of the service were offered a chance to serve one year overseas with a guaranteed "out" at the end of that time. I opted to not do that.

I was sent back to San Antonio, Texas, as a Flight Chief on the single-engine AT-6. That was an unarmed plane used for training. We kept the plane maintained and operating for pilots coming back from overseas so they could get their necessary hours of flying time in. That way they would be able to collect flight pay for their last month of service before they were discharged. I stayed in San Antonio another six or seven months until I was honorably discharged. I entered the service as an Aviation Cadet and came out as a Private. They gave us separation money and I returned home.

I had good training in the military and enjoyed what I did. I didn't seem to have any ill effects from my military experience.

—Interviewed by Marcus McLeroy, August, 2001

GEORGE W. "BILL" HAYNES

I was born, December 28, 1925, in Sylacauga, Alabama. My mother said that day was so cold that water being heated on the wood burning stove froze. I grew up in Sylacauga, playing tennis, basketball, football, and baseball.

While still in high school, I had joined the Enlisted Reserve Corps (ERC) of the Army Air Corps, so that I could finish high school. They were drafting people even before they finished high school but by being in the ERC, I was able to finish. I graduated on a Wednesday, in May of 1944. The next day, Thursday, I had my papers, and the following Monday, May 31, I was in the Service.

I was inducted at Ft. McPherson in Atlanta and was then shipped to Keesler Air Force Base in Biloxi, Mississippi. They put us in a black tar-papered building with no air conditioning and turned off the fans while we took a battery of tests that lasted eight hours. The water was just running off our faces. Out of 200 people, five passed the tests. They ended up spending the rest of the War washing air planes in Columbus, Mississippi. The rest of us went into Gunnery training.

The training consisted mostly of two hours close-order drill, two hours of extended-order drill, two hours of physical training, and two more hours of drills. I weighed 185 pounds when I sent into the Service and was pretty fit, but they dropped me to 155 pounds. The food wasn't exactly like my mother's cooking. I particularly remember the breakfasts at Keesler—little brown balls of green syrup that didn't hold you very long in that hot sun and exercise.

From Biloxi, we were sent by train to Kingman, Arizona, where we were trained to use 50-caliber machine guns, both turret driven and hand held. There would be a plane towing a sleeve and we would fly and shoot at that sleeve. We had one hot shot pilot and he liked to fly us into the Grand Canyon. If we fussed about it, he would make us sweep the floor while we were flying.

A really tragic thing happened while we were training on those guns. They had a row of 50 to 60 hand-held machine guns with the yoke dropped into a pipe. You had to learn to fire them. One young guy froze. He rode the gun up out of the turret and killed fifty people. He just blew them down. There were more people killed in that incident than the two months I was in World War II.

From Kingman we went to Flatpark in Tampa, Florida, which was a staging area. En route, I got to spend seven days at home. From Flatpark, I went to Avon Park, Florida, then on to Hunter Air Force Base, and finally to New Jersey.

We crossed the Atlantic on the *Queen Mary*. There were about 25,000 of us, including 400 black women in the Women's Army Corps (WAC). English food has never been very highly rated, and I ate so many of those sugar wafers that I can't stand them to this day. We arrived in Glasgow, Scotland, to a big band playing. We thought it was for us, but it was for the English soldiers coming back from Africa. Interesting how you think only of yourself, but then you grow up pretty quickly.

We were shipped down to an airbase where I was stationed with the Eighth Air Force, 306th Bomb Group, 423rd Bomb Squadron. Our squadron was called the "Clay Pigeon Squadron." Later they made a movie about it, called "Twelve O'Clock High." We were there approximately two months before VE-Day.

We were actually in London the night before VE–Day. They sent us all back to our bases, knowing that they were getting ready to sign the papers. They didn't want problems with the English and Americans celebrating too much.

Our next assignment was to do photo mapping. A "top secret" mission, it was called the "Casey Jones Project." We photo mapped at 20,000 feet all of Europe, Africa, the Azore Islands, Sweden, and Norway. We tried to map Spain but they shot at us even though the War was over. Spain was not our friend during the War. The pictures were so good that you could see a person smoking a cigarette from 20,000 feet. The purpose of the mapping was in case of future wars they could fly over and tell if there were any underground changes or silos.

After two months in England, they sent another staff sergeant and myself to a Luftwaffe base in Gieberstadt, Germany. We were supposed to maintain order while we were there. I was in charge and we had all these Luftwaffe barracks. The people who had lived in those barracks would come back at night and try to steal the furniture. One night we caught a guy and we were going to turn him over the Yugolsavs who were holding the German prisoners. When we found out he was the only one who could keep the generators running to supply electricity for the whole city, we had to let him go.

Then they brought us back to England and we started flying down to the Azores to photograph those islands. One day in November, 1945, I was flying on a B-17 from Bedford, England, to the Azores. Although the official reason was to do photo mapping, the real purpose was so the high ranking officers could buy watches at $5 each and then sell them (for $350-$500 each) to the Russians in Berlin. Because of the long distance it was necessary to carry two extra 500 gallon tanks of fuel in the bomb bays. Four hours out our right in–board engine blew up, cutting a big gash in the horizontal stabilizer. We would get the fire stopped with the fire extinguisher then it would start up again. I promised God that if He would get us out of that, I would live my life for him.

I believe that my mother's prayers saved us on that plane. On that island I could see her as clearly as I saw her in 1948. She had on a white skirt. I can see her as clearly today as I did then.

It took seven years and many prayers and heart tugs but I finally joined the First Baptist Church in Sylacauga. When you truly believe in Jesus Christ and let the Holy Spirit enter your heart you join a larger family. Mark 3:35 says, "For whosoever shall do the will of God, the same is my brother, and my sister, and mother."

The Azores were beautiful but there wasn't much to do. We didn't even have church services. The food was plentiful. We used to take stalks of bananas back to London and sell each banana for $5 because the English hadn't had bananas in four or five years. We also spent time in Meritec, mapping the Sahara Desert. We would photo map and then they would tell us to go back and do it again because the sands would keep shifting. We also went to Dakar. One of the saddest sights at Dakar was to see the malnourished children with their bloated stomachs, smoking marijuana. You could smell it when you walked down the streets.

I spent the remainder of my service based outside of Marseille, France. I was able to take the train and visit places like, Nice and the Riviera. I would also take a jeep and drive up to Avignon. That City was the seat of the Roman Catholic Church when it moved out of Rome. One of my English teachers had always told me to try to see all the churches and I think I've seen almost every church in England, southern France, Germany, and Africa.

One of our last missions was a flight photographing from Istriss to Paris. Just before we got to Paris we had an engine catch fire. We were able to put it out but coming back it flared up again. Normally on a B-17, if you can get the fire out everything is OK, but if it's a hidden fire then when you cut the engines the plane blows up That was not uncommon. As we landed, doing 80-90 miles per hour, all of the crew except the engineer and pilot were to jump out of the plane before they cut the engine.

When it came my turn to jump, I kept looking down at that blacktop and hanging on to that door. You really had to dive and roll so that the stabilizer wouldn't hit you on the head. Our volunteer gunner kept yelling, "Get out!" Finally I turned loose. We were all skinned up pretty badly from one end to the other. They taxied on down to the end of the runway before they cut the engine but nothing happened. It's funny now, but it wasn't funny then.

Flying in those B-17's was quite an experience. They weren't pressurized so you were flying with oxygen masks the whole time. A lot of people got frost bite in Europe because when you were flying at that altitude it was anywhere from 20 to 60 degrees below zero. If you opened the windows to stick a gun out, and didn't have your hands and face covered, and your electric suit functioning, you could freeze pretty quickly.

We came home, then, from Le Havre, about 3,500 of us on a Liberty ship. It was a rough crossing and a lot of people were sick. But we made it across and docked at New York City. I never will forget seeing the Statue of Liberty. We had two or three days in New York City. I remember going to Times Square and Doris Day was singing in the restaurant we went to. Then it was home to Sylacauga. I was discharged from the Service, June 15, 1946, having been awarded the EAME Service Medal with Bronze Star, the American Theater Service Medal, the Good Conduct Medal, the World War II Victory Medal, and the Occupation Medal.

My military service changed my life. Had I not gone into service, I probably would have gone into sports. When I did come back after the War, I had several calls from different colleges, wanting me to play football. Somehow, it didn't interest me. I wound up at Georgia Tech. I met Eleanor on a blind date, in 1948, while I was a junior at Tech. We were married August 27, 1950. We have two children, Steve and Lisa.

—Interviewed by Harland Armitage, July, 2001

Bill Haynes

OTIS CALLEY (O.C.) HUBERT

O.C. Hubert was born in Allen's Mill, Alabama, in 1906. He attended Chambers County High School in Milltown, Alabama. Later he attended evening school at Georgia Tech and at Woodrow Wilson School of Law. He married his wife, Ruth, July 1, 1933, in Birmingham, Alabama, at Ruth's sister's home.

At the outbreak of World War II, O.C. was working at Georgia Power Company. Because of his age (36), he had to pull some strings to get into the Service. In 1943, he sought a commission in the Navy Air Corps. Following his basic training at Quonset Point, Rhode Island, O.C. was commissioned as a Lieutenant. He was then sent to Corpus Christi, Texas, for further training. In 1944, O.C. took his family with him to Texas, where they lived near the Base. While in Texas, O.C. bought some cotton acreage and some citrus groves. This provided him a "stake" to get started in the real estate business after the War.

O.C. Hubert was loyal and dedicated but he was not a combat sailor. Because of his age, he felt he was not strictly needed or essential. Nevertheless, he was anxious to serve and volunteered at every opportunity. In early 1944, he again volunteered to go overseas and was sent to the South

Pacific (New Guinea), where he was assigned to the staff of Admiral Kincaid of the Seventh Fleet. O.C. used to tell how his office was down the hall from General Douglas MacArthur's office. He would frequently see the General walk by his door.

Later, O.C. was sent to the Philippines, near Luzon. While there, he discovered a large cache of materials, food, and bedding, which had been stockpiled at some remote place and forgotten. O.C. was then put in charge of marshaling the food resources before an important battle. For this effort he received a commendation and medal.

O.C. was in the South Pacific for both VE-Day and VJ-Day. Later that year he contracted pneumonia and was evacuated to Perth, Australia, to recover. He returned to the U.S., slim and trim, in September, 1945. To get home, O.C. caught a flight from Australia through Hawaii to San Francisco, and from there to the house at 492 Hardendorf Avenue, Atlanta. To the surprised delight of his family, he showed up wearing a new blue uniform and his service medals, and declared the only things he wanted were a glass of milk and some real eggs. The family remembers that he hated Spam the rest of his life.

In late 1945, O.C. Hubert mustered out of the Navy as a Lt. Commander and returned to his job with Georgia Pacific. With his two brothers, O.C. soon formed his own real estate company. After his oldest child, Richard, graduated from Bass High School in Atlanta in 1952, O.C. moved his wife and his daughters Marilyn, Judith, and Deborah to Skyview Drive in Marietta.

O.C. Hubert died on June 2, 1986.

—Information furnished by O.C. Hubert's son, Richard Hubert, September, 2002

O. C. Hubert

HARVEY N. HYATT

I was born at Georgia Baptist Hospital, grew up in Atlanta, and graduated from Fulton High School. I remember the day the Japanese bombed Pearl Harbor. A buddy and I were down at the rifle range near the Federal Penitentiary, digging metal slugs out of the bank. When we got home, we heard on the radio about the bombing. We never went back to the rifle range because it was federal property and they closed access to it.

On January 23, 1945, a friend and I joined the Navy. It was either join or get drafted into the Army. We had Army ROTC in high school and we didn't want any part of the Army. It was about a month before my eighteenth birthday when we joined.

We did ten weeks of boot camp at U.S. Naval Recruiting Depot at Bainbridge, Maryland. I was in the medical corps school when Germany surrendered. Then I went to the U.S. Naval Hospital at Quantico, Virginia, and was there when Japan surrendered in August, 1945. We didn't see any combat service.

Several of us got tired of hospital duty so we applied for overseas. We were sent, first, to the U.S. Naval Air Station at Patuxent River, Maryland. Then they sent us to the Armed Guard Center in Brooklyn, New York. To give us something to do they put us on shore patrol duty in Brooklyn. Finally, in March, 1946, we went by Liberty ship to Camp Home Run in Le Havre, France. From there, we caught a ferry to

Southampton, England. I had my first taste of English mustard there. It was so hot it almost knocked my head off. I don't remember what I ate but I sure remember that mustard.

We went on to London to await orders. After two or three nights in a great big mansion which had been taken over by the USO, we took an overnight train to Stanrock, Scotland. Then it was another ferry to Laurene, Northern Ireland, then a train on to Londonderry. I was a Pharmacist Mate Third Class at a radio relay station. We had one doctor, one chief pharmacist and three or four of us seamen.

When it was time for us to come back home, we just reversed course. I got home on July 4th.

After getting out of the service and attending Georgia State College for a while, I went to work for Standard Oil Company of Kentucky. I stayed in the Reserves though. Then the Korean War started and every time the phone rang I thought, "One of these days that call will be for me." And soon it was. I spent twenty-one months as a Pharmacist Mate at the West End Dispensary, Marine Forward Recruiting Depot, Parris Island, South Carolina. We took care of a lot of feet there. One fellow came in and when the doctor told him to take his shoes over to the Sitz bath (meaning for him to soak his feet), he soaked his shoes instead. Great big fellows would come in with foot problems. We would get a knife and whittle a little on them, not even drawing blood, and some of them would pass out. I stayed in the service, then, until 1954.

Would I do it again? I think I would. Everybody wanted to be in. They wanted to fight for their country. Back then you were a coward, or 4F, or everybody looked down on you if you weren't in the Service.

After my military service, I went back to working for Standard Oil. Altogether, I worked 35 years for them. The last job I had was driving a transport truck with a tractor trailer delivering diesel fuel and gasoline. I retired in January, 1982.

I met my wife, Mary Jane Camp, at First Baptist Church of Atlanta. There wasn't a Singles program at Marietta First Baptist then so she and Imogene Keck would come to Atlanta. I was secretary of the training union and I got to introduce them. I said, "We have two visitors, Imogene Keck and Mary Jane Camp." It was three months before I knew which was which. We dated for about three years and were married on July 3, 1969.

—Interviewed by Harland Armitage, September, 2001

Harvey Hyatt

JAMES, JOSEPH, BILLY, AND PHIL INGRAM
With
Ellen Ingram

James Ingram—

Altogether, I had six brothers and four of them fought in World War II. My oldest brother, James, was born in Nelson, Georgia, in 1919. He graduated from high school during the Depression and Dad got him a job at a textile mill in Chicopee, Georgia. He eventually became a Master Welder and worked in the textile mills until he retired.

Although James was the oldest of my brothers, he was the last to go into the Service because he was married and had two children. I think he was 25, in 1944, when he entered the military at Fort Leonard Wood, Missouri. He was a foot soldier in the Army and was in hand-to-hand combat in France and Germany. He really had it rough.

James didn't talk much about his experiences in the War. I did hear him tell about having to kill a German soldier. The Germans started advancing on his foxhole and the commanding officer told them to fire. "They're going to kill you if you don't," the officer told them. James looked up and was looking into the barrel of a gun. He said, "I had no choice." I'm sure he had killed others but this one was so close it really affected him. In reading over his letters to my mother, he simply said that he was in some big battles and had two narrow escapes. Then he began to write about how he appreciated what God had done for him, and what a help it had been that he could pray and believe. And he thanked Mother.

He was in Europe when the War ended. He had been told that he would be sent back to the States to train for combat in Japan. Fortunately, he didn't have to go.

James is widowed and lives in an assisted living facility in Gainesville, Georgia.

Joseph Ingram—

Joe was my next brother. He was born in 1920 and he was the first of the boys to go into Service. He had attended Georgia Southern College (formerly Georgia Teachers College) with a major in Industrial Arts. He was in his first year of teaching and they allowed him to finish the year before they took him into active duty. That was August 22, 1942. Joe attended Air Force Officer Candidate School (OCS) but they found out he was color blind so they wouldn't let him continue.

Joe spent most of his War duty time in England. He was there throughout all the bombing—the Blitz every night. I think, as a result of that and the weather, he never wanted to travel overseas. He was part of the Air Service Command Depot and worked on the repair and inspection of almost every type of aircraft used in the European Theater. While Joe was overseas, he was able to get together with a couple of our other brothers. It meant the world to them.

When Joe got out of the service, he worked, first, in the fertilizer business and then formed his own insurance agency. He was very active and civic minded and served as Mayor of their little town. He and his wife had three daughters.

Joe died from a massive heart attack at the age of 58, in 1978.

Billy Ingram—

Next was Bill, who was actually named Billy. The military wanted to put his name down as William, but he said, "No." Bill entered the Air Force on November 21, 1942, at the age of 23. He went to OCS and became a navigator. As a navigator, Bill was part of the India-Burma Theater of War. He "flew the Hump," (missions over the mountain range there) in a B-24.

Bill's plane was shot down and all of the crew, except for Bill and the tail gunner, were killed. The last thing Bill saw after he bailed out was the plane crashing into the mountains. It was pitch black night. Bill didn't know where he was so he lay down and went to sleep. The next morning, he buried his parachute as he had been taught to do and had started walking out of the mountains when he saw some soldiers coming. Fortunately, they were friendly and got him across the line, back to the camp where he was stationed. The air crews had some sort of system that allowed them a certain number of hours to get back to base if they had been shot down. Bill got back two hours before his deadline was up. Otherwise, Mother and Daddy would have gotten a telegram that he was missing.

Bill had a hard time dealing with all of that, especially the loss of his crew. They sent him back to Miami for R & R. It was six or eight months before he was actually able to go and talk to the families of his crew members.

Bill decided to make the military his career. He had 30 years and retired as a Lt. Colonel. He loved the military. During the Korean War, he met up in Korea with one of my other brothers (who had stayed in the Reserves and was called back up). Bill spent two tours of duty in Japan. He was also in Hawaii. Then he headed up the ROTC program at the University in Scottsboro, Mississippi. Bill was awarded the Distinguished Flying Cross and the Air Medal with Oak Leaf Clusters.

Bill is 80 and lives in Lakeland, Florida. He and his wife have four children.

Phil Ingram—

Philip was the third brother, born in 1923. He went into the Service in 1943, at age 21. He, too, was a foot soldier and had it pretty rough. He was in communications and radio. Phil is the one who got to see Joe more often because Phil was in Germany and France. Phil was the brother who was recalled for the Korean War and met Bill several times in Korea.

Following the War, Phil worked mostly in retail sales. He managed a Woolworth store and they were transferred a good bit. He and his wife had three children. Phil is retired and lives in Florida.

My two younger brothers, Bobby and Jack, were also in the Service but that was after the War. Bobby was in the Air Force and Jack was in the Army.

Ellen Ingram—

Our father was a stone cutter with Georgia Marble Company. He worked many years in Nelson, Georgia. Because of the nature of his work, we moved a number of times. When I was eighteen, in 1944, we moved to Marietta. My parents and I joined Marietta First Baptist Church in 1945. I had finished high school by then and because of my mother's poor health, I didn't go away to college. Instead I took business courses locally.

My first job was at Bell Aircraft during the War. I started out as a mail clerk. We delivered the mail throughout the plant by bicycle. Then I got promoted and delivered confidential mail (on foot, and dressed to the hilt) to the executive offices. When the War ended, everybody was terminated. I've also worked at Stephens Lumber Company, and for the Tax Collector. My last job, at which I worked for twenty-eight and a half years, was as Payroll Supervisor for the Marietta Board of Education.

During the War, the rationing didn't bother us too much. Shoes and gasoline were scarce, but we felt we had so much more than many people. We managed to still have fun. We would have scrap iron drives where we would go out and collect any kind of scrap metal that could be recycled.

When we first came to Marietta, we couldn't find a place to live, so the five of us had a two-bedroom apartment in the basement of a house on Hill Street. There was another family of four in another apartment in that basement and we all shared one bathroom. That was kind of wild. After three months, we found this house on Stewart Avenue, and I have lived here ever since. My parents died in 1977, eleven weeks apart. They were very devoted to each other. I'm glad that it worked out that I could take care of them.

—Interviewed by Ruth Miller, September, 2001

James Ingram

Joe Ingram

Billy Ingram

Phil Ingram

WILLIAM C. INGRAM
With
Mrs. Will Ingram and
Mary Ingram Wheeler

William C. Ingram entered the Army at Ft. McClellan, Alabama, in the spring of 1942. He was 25 years old at the time, eager and ready to serve. The day he left for the service, he had the record player volume turned up as loud as it would go, playing "Down Yonder," his favorite song.

After doing postal work at Camp Stoneman, California, Will went to Officer Candidate School at Fort Benning, Georgia. He was commissioned as a 2nd Lieutenant, then served at Fort Leonard Wood in Missouri, and Camp Laguna, Arizona. He was eventually stationed in Northern Ireland. While fighting in France in July and August, 1944, he was wounded in the arm and chest. Following initial treatment in a hospital in England, he was sent to Baker General Hospital, Martinsburg, West Virginia. He was a patient there from April, 1945 to February, 1946.

Will Ingram married Frances Hubbard of Newnan, Georgia, on August 12, 1945, while he was still a patient at the hospital. The war ended while they were on their honeymoon in Atlanta. There were people celebrating in the streets.

Will Ingram attained the rank of 1st Lieutenant. He was awarded the Bronze Star, the Purple Heart, and other medals and ribbons. His younger brother says, "There was no one prouder than Will to be a soldier."

After the War, Will worked for the United States Postal Service until his retirement at age 55. He died August 12, 1977, at age 60.

—Information furnished by Mary Ingram Wheeler

Will Ingram

ANDY JANSAK

My parents came to the United States from Czechoslovakia in about 1914. I was born in Corinth, New York, in 1917. We then moved to New Jersey. My father died in 1924, leaving my mother with five kids under the age of nine—two girls and three boys. When my mother couldn't handle bringing up five children, the State placed us in foster homes. The girls were sent to Camden, New Jersey. The boys were given to a nice lady, Mrs. Archer, in Adelphia, New Jersey. In 1932, we were able to get back with my mother in Bronx, New York. We went to school there.

I was drafted into the Army in 1941 and served for 27 years. I didn't really want to go but the War hadn't really started so it wasn't too bad. I took basic training at Pine Camp, New York (which is now Fort Bluff). In September, 1941, I went to Ft. Knox, Kentucky, and stayed a couple of years. I made First Sergeant in 1942. My Division transferred to Fort Campbell, Kentucky, and I was promoted to Warrant Officer in December, 1943. Late in 1944, we went to Boston, Massachusetts, and from there to Europe. I stayed in Germany until the War in Europe ended.

We didn't see too much action where we were based. We landed in Le Havre, France, and went across into Germany. I was in a reconnaissance battalion which was far ahead of the Division. I was Supply Officer so I didn't do much of the shooting.

In February, 1945, we went into what looked like a

deserted town. From one house the Germans opened fire, and one of my good friends, a Lieutenant, was knocked out of the turret of the armored car but he survived. We backed off then. Another time we came up on a bridge and a couple of soldiers there from the Third Infantry Division (they were about the best over there) said, "What are you going to do here?" I said, "We're going take this bridge." They said, "We took it three days ago."

Another time, I confiscated a Mercedes. I put it behind my jeep. One day the Colonel said, "Andy, get rid of that car." I said, "What car?" He said, "You know what car." We had a lot of memories like that—fellows raiding the wine cellars... other than that, it was pretty normal.

I had a brother who was a B-26 pilot. We had been trying to get together. Finally, he flew into Salzburg, Austria. We were just outside Salzburg. He went up to the driver of this two and a half ton truck and said, "Do you know a Warrant Officer by the name of Jansak?" The kid said, "He's my boss." When the fighting was over we flew back to Benlow, Holland, and I stayed with my brother for about twelve days. Then he flew me back to Austria.

When the fighting ended in Europe, we were given 30 days R&R (Rest and Recuperation) leave back in the States. Then we were supposed to go to the Far East but VJ-Day came so we didn't have to go. I went to California with my unit to be discharged. I was having a little medical problem and decided to stay in until I got it straightened out. I got better and I got orders for the Philippines, so over I went. I stayed there twenty-six months. I found the Filipino people very nice. By the time I got back I had almost ten years so I decided to stay in the Service.

I came back from the Philippines in 1949 and was sent to Fort Jackson, South Carolina, where I met Lee Threlkeld. We were married at Fort Jackson in 1950 and were sent to Germany for three years. From there we came back to Fort. Gillam here in Georgia. Then I did three consecutive overseas assignments in Korea, as a squad officer. The last tour, in 1965, I was up on the border DMZ (De-Militarized Zone). I was discharged as Chief Warrant Officer (W-4) at Fort McPherson on March 1, 1968. During my career in the Army, I was awarded the Bronze Star for Occupation of Germany, European African Medal, Eastern Campaign Medal, World War II Victory Medal, American Defense Service Medal, American Campaign Medal, Armed Forces Reserve Medal, National Defense Service Medal, and the Army Communication Medal.

Most of my Army career was spent doing engineering supply work. I had a lot of other jobs, too, including Administrative Assistant. I ran a golf course for a while at Fort MacPherson. I spent 27 years in the military service.

(Andy Jansak died on April 28, 2002)

—Interviewed by George Beggs, June, 2001

Andy Jansak

LEE THRELKELD JANSAK

I grew up on a farm in the Piedmont section of South Carolina, graduating from high school in 1937. My father had died when I was sixteen, leaving my mother with four children to raise. I was aided in school by President Roosevelt's National Recovery Act, specifically the National Youth Administration. In exchange for this aid, I was required to perform light tasks at my high school.

College was not an option because funds were not available. My grandmother was a midwife so it just seemed to be my calling to be a nurse. I entered nurse's training in Anderson, South Carolina, in January, 1938. Books were furnished and tuition was not charged. We received $10 per month during our first and second years, and $12 per month for the third year. There were ten trainees in my class and we lived in nurses' quarters under strict discipline. We ate our meals in the hospital dining room where absolute decorum was required. Our classes were taught by the staff doctors and nurses. We were "on probation" for the first six months. I completed the three-year diploma program in February, 1941.

After passing the State Boards in June, I joined the Red Cross. I also did a little private-duty nursing. One patient I nursed was a racketeer in Atlanta. He had been shot and was in the hospital in Anderson. He was a young man and very impolite. As I sat in his room one evening, I read my mail. In it was a letter from the Red Cross saying, "We need you."

When I read this letter a smile came over my face and I thought, "I'll go into the Army. I won't nurse people like you." I volunteered for the Army Nurse Corps and reported for duty at Fort Bragg, North Carolina, on August 2, 1941.

At Fort Bragg, I did hospital duty and learned about Army life—how, when, and whom to salute, marching in formation, bivouacking, pitching pup tents, eating out of mess kits, drinking from canteens. The Army furnished our blue dress uniforms and our white hospital uniforms. We lived in barracks (crude by today's standards); however, the rooms were private. We were paid $70 per month (the average civilian pay was $50). Bottled Cokes at break time cost five cents.

I was honored to be asked to join the 65th General Hospital Unit, affiliated with Duke University. In order to join the unit I had to receive permission from the chief nurse—a Captain with 26 years Army service. She was not enthusiastic over the idea because I would be joining a unit composed of nurses with no Army background. She ultimately relented, gave permission, and I was to learn later how fortunate such a move was in being assigned to a general hospital rather than an evacuation unit. Our unit consisted of 500 enlisted men, 50 doctors, 120 nurses, three Red Cross personnel, three physical therapists, three dieticians, and six administrative Army officers. Our commanding officer was a World War I veteran, and a full Colonel with 27 years of military service.

We departed Fort Bragg in *winter* uniforms in August, 1943, by un-air-conditioned troop train. Three days later we reached our destination, Camp Shanks, just outside New York City. There we changed our uniforms from navy blue to olive drab. Due to a shortage of uniforms our departure for overseas had to be delayed. We were sent to Fort Devens, Massachusetts, until we could be re-supplied. While there we had further training, including ship evacuation procedures and negotiating obstacles courses. Our gear was a helmet, gas mask, mess kit, and canteen.

We sailed aboard the *Queen Elizabeth* from New York to Scotland in October, 1943. As we marched up the ship's plank, the band was playing "Pistol Packin' Mama." Suddenly the music stopped and they started playing "I Want a Girl Just Like the Girl that Married Dear Old Dad." We later learned that a World War I Army nurse, sister to then-Secretary of War, Henry L. Stimson, was an official greeter for the nurses boarding the ship. She told the band leader that the music was inappropriate for nurses boarding a ship for overseas duty in time of war. Thereupon, he abandoned "Pistol Packin' Mama" for the latter selection.

We zigzagged across the Atlantic Ocean in a record-breaking three days, dodging enemy submarines all the way. The *Queen Elizabeth* was, and still is, the fastest ocean liner on the seas. Designed as a luxury liner, the ship was converted to a troop carrier. Only two ports in the world could accommodate the ship: New York City and Southampton, England. The ship docked in the Firth of Clyde off the Scottish coast near Glasgow. Before anyone was allowed to leave the ship, the British Air Commodore came aboard to address us over the loudspeaker. After welcoming us to British soil, he told us that although there was class distinction in his country, there was no color distinction, and that we would remember that at all times!

We were then ferried to land where we boarded the troop train for an overnight ride through Scotland. People throughout the countryside lined the railroad tracks, displaying the "V" (victory) sign. The gesture, which was initiated by Winston Church, was a great morale builder.

Our first duty assignment was in a mountainous resort near Great Malvern, Worcestershire, England. Many wealthy Londoners, the elderly, and children had been evacuated to there to escape the Blitz. I had my first experience owning and riding a bicycle, the most common form of transportation there.

The English were great hosts, freely sharing their

homes for afternoon tea and occasional evening meals. One family, who were very proud of their Royal Air Force son, invited four of us to dinner. The son had been seeing an American girl, and the parents were anxious for their daughter to meet an American soldier. Our foursome included a prospect who was heir to large textile mills in North Carolina, and a staunch Republican. As we gathered around the fire after dinner, the young man expressed a negative opinion about President Roosevelt. Our host practically ushered us out of the house, signaling an abrupt end to the soldier's future with the daughter! I would also like to mention Peter and Don, child refugees from London, who often ate their meals with our unit.

We established a general hospital at Great Malvern, and received casualties from North Africa, Sicily, and Italy. The majority of our patients were rehabilitated and returned to their units in preparation for D-Day. In March, 1944, the Air Corps was suffering heavy casualties, and their nearest medical facility was a station hospital with minimum staff and surgical expertise. The 65th was requested to replace the station hospital, and I was selected for the advance cadre of hospital personnel.

Our hospital was formed at Bottesdale in Suffolk, England. It served the Eighth Air Force casualties and thousands of others. My first patient on the neurosurgical ward was a young Lieutenant fighter pilot who had crashed on trying to land at the air field. He had lost a portion of his frontal skull. He was awake during the surgery while bone fragments were removed from his skull. After the surgery, his head and face were bandaged to include his eyes, with his nose and mouth as the only openings. The patient was warned that he should not cough or sneeze and should be perfectly still for fear of spinal cord rupture. He remained under our care for six months then was sent to England Hospital in New York, where they put a silver plate in his skull. The silver skull plate had been crafted in London and was sent to the States with the patient. This was considered quite revolutionary at that time. After the war, I enjoyed a visit with this patient. He had often commented during those months of recovery, that he could picture me in his mind's eye. When his bandages were removed, he said that I looked exactly as he had imagined!

We experienced numerous air raids, and were required to don our helmets, take a gas mask, and return to our duty station in complete darkness, with only a flashlight to guide our way. On one occasion, a bomb fell just outside of our compound, leaving a large crater in the ground. As the war was winding down and blackout conditions were less observed, German aircraft strafed our village, mistaking it for an Air Corps runway. Two enlisted men were injured during that episode and given Purple Hearts—even though they were actually in a pub at the time.

At the close of the war in Europe a point system based on length of service determined who would return first to the States. Due to my longevity, I soon boarded the *Queen Elizabeth* for what proved to be its last voyage from the Firth of Clyde. Afterwards, the ship returned to its home port in Southampton and became a luxury liner again.

The plan was for me to return home for 30 days leave with family, and then be redeployed to the Pacific. However, the atomic bombs dropped on Nagasaki and Hiroshima brought the war to a close and my services were no longer needed. Following my leave, I reported to Fort Selbert, Alabama (long since deactivated), the temporary home to 6,000 nurses awaiting a return to civilian life. Since I was in the Reserve, I received a discharge.

I worked for a year at the VA hospital in Columbia, South Carolina, then returned to the Army Nurse Corps. I was assigned to Fort Jackson, South Carolina, where I met the officer who was to become my lifelong mate. Shortly after Andy and I were married, I was given orders for

Korea. These were later changed and I went to Fort Gordon, Georgia. My Army career was interrupted by the arrival of the first of our three children. I resigned from the service in October, 1951. Several years later I resumed my nursing career as a civilian nurse with the Army at Fort McPherson, Georgia. I served there for 21 years.

In May, 2001, I attended a reunion of the 65th General Hospital, a yearly tradition since the end of the war—52 years! Held this year at Duke University, we were hosted by the Medical Alumni Association, whose representative expressed much appreciation for our wartime contributions. Regrettably, only two of our unit's physicians are still living, but they both attended the reunion, along with 70 others, including ten nurses. Although our numbers thin with each passing year, we still have a great spirit of unity and enjoy reliving many of our World War II experiences.

As I look back on my Army days, I have a deep sense of appreciation for all who served in the Armed Forces. It was a period of great adventure and a remarkably character-building influence in our lives. It was an honor and experience that I would not exchange for anything... yet I would not like to repeat it. I shall always be grateful for the opportunity to serve my country and to work alongside some of the finest personnel the medical community had to offer.

—Written by Lee T. Jansak

Lee Jansak

CHARLES B. JOHNSON
With
Kathleen H. Johnson

Charles B. Johnson was born in Atlanta, Georgia, September 3, 1916. He graduated from Boys' High School. Upon his graduation from Georgia Tech in 1938, he received a reserve officer commission in the Army. He was called into service on December 26, 1941 (at age 25). He reported to Fort McPherson. After taking a refresher course at Fort Monroe, Virginia, he was sent to the Bermuda Base Command where he served as a Battery Commander. He was in Bermuda for three and one-half years, during which time he had one two-week leave.

Charles and Kathleen were married two years before he went into the Service. For the first two years of Charles's military service, Kathleen lived with her parents in Atlanta and worked as a secretary. She wrote to her husband almost every day. In February, 1944, Kathleen joined Charles in Bermuda. She worked as a secretary in the Army Headquarters. They rented a house, "Atlanta By the Sea" in Tucker's Town and enjoyed being together until the Base closed in the spring of 1945. Kathleen remembers VE-Day as "thrilling." They were back in Atlanta by the time VJ-Day came along.

Charles was separated from the Service in October,

1945, at Ft. Monmouth, New Jersey, and took the train home to Atlanta. During his time in the Army, he attained the rank of Captain and was awarded the Atlantic Theater Ribbon. Charles was lucky not to see any combat but he helped defend Bermuda as an important Army, Navy, and Air Force Base.

After the War, Kathleen remembers going, with Charles, to Muse's Men's Store in Atlanta, where he bought three suits because he had no civilian clothes. Following his military service, Charles owned and managed a soft drink bottling company. Later he became a real estate appraiser.

Charles B. Johnson died on July 28, 2000

—Information furnished by Kathleen H. Johnson. Charles B. Johnson was the father of Charles B. Johnson, Jr.

Charles Johnson

George Johnson

GEORGE JOHNSON
And
Evelyn Stephenson Johnson

George Johnson

The biggest thing I remember about Pearl Harbor is coming home when I was about sixteen and seeing my daddy crying. He said, "They just announced on the radio that Pearl Harbor has been attacked and that we are at war." Born in 1884, my daddy had known a lot of veterans (even Civil War veterans) and he realized how awful this was.

I wanted to enlist immediately, even though I was just in the eleventh grade. My dad wouldn't sign for me to do that. So I took the Air Corps test to become an aviation cadet. I passed that and was sworn in, put in the Reserve, and went back to high school. Two days before graduation I was called to active duty. My high school principal, W.O. Chaney, had to talk the Commandant at Fort McPherson out of an overnight pass so I could attend my own graduation.

Two days earlier, I had attended Evelyn's graduation from Girls High in Atlanta. We had been going together about two years. The night of her graduation, I had given her an engagement ring.

I entered the Army Air Corps at Fort McPherson and was sent to Keesler Field in Biloxi, Mississippi, for basic training. I remember riding the train and having to stand up most of the way. The reason for basic training was to harden you and shape you into a person who would do what you were told, to prepare you for military life. It seems like it rained all the time. It was a hot, muggy, miserable time.

During basic training another fellow, Charlie, (from Stone Mountain) and I got a lot of kidding (about being from Georgia) from the New York and New Jersey Yankees. They wanted to know where our red suspenders were and how it felt to wear shoes for the first time. They were never able to tease us about our shooting, though, because Charlie and I scored 197 out of a possible 200 points on the firing range.

Once, on my day off, I went fishing, wearing just a pair of shorts, and got thoroughly sunburned. The next day we were to do gas mask training. After marching ten miles with field packs and full equipment, I was pretty raw. We were to stay in a bunker while they pumped tear gas in to test our gas masks. That gas just ate into my sunburn blisters and ruptured them on the way out. I almost bowled over a staff sergeant at the door as I left. The next day there was a general order issued that anyone who was foolish enough to get sunburned would be court marshaled.

After basic I was to go into aviation cadet training but this was late in the War and they decided they had enough cadets. While I was at Keesler, waiting for an opening in cadet training, I had gone to aircraft engine mechanics school and to B-24 specialist school. Essentially, I had been trained to be an aerial engineer on a B-24 so I was sent to Tyndal Field, Florida. My orders actually read, "Temporary Permanent Party." On my way to Tyndal I had a ten day pass so I went to Atlanta and married Evelyn. It was December 19, 1944.

At Tyndal we were assigned to taking care of and training gunners. We would take off in a B-24 at 6AM, fly out over the Gulf of Mexico and run either pro-target training sessions or live ammunition frangible bullet assignments. A P-63 would come in and attack us and our gunners would fire at the P-63's with the frangible bullets.

On one of these missions the number three engine on our plane caught on fire and flames were going back past the vertical stabilizer. I started for the fire extinguisher system which is behind the upper turret. At the same time a student gunner in the upper turret pulled his seat latch and dropped back and got stuck between me and the hose. It was a hairy situation. I finally put both of my feet on his shoulders and pushed to get him unstuck so that I could get to those hoses and cut off the fuel going to those engines, and to lighten the load on that side. Then I remembered that my parachute was down in the nose where I had stored it because I had to move around a good bit.

I immediately went down and got my parachute and we prepared to abandon ship. Fortunately we had a very experienced combat pilot that day. He side-slipped the plane and blew out the fire. We came back and landed and I couldn't believe all the fire trucks. When we stopped and got out I saw that the engine was burned almost completely away from the mounts and the skin on the bottom of the wings was horribly wrinkled. I began to get awfully weak-kneed after seeing that damage.

After several months at Tyndal the cadets opened up for flight engineer training on B-29's to go to the South Pacific. I volunteered and was sent to Maxwell Field. After that came the atomic bombs and the Japanese surrender. It was a great time of celebration, of course, but nobody knew what was going to happen to us. It seemed like we had 24-hours-a-day PT (we called it "Political Punishment"). And that's how I ended my military career—At Maxwell Field on November 9, 1945. I went in as an aviation cadet and came out the same rank. The day I was discharged, we found out Evelyn was expecting our first child. The government covered all the costs for that first baby.

We had a difficult time after the War—only a high school education and no experience. We lived with Evelyn's parents the first two years. I worked at a variety of jobs including rebuilding streetcars and buses, and as an elevator mechanic. Eventually I went to work for Lockheed and stayed there thirty years.

Evelyn Johnson

I was born at Grady Hospital in Atlanta and George was born at home. His folks lived so close to Grant Park that they could hear the lions at the zoo roaring when they were fed. While the Cyclorama was being built, George as a little boy would go play on the mounds of dirt that had been brought in to create the Cyclorama. We haven't strayed too far from our birth places.

I remember the war and the rationing of shoes, gasoline, and tires. My daddy's car was stolen and we found it jacked up with all the tires missing. Daddy got some more tires so that we could go and see his parents in south Georgia. Those tires were known as "May Pops" because they might pop before they got you where you were going.

After we were married, we lived on the base at Tyndol Field in a furnished apartment. We paid $25 a month for the place. We were young and we loved each other and I knew that George would look after me so I wasn't afraid to go with him.

After the War I worked at various jobs—Rich's, Internal Revenue Service, Lockheed. But I usually tell people that George made the living and I made the living worthwhile. We have three fine sons and are fortunate to have them living close by.

—Interviewed by George Beggs, November, 2001

EMMITT CLINTON JONES
With
Lucille Jones

Although my husband, Clinton, and I were both born in Cartersville, Georgia, we didn't know each other. He was born August 6, 1908, and was ten years older than I. We actually met in Atlanta, in 1939 or 1940, while I was attending Crighton Business College. We were dating at the time the Japanese bombed Pearl Harbor and that's when Clinton enlisted in the Army Air Corps.

Clinton entered the Service at Fort McPherson and was sent to Ogden, Utah. After that, he went to Fort Dix, New Jersey, and was shipped overseas to England as part of the Eleventh Air Special Group. Although he trained as an aircraft mechanic he also had a little medical training and almost always wound up in a doctor's office. Part of the time, he drove an ambulance.

Clinton took part in the invasion of North Africa and was stationed there for a long time. Just before he came home, he was sent to Italy for a while. He was actually on a ship coming home when the D-Day invasion took place.

We had corresponded all the time Clinton was overseas. When he came back home, we decided to get married. That was June 14, 1944. We lived in Miami, Florida, while Clinton finished out his time in the Service. He held the rank of Corporal when he was discharged.

Following the War, Clinton started working for Dixie Steel in Atlanta and worked there until September 10, 1956, when he was killed in an automobile accident. We had two small sons at the time.

I had started working at the Cobb Exchange Bank in Marietta, in 1954. The bank merged several times and was called First Bank and Trust when I retired in 1983.

I started attending First Baptist Church about 1950, when the children were young. I think I joined right after Clinton died.

—Interviewed by Ruth Miller, March, 2001

EMMETT C. JONES
674 Gaskill St.
Air Corps, Abroad

Clinton Jones

THOMAS DAVID JONES, SR.

I was born, October 22, 1918, in the front bedroom of my Grandmother Dickson's country home in a farming community near Madison, Georgia. We moved to Atlanta when I was about four years old and I attended schools there. I went to Bass Junior High School and then on to Tech High School, where I was on the tennis and track teams. I also played in the ROTC Marching Band.

After finishing Tech High School I attended Georgia Tech as a co-op student. I got a job with Georgia Power Company in the Appliance Repair Department. When the Japanese attacked Pearl Harbor I immediately quit my job and volunteered as a Navy pilot. However, I didn't pass the physical exam because my vision wasn't perfect. So I asked Georgia Power for my job back and they immediately returned me to the payroll.

About a year and a half later, I joined the Navy, again, as a Seabee (a construction unit). The Navy turned us over to the Marines for our basic training at Norfolk, Virginia. Although the Seabees were a non-combat unit, we still trained in combat techniques. I won the sharpshooter award and was given a war bond and a case of beer. The Marines hated the Seabees because of our guaranteed third class rating, which we received as a recruitment incentive. Consequently, our boot camp was rough. Our drill instructor was a many-times–demoted Marine PFC who deeply resented that our rating was one notch above his.

Following boot camp and a thirty-day leave, we were sent to Davisville, Rhode Island, where we learned to construct 10,000-gallon fuel tanks in just a few hours. The completed tanks were sent by ship to Freetown, South Africa, where we were to build a tank farm for refueling ships. These unusual tanks would float just below the surface. We were scheduled to join a convoy, aboard another ship, to South Africa. Our assignment ended when the Germans sank the transport carrying our tanks.

Next, the Navy loaded up 10,000 of us aboard the *Queen Elizabeth*. Because of a shortage of fresh water, they had boarded up the showers and bathrooms. We pulled out on Thanksgiving Day and were fed the traditional Thanksgiving meal. Unfortunately the food was contaminated and everyone got diarrhea. The Navy had a 10,000 man problem. They responded quickly with medication and we were soon back to normal. Since all the showers were boarded up, we stripped off our clothing and the Navy hosed all of us down with sea water. We solved our clothing problem by tying our clothes to ropes and throwing them overboard behind the ship until they were clean.

It took us ten days, along with a convoy of Battleships, Cruisers, and Destroyers, to reach New Caledonia. We immediately began constructing a landing strip, right behind a Japanese occupied island. It was here that we began to see the full impact of being issued a full sea bag of Navy gear plus a full set of Marine or Infantry gear, including the weapon, which in my case was a heavy Browning Automatic Rifle (BAR). Many men ruptured themselves climbing down the cargo net with this excessive load of equipment

Due to my sharpshooting skills, I was made the BAR man. I am grateful that I never had to use my skills because the BAR, due to its special effectiveness, usually drew immediate and intense enemy retaliation.

I worked in the Post Exchange (PX), issuing clothing. New Caledonia was a Navy supply base and receiving station and was often the target of Japanese undercover operations. They would sneak in at night to blow up stuff. We lived in Quonset huts and tents while the natives lived in wood houses with thatched roofs.

The food was good and nourishing but, according to tradition, we complained loud and long about everything except the coffee. Our coffee helped us to win the War. We ate an awful amount of Spam and fruit cocktail. We did get excited about the rumor that fresh meat was being shipped from New Zealand. It turned out to be goat meat. When it was being cooked, it smelled up the whole island. So we bought ourselves a soda and a can of peanuts and called it dinner. We should have received a medal for enduring the smell.

We were returned to the U.S. through San Diego. I had entered the Navy as a Third Class Ship Fitter and received just one promotion, to Second Class during the time I was in the Service. I was stateside on leave when VE-Day and VJ-Day occurred. It was a fantastic feeling to know the War was over.

At the end of my leave, I reported to Rhode Island and was then sent to Jacksonville, Florida, to be discharged. About twenty or twenty-five service men boarded the train in Rhode Island and since I was the senior ranking man, I was given charge of the records for all those men. When we crossed the state line into Georgia, the conductor made the black service men go to the back of the train. I was responsible for the men and we were supposed to stay together but I had to comply and send the men to the back. After my discharge, I took the train home to Atlanta.

I was, and still am, a patriotic person and am proud of my service. With three years and seven months, my only decoration was the Foreign Service Award. I am not a gambling man so I sent most of my pay home and my mother banked it for me. I had a really nice nest egg when I returned home to Decatur, Georgia. I went back to my job at Georgia Power Company and retired from there on May 1, 1981, to our farm in Rutledge, Georgia.

I met my wife, Dorothy, after discharge from active service. We married in February, 1947, and have been married almost 55 years. We have two sons and four grandchildren.

—Thomas Jones is the father of Rev. David Jones. Information supplied by Thomas Jones, January, 2002.

Thomas Jones

SAMUEL WALTER KELLY, JR.
With
W. Joe Kelly

My late brother, Walter, and I were both born in Seneca, South Carolina, but because our family moved to Atlanta when we were very young, we have always called Georgia home. We both attended S.M. Inman Elementary School, Bass Jr. High School, and Boys High School.

Walter graduated from Boys High in June, 1942, and was just living to get into the Army. However, our father persuaded him to go to military school at Clemson University. He stayed for one school year then, in June, 1943, enlisted in the Army. Walter had ROTC training both at Boys High and at Clemson and could have gotten a deferment but he wanted to be where the action was. He took his basic training at Fort Leonard Wood, Missouri, and then went into demolition work at another camp.

While Walter was working with an officer in a demolition demonstration, the officer evidently made a mistake and there was an explosion which killed the officer. Walter was standing close by and parts of the other man's body and skull were blown into him—a memory he carried to his dying day. Walter had severe trauma and was hospitalized for quite some time. His hearing was also affected. But he came out of that with one goal—to get back into the fight.

Walter then became a paratrooper and jumped in demonstration units as part of his training. He told me about one jump where he passed three other fellows who had jumped ahead of him. He hit pretty hard, but he was tough. Next he was sent to OCS at Fort Benning, Georgia, and still hadn't gotten to fight. He graduated and was commissioned a 2nd Lieutenant in 1944. I attended the ceremony. Walter was with the 82nd and they were training for the invasion of Japan. The world changed when the atomic bomb was dropped.

Walter got to go to Japan but he was part of the occupation forces. Although he was just a Lieutenant, he felt like Supreme Allied Commander of the little town where he was stationed. As part of his paratrooper training he had to learn to ride a motorcycle. He used to say they had more paratroopers who were hurt riding than jumping out of airplanes. In Japan he didn't have a motorcycle, he had a horse. It was always cold in northern Japan so the photos of Walter on his horse all show him bundled up.

Walter had a good sense of who he was. He was an Eagle Scout and a leader. He enjoyed telling about the day he inspected a bunch of new troops. Walking up and down the line, Walter saw a soldier who had been his ROTC officer at Boys High. The boy had given Walter a hard time because Walter had been a football player. Walter enjoyed walking up to him and saying, "Stand at attention, Soldier!"

Walter was proud of his World War II service and happy to be a part of it. He was disappointed that he didn't actually see action in either Europe or Japan. He had trained hard for it.

In 1946, Walter came home. After graduating from the University of Georgia, he returned to Marietta and joined Daddy Kelly in the car business. He was very active with the Salvation Army and the Boy Scout movement. He was also instrumental in the formation of the Honorary Commanders Association, which brought together the civilians of Marietta and the military people at Dobbins Air Force Base. Walter married in 1950. He and his wife, Elaine, had two sons: Samuel Walter Kelly III, and Michael Grant Kelly; and one daughter, Krissy Kelly Gibbs.

Walter's wife, Elaine died December 28, 1992. Walter Kelly died August 11, 2000.

—Interviewed by George Beggs, July, 2001

Walt Kelly on the left, in Japan

WILLIAM JOSEPH KELLY

While my brother, Walter, was serving overseas, I was finishing Boys High and hoping to get into the War before it ended. We at home coped with shortages. We rode buses and street cars and hitchhiked, which was quite safe at that time. No one complained. We just all supported the War effort, even the newspapers did. You would walk down the street, see a gold star in a window and know that someone in that household had been killed in the War. We had blackouts and, as a ninth grader, I was an air raid warden, making sure that everybody turned out their lights.

A lot of my friends volunteered for the military. Some of them had to lie about their age or get their daddies to sign so that they could go in. One of the most athletic and versatile tough young man I knew, was shot down on his first parachute jump.

We had a strong ROTC unit at Boys High. In fact, former Secretary of State, Dean Rusk, was a Colonel there. We had good military training. On VJ-Day, August, 1945, I enlisted in the Army. I saw the War missing me and wasn't happy about it. I was happy that the War had ended but not happy that I didn't get in. That fall, I went to Georgia Tech and played football. I turned eighteen on November 2, and January 16, 1946, I entered the Army at Fort McPherson.

I went to Fort Belvoir, Virginia, for basic training. Then my Colonel informed me that he was sending me to OCS. I said, "No, Sir, I have not signed up for that. I understand that the class has been going for three weeks already." I knew that the class had started several weeks earlier and I had been relieved that I wasn't going to go. His reply was, "Private Kelly, we have looked at your records and you're an Eagle Scout and a Georgia Tech man and you can certainly catch up. You will report on Monday morning." I said, "Yes, Sir. I will report." And I did.

I graduated from OCS on December 20, 1946, and had orders to report to San Francisco for duty on Iwo Jima. I boarded the *U.S.S. Admiral Evelee*, the largest troop ship that the Army owned. There were twelve of us in one small room. We stopped at Manila and then went on to Iwo Jima.

It was early February when we arrived there. It had been raining for weeks. The beds were wet, the food was wet, the salt was wet, the bread was wet. Three of us were assigned to the MOS, Post Engineer. We were eighteen-year-old soldiers and post engineers usually have 30 years experience. We reported to the General. He looked at our shiny lieutenants' bars and just shook his head. He very kindly told us that he needed engineers with experience. He apologized for having to reassign us.

We stayed around there for three weeks. The bed never got dry, the food never got tasty, and the weather got worse. In addition, there were land mines with signs saying, "Ten Americans have been killed here in the last twelve months from land mines. Be careful where you walk." There was some rioting among the troops and, as officers, we had to wear side arms everywhere we went. Finally, they cut our orders and put us on a plane to Guam. It was like going to heaven. It was sunny and warm, nice beaches, friendly people, great food. That's where we spent the rest of our time and we were happy.

We arrived on Guam in early February and left around November or December. During that time we were assigned a unit with a thousand soldiers, all of them black. We were on one side of the runway and the white unit was on the other side. We had eleven officers: one Captain, ten 2nd Lieutenants, and a 1st Lieutenant. We had our own barracks and mess hall. We had a chapel and a black Chaplain. Two of us worshiped with them on Sundays and it was a rich experience. You couldn't always understand the preachers but you could always understand the gospel music. It made me homesick.

Ours was the only place on the north end of the island that had indoor plumbing. We scrounged a toilet and hooked it up but we had no water. One of our air support fellows said he knew where there was a tower and if we could get a tank, we could hook it up on the tower. So he flew over Tinian, which was nearby, and hooked a cable to this big tower and flew it back over and put it down by our cabin. We put a water tank on top and had plumbing. Six of us lived in that little house.

The title of my unit was 811 Aviation Engineer Unit, Twentieth Air Force. I did all kinds of work. I had my own asphalt plant, my own rock quarry, bulldozers, motor graders, concrete mixers, and a rock crusher. I had 100 men assigned to me and we did airport maintenance and construction work. We built houses and put in water systems, We were essentially trying to rebuild the island. Because of the heat, we only worked from 7 AM to 1PM. That left us plenty of time to practice football in the evening when it was cooler.

Our football team was all black, except for the one white quarterback named Joe Kelly. We didn't have any grass; all the island was coral. You couldn't play tackle because the coral would cut you to pieces. I got hurt a lot more by my own team than by the opposition

In 1947, there were still Japanese running around on Guam. They would not surrender because they didn't believe their own people that the War was over. They really were not dangerous. Their ammunition had either been dampened or their rifles were so rusty that they couldn't shoot anybody. We figured there were 27 still alive on the island. The jungle was so thick that you couldn't see three feet in front of you so you wouldn't know if they were there.

I did find one Japanese while we were putting in a water line from Turracki Bay up a 300 foot coral cliff. As we cut through the jungle I came to a little clearing where a Japanese had evidently spent his last moments. He had very neatly taken off his shoes and arranged his belongings in a neat little clearing. His skeleton was there.

When our time was up and it came time to go home, they said they would send us back by air, but when the planes came in from Okinawa and Japan, there was no room for us. There was an old plane out there that needed a part put on it but they didn't have the tools, so we volunteered to help them. We really didn't know how to repair an airplane. After about four days of trying, we finally got lucky and had all of the bolts in the right places, the fellow tightened it up, cranked the engine, and we flew about 10,000 miles back home.

We flew first to Hawaii, where I had my first milkshake in over a year. Then we flew on to San Francisco and Dallas. The family of one of the officers met us in Dallas and took us to their house. I showered, put on my best uniform, and flew home to Atlanta. That was the end of my military career.

I was assigned to a Reserve unit for a couple of years. Every summer I had to go to summer camp at Fort Rucker, Alabama. A lot of guys in my group ended up in Korea. When that war started they started calling people alphabetically. They were down to the H's and I was packed, sure that I was going back in. But they never called another person from that unit.

I really enjoyed my military experience. Like my brother, I'm sorry that I didn't get in on the action. I'm proud to have served. It was certainly beneficial to me. I gained in maturity and experience. I also saw, firsthand, the terrific sacrifices that my friends and neighbors made on those islands in the Pacific.

I re-entered Georgia Tech and when I graduated, I worked for my father at Kelly Motor Company. At the same time, I studied law at night at John Marshall Law School and graduated from there in 1965. In 1962, I bought Perkerson's Corn Mill. Then several local people and I started a bank, which we eventually sold to the Trust Company of Georgia. After I sold the corn mill, my son and I operated a few Ace Hardware stores. Then I went to work as public relations director for Life College. I created the Christmas lights program that is still popular today.

I have been retired for about a year. I stay active in church and community affairs and have enjoyed my alumni association at Boys High School.

I have three children: Bob, Pepper, and Kathy.

—Interviewed by George Beggs, July 2001

Joe Kelly

DAVID KILE
And
Kitty Kile

David Kile

I was born in Marietta, Georgia, in 1922. After graduating from Marietta High School, I went to work for Bell Aircraft. The War had started and as the draft got closer, I decided I'd better join up. I didn't really have to go. I was exempt because I was an only child. Also my job would have allowed me to get deferments but I felt I needed to go.

In December, 1942, I arrived at Great Lakes Naval Station. I had been told that it was warm and to just wear a sport coat and slacks. When we stepped off the train at Great Lakes it was 15 degrees below zero and snow up to my knees. And I wasn't the only one in that fix. I learned right quick not to believe everything I was told in the Service.

Boot camp was mostly marching and learning how to obey commands. We marched all day, even in the snow. We had a little Chief Petty Officer (about 5 foot 3 inches tall) and he was an atomic bomb. He was rough and he really put us through it. He taught us a lot of things. Our basic training lasted ten weeks. We got a seven-day leave and I came home. Then I went to Green Bay and from there they sent me to Miami University in Oxford, Ohio, to learn Morse Code and all about operating and maintaining radios. At the end of August, we got a 23 day leave and I came home again. Then we all met in Cincinnati and went west by train to a base near Heyward, California.

After about two weeks, we went by a banana boat that had been converted to hold 3,000 sailors, to Brisbane, Australia. The trip took about two weeks and part of that time we spent circling to avoid submarines in the area. We stayed in Brisbane about a week, living in tents on a horse race track. Then we went to Sydney, and on to Canberra, the capitol. They sent us there to listen to how people talked on the radio in that part of the world. Somebody might radio, "HW", That meant how's the weather. They would come back with "C" or "CL" (cloudy or clear). Then he'd want to know who the person was and that person would come back with "JT." That meant "Jo time." He'd say no "TT" (tea time). He wanted us to know that he was English and we were Yanks.

We then went back to Sidney and I had the pleasure of touring all the way across Australia to Fremantle on the west side. For 24 hours we rode a modern train, the one the president of their country used. Then we got on another train. It looked like something out of the old western movies—three people sitting on a bench on one side facing three on the other side. We spent the next seven days on that train. The train would stop every now and then at what they called a station, but in most cases it was just a farm. They fed us twice a day. The train would stop, the cooks would set up tables and fix breakfast. You would stand around to eat. Then, it was back on the train and ride until afternoon, and do the same thing.

The landscape was really barren. But after the evening meal the Aborigines would come around to get the food we had thrown away. They all seemed happy. You would hear them saying, "Hey smokie, Hey smokie." They wanted cigarettes but they didn't smoke them. They would peal them and put the tobacco inside their lower lip.

At Fremantle, I was assigned to the submarine division and put on a patrol yacht, PYT. Mine was the PY-10. That particular yacht had been built at the beginning of World War I. The government wanted it and the owner said they could have it if they would name it after his daughter Isabelle. We took a lot of "ribbing" about serving on a ship named for a woman. It had served in the north Atlantic during WW I and when the war was over it went to Pearl Harbor. It was an admiralty yacht, painted white, and worked from Hawaii to the Yalu River in China, to the Philippines, to Guam, and all those islands. The Chinese named it "The Galloping Ghost of the China Coast" because it was painted white. I was on that ship as a radio operator from December, 1943 until November, 1945.

We never did see any true action. We were scouted once by a Japanese plane. Basically, we escorted our submarines when they came into confined waters for cleaning and provisioning. In the first part of 1945 the Navy assigned me to a submarine. I was all packed and ready to go and my orders were canceled. It seems there was a radio man about a year younger than I who started objecting, saying he had been there longer and should be the one to go. So, finally they changed his orders. I told the Captain that I didn't like what he had done and he could tell the Admiral that. Well, he did.

Soon, I was told to go see the Admiral. When I got to the Admiral's office, he told me to have a seat. Then he said, "I understand that you are upset with me because I changed some orders." I told him why I was upset. He said, "Wherever we put you, you are needed or you wouldn't be there." I said, "I understand, Sir." He was very pleasant. He explained the Navy to me a little bit more, where I was needed, and what I was to do. So, I went back to my ship.

We found out later that the man who went on the submarine in my place went all to pieces in 30 days. Later that sub was lost. That Admiral got to know us pretty well. He would come on board often.

One time a sailor on the sub tender was trying to anchor it better to the pier using a cable. We had 125 mile an hour winds and breakers coming over the ship. The Captain of our ship and another guy were watching when the cable popped. It hit the sailor right across the back and threw him about 300 yards. The old man hollered, "Get me a yacht!" Another guy and I jumped in a boat and took off. We rescued that guy. He was alive when we got him into the boat but he wasn't in the best shape.

Sometime around late July or early August of 1945, we received orders to head out to the Philippines. We understood they were collecting every ship they had so that if the atomic bomb didn't work they would send all the ships in. About the time we got up to Darwin, they dropped the bomb. After about three days we received orders and the message was in plain language. I took it all down and gave it to the Captain. He said, "Are you sure this is for us?" He asked me to get a repeat on the message and I did. We were heading back to the U.S. When we got to San Francisco we decommissioned the ship. We stripped it, took it out to Hunters Point and cut it up.

When we got ready to go home, they pulled me out of line and said, "Kile, you go back on board." They said the records showed that I didn't have enough points to get out because I had taken leave. I told them to get the yeoman who entered that in my record and I'll show you a nut. It should say "R&R, five days." They kept pushing so I played the baby. I asked, "Is there a chaplain on this base?" Even though it was 2 AM, I said I wanted to see him. So they woke him, I told him my story, and he came down and said, "This man is going home." They said, "OK."

We took the train from California to Chicago, then on

to Marietta. The only problem was, the train wasn't supposed to stop in Marietta. That meant I would have to go all the way to Atlanta then try to catch a bus back home. When we got to Marietta, with the encouragement of some of the other boys on the train, I pulled the emergency stop cord. When the train stopped, I got off and took a taxi home. The taxi driver was an old friend. You could ride a taxi for a quarter but I gave him a dollar.

    I was in Marietta for two or three weeks, then I had to report to Charleston, South Carolina, on Christmas Eve day to get my discharge. I went to the designated office and handed my orders to the Petty Officer. He said OK and put them back on top of the file cabinet. I asked where to go next. He said to go to such and such barracks. He said, "You're going to be out of here in about four days."

    About eleven days later, I asked what they were doing. They said they had no record of me. We looked everywhere but couldn't find my papers. I got in trouble while I was there. I was standing around with nothing to do when a big officer walked by and told me to start picking up cigarette butts. I said, "Wait a minute, Admiral, they didn't get me in the Navy to pick up cigarette butts." He said, "You do what I tell you." I said, "You don't even know my name." He said, "What do you mean?" I said, "No one around here knows my name." He looked at me like I was nuts and just walked off. Nobody knew me. How could they do anything? Finally, they had me retrace my steps. I showed them what office I had gone to with my papers. They found the papers behind the file cabinet and I was out of the Navy in twelve hours and headed home.

    I left the Navy as a Radioman Second Class. I had about five ribbons, I think. Good Conduct, South Pacific, some others. After I got home, I walked the streets of Atlanta for thirty days trying to find work. Then I was given the opportunity to help restart an automotive wholesale supply company. I stayed with the company 25 years. After that I went into business with two other people. We had three auto parts houses—Mableton, Smyrna, and Powder Springs. I stayed in the auto parts business 41 years altogether.

Kitty Kile

David and I started dating during my junior year in high school. We had a little "understanding" but didn't become engaged because of the War situation. We waited and we wrote. While David was overseas, the letters would be V-Mail (that flimsy little paper), censored of course, and come in batches. After David left for California, I didn't see him again for three years.

Meanwhile, I worked in Atlanta as a bookkeeper, earning 35 cents an hour and riding the streetcar back and forth. Then I started working at Bell Bomber and made lots of money—75 cents an hour. I don't remember rationing and shortages bothering me too much. We were very careful.

When David came back home from overseas, he sent a telegram saying he would arrive on the Dixie Flyer. We had a Dixie Limited and a Dixie Flyer. The Dixie Flyer was supposed to come in late afternoon. David's mother and I got dressed up to meet the train but David wasn't on it. They had apparently missed the connection in Chicago. He came in at 7AM the next day and no one was there to greet him. He had to take a taxi home.

David got home in January of 1946. We were married in April of that year.

—Interviewed by Charles Miller, March 2001

Kitty and David Kile

HORACE KILLEBREW

I knew that I was eligible for the draft on my eighteenth birthday in July of 1944, so I tried to enlist in the Navy. They rejected me because of my red-green color blindness. I had been attending Georgia Tech, so I came back home until the draft called me in November, 1944. I had taken and scored well on a test to see what I knew about electronics, so the Navy decided they wanted me after all—despite the color blindness.

I was inducted at Fort McPherson and wound up at Great Lakes Naval Training Center. That training facility is in Chicago, and I arrived there in January, 1945, in seventeen degrees below zero temperature. I was a country boy, born in the little dirt-street town of Damascus (Baker County), Georgia, who had never experienced cold weather. We were issued our uniforms and gear. One of the buckles on the leggings I was wearing was not secured properly. I slipped on some ice, literally overturned, and woke up three hours later with an old Navy Captain doctor asking me if I knew my name and where I was. I spent the first two days of Navy boot camp in the sack.

Following a month in an electronics training center, we were next assigned to Gulfport, Mississippi. Three months later, I was sent to San Francisco. I was there when the War in Europe ended. There was no particular celebration because we knew we had Japan to deal with. I was still in San Francisco on VJ-Day.

For some reason, on that day, the military services released all personnel for shore leave or "liberty." We went into San Francisco and I witnessed the most horrible destruction of private property I have ever seen. The military people literally took San Francisco apart that afternoon. Store fronts were broken. The streets were littered with glass. People were walking out of department stores with looted merchandise. In my opinion, all that could have been avoided because about 10 PM the MP's and Shore Patrol cleared the streets.

I didn't have enough points to be discharged from the Navy, so they sent me to Camp Elliott in San Diego. Now that was a literal hell hole. The barracks were really something like Celotex siding back. Then they put me on a troop ship to Hawaii. I was in Hawaii for six to eight weeks, doing basic scullery kitchen duty. Then it was on to another troop ship and back to San Francisco for me. I was discharged in Jacksonville, Florida, in May, 1946. I rode a train back to Damascus.

I had entered the Navy as a Seaman First Class and came out with the same rank. My military experience was a good one. As a result of the navy training I aced my electrical engineering courses at Georgia Tech when I returned to school.

How do I feel about World War II? I approve of what we did. The free nations of the world were lax in their duty in not coming to grips with Hitler before he achieved that much power. We sat by too long and let him get away with his ambition to rule the world.

My two older brothers, twins, were in the Service before I was. They both wound up in the China-Burma-India (CBI) theater. One brother, with the Corps of Engineers, laid pipelines across Burma so that Chenault and the Flying Tigers could have gasoline. My other brother flew on C-47's and became part of the Air Force's earliest attempts at air-dropping supplies. He flew about 240 missions across the Himalayas and areas like that.

After the service, I returned to Georgia Tech and graduated in 1949. I met Barbara at the home of a friend in 1950. We were married 70 days later. That was 51 years ago.

I have worked for the U.S. Geological Survey; for Lockheed; for Brown Engineering in Huntsville, Alabama; and for IBM. I finished my career in Atlanta, with IBM, and retired on April 1, 1990.

I think all the good things in my life can be attributed to God. I wasn't much of a practicing Christian until after Barbara and I were married. At that point, we made a commitment of our lives to Christ, and a commitment to tithe. Church has always been an integral part of our lives—not just membership, but fellowship, support, and love. I was ordained as a Baptist Deacon in Madison, Alabama, in 1964. I am a deacon at Marietta First Baptist Church, sing in the Chancel Choir, and serve with the Disaster Relief Team. Barbara also sings in the Chancel Choir.

—Interviewed by Harland Armitage, September, 2001

Horace Killebrew

HUGH KINARD

I was seventeen years old when I graduated from high school in Meridian, Mississippi. That was in June of 1944. I tried to enlist in the Navy but they wouldn't take me because I wore glasses. Then I tried the Air Force but they wouldn't take me either. So I had to wait until I was drafted at age eighteen. Nobody wanted to be in the Infantry, so we all tried to enlist in the Navy but I still wound up in the Infantry. In the meantime, I enrolled for a semester at the local junior college.

It was March, 1945, and the War was winding down, when I was sent to Camp Shelby, Mississippi. From there, I was sent to Camp Wheeler, near Macon, Georgia, where I spent eighteen weeks in basic training. By then the military had that training down to a science. It was extremely well organized. We were training to take part in the invasion of Japan which was scheduled for October, 1945. They were teaching us to speak Japanese. All the targets had Japanese faces, and the little villages on our problems had Japanese buildings.

Our training was tough. I was there as a green, naive eighteen-year-old from Mississippi who had seldom been out of the state. The trainees were either eighteen and unmarried, or thirty-six and married, with children. The draft boards were taking both ends of the spectrum because they had already taken the in-between ages. The older guys often had a bad attitude. They didn't want to be there. They said, "No, Sir. I'm not here to volunteer for anything and I won't do anything unless I have to." They spent most of their evenings in the Post Exchange (PX) drinking beer, and their weekends getting drunk. It was a real education for me. On the other hand, I thought it was something of an adventure. Everything was new. I didn't mind volunteering. Although I was small and not strong, I managed to do what I needed to do. I qualified for OCS but there weren't any openings.

We were getting ready to go to the Philippines to fill out the units that had vacancies from the battles there. The Eighth Army was getting ready for Japan and we were the replacements. The last week of our basic training, Germany surrendered. We were headed to the Fourth Replacement Depot in Manila. Just as we were ready to ship out of Fort Ord, California, they decided to move the replacement depot to Japan. Ours was the first ship that went directly from the U.S. to Japan with troops. A lot of men got seasick but I never did. I never missed a meal. They found out I could type (50 words a minute, easily) and had some college so they gave me a special classification. I would type materials for the officers.

We got to Tokyo Bay in October and they were still not ready for us. They sent us by train to where the Replacement Depot would be, and marched us by squads out to a vacant field. A big truck came by with bundles which contained a twelve-man tent and twelve cots. "Fellows, this is your home," they said. It was raining, we were standing in the mud, and they said, "Put up the tent because this is where you sleep tonight." We stayed in those tents about two or three weeks. There was no such thing as hot water. The first few days the only thing they found in the big barrels of food was biscuits and beans. We had biscuits and beans for three meals a day. They had all these supply ships out in Tokyo Bay. They would unload the ships and pile the stuff on the dock. Then they would find out what they had. We could tell what they were unloading by what we would have for supper that night. Sometimes we would get sliced peaches or some stew.

They had gotten in a request for an editor from the 185th Regimental Combat Team that was stationed a hundred miles north of Tokyo. The unit was made up of a National Guard unit from Arizona and New Mexico and included a lot of Indians. They were called The Bushmasters and two men from that unit put out a regimental newspaper. They had carried a little mimeograph machine, a portable typewriter, a package of stencils, and some paper and ink all through the Philippines. They were seasoned veterans with enough points to go home so I was sent up there to learn how to publish their newspaper.

The unit was stationed at what had been the officer training camp for the Japanese army. It was terrible—filthy and vermin infested. They finally got it cleaned up and I began working with these two experienced men. They gave a fellow from New York the job of artist and I was to do the editing of the "PFC Times"—later the "T-5 Times." We had a lot of fun putting that together, writing about all the guys going home. Then they began to send us information on colleges—how to apply, courses available, that sort of thing—for the men going back home. After a month, the two seasoned veterans went home and we continued publishing. We had to send a copy of everything to Corps and Army headquarters, as well as a copy to the Pentagon.

On the basis of what we were doing, when that unit got ready to come home in December, the Eighth Army requested that I be assigned to them to edit a magazine. They wanted to provide all the veterans who were leaving to go home with information on education. I didn't know a thing about publishing a magazine but they gave me the job as editor. I was stationed in Yokohama and running back and forth to Tokyo. One time I wound up in an elevator with General MacArthur, in his headquarters building. At that time I was still a PFC. Then they decided my job was worth more so they promoted me to Corporal. The next day, I got another promotion to Sergeant.

They assigned me five professional writers whom they had hired from the U.S. They put me in an office with a big desk and all this equipment, reference books, etc. I didn't know what to do with all that stuff so I had to learn in a hurry. We called our magazine the "Octogram Digest," because the Eighth Army insignia was an octogram. We got a commendation from General MacArthur's office for the work we were doing.

I stayed there until July, 1946, when I was in an accident. A weapons carrier overturned and I was underneath. I spent two months in the hospital there. Then they flew me home and my magazine career was cut very short. I had nerve damage to my arm and they gave me three months furlough to come home to convalesce. I worked in the garden and my arm healed. I left the service in March, 1947.

The GI Bill was in effect by this time and I had to decide on a college. I wanted to stay with magazine work so I decided on a double major—education and art. Most of the colleges were full but the University of Miami and the University of Cincinnati both accepted me. I thought that if I went to Miami that I wouldn't have to buy a lot of winter clothes as I would have to do for Cincinnati. So that's where I went. While at Miami, I met Lois Farrar. She was in nursing training. When I graduated, we were married.

I had felt the call to do full time Christian work, so we spent the next four years at Southwestern Baptist Theological Seminary in Ft. Worth, Texas. I graduated with a master's degree in Religious Education. I worked as a Minister of Music/Education at several small churches.

By this time, I had a family (daughters, Laurel and Carol) and I decided to get a degree in public education. I earned a master's degree and then a doctorate and went to work in the public school system. I worked in education until I retired.

My war time experience wasn't terribly exciting and dangerous, but it was interesting. In a lot of ways, it prepared me for my future life.

—Interviewed by Charles Miller, August, 2001

Hugh Kinard

CLEVELAND KIRK
With
Janette Kirk

My late husband, Cleve Kirk, was born in a house on Burnt Hickory Road, Cobb County, Georgia. He attended New Salem School. Cleve joined the Marietta National Guard on December 14, 1938. They were mobilized and sent to Fort Stewart, Georgia. A week before they were to come home, Pearl Harbor was bombed, so they were put into the regular Army.

While at Fort Stewart, Cleve was a Fire Control Instructor. He could fire and hit the target 171 times in 200 rounds. Living conditions at Fort Stewart were difficult. Cleve said that on Christmas Day he got a hot bath and got to use the bathroom.

From Fort Stewart, Cleve was sent to Greenland, where they trained for one year. He and his brother both went into Germany on D-Day—Cleve with the Anti-Aircraft Artillery, and his brother with the Security Section. His brother was wounded and sent back home but Cleve had to keep going. He fought in three battles and in June he received a battlefield commission from Sergeant to 2nd Lieutenant.

Cleve was then assigned to a camp where the Germans had been holding the Jewish prisoners and starving them to death. He had to work until all the prisoners were liberated and sent back to their homes. Cleve had to sign the discharge papers for every one of them. He said that the first night they were there, they thought they would be good to the prisoners so they gave them steak and potatoes. The men sat down and cried. Their stomachs wouldn't handle that much food. About five years before Cleve died, the government asked him if he remembered a Dr. Mittshler. He was the man who was so cruel to the Jews. Cleve said he remembered seeing the man but didn't know whether or not he had signed the man's papers.

Following the War, Cleve came home and worked for about three months with North Carolina Electric Company. He didn't like the work so he re-enlisted in the Army. They assigned him to an Anti-Aircraft Artillery (AAA) school at Fort Bliss, Texas. Next, he did recruiting for the Army at Stone Lake, Iowa. We married during that time.

Cleve's next assignment, at Fort Benning, Georgia, lasted just three months. He said, "This is wrong; this is for foot troops, and I'm Artillery." So they sent him to Fort Sill, Oklahoma, where he taught automatic weaponry. After five years, we went back to Fort Bliss, Texas, where Cleve again was an AAA instructor. Then he was sent to Korea where he, again, was in Anti-Aircraft Artillery.

After Korea, Cleve spent several years with the Missouri National Guard at Joplin, Missouri. He had 40 units under his command. Then it was back to Fort Bliss again. At that point, Cleve asked for an assignment closer to Marietta because his parents were getting old. The Army sent him to Fort Gordon, Georgia, and we lived there about four years until he retired. While at Fort Gordon, Cleve was with the 41st Civil Affairs Office.

Cleve retired from the Army as a Major. During his military career, he had been awarded the Bronze Star Medal; American Defense Service Medal; the American Campaign Medal; the European-African Middle Eastern Campaign Medal with three stars; World War II Victory Medal; Army of

Occupation Medal; National Defense Ribbon; Korean Service Medal; United Nations Service Medal; Presidential Unit Citation; U.S.A. 1940-1945 Freedom from Tears and Want, Freedom of Speech and Religion Medal. He also received a medal from the President of South Korea.

At Cleve's retirement ceremony all the men marched past in a full dress parade. His parents got to see that. Cleve said he had marched in many of those parades.

When Cleve died, I requested a full military funeral. They told me that because of budget cuts that it couldn't be done. I told them that they could keep the body until they could do it, then I went home and made some phone calls. The next day they called and said it was all set. I have never seen a cleaner set of men than those who came to carry Cleve's body to its final resting place. The three soldiers who folded the flag were crying as they did so. Roy Smith from the Church made a display holder for that flag and it rests on our mantlepiece.

When we came back to Marietta, we went down to the 214th AAA, which was the old fall out of the Marietta National Guard. Cleve became president of that group and when he died I became president. There aren't many of them left now. I enjoyed every minute of being with Cleve in the Service.

Cleve Kirk died September 27, 1997.

—Interviewed by Marcus McLeroy, June, 2001

Janette and Cleve Kirk

PAUL KOCH
And
Eileen Koch

Paul Koch

I was born, raised, and attended high school in Quincy, Illinois. For a while, I had an exemption from the Draft because I was working on a farm. The Draft Board determined your classification by adding up the points for the farm—each milk cow was one point and you got points for the number of acres of corn or soybeans you had under cultivation. My classification was 2-C. I worked on the farm for two years but then began to feel like I should go into the Service. I turned in my 2-C classification and the Draft Board was happy to take care of it.

I was drafted into the Army in March, 1945, at the age of twenty. I took basic infantry training at Camp Robinson, Arkansas, and in July, 1945, I was shipped through a series of assembly centers—Fort Riley, Kansas; Camp Adair, Oregon; and Camp Stoneman, California.

From Camp Stoneman, we sailed out, underneath the Golden Gate Bridge, headed for points in the Pacific. We were transported by the Merchant Marines aboard an old ship that had been a fancy ocean liner in its day. We were transporting Red Cross personnel (officers) and a group of enlisted men—all privates. The enlisted men were only allowed on one open deck. We soon found that running along next to the ceiling on that deck was a rod about an inch and a half in diameter. It turned out to be the steering gear of the ship. Naturally, guys being guys, they would get up and hold onto that rod. Then the loudspeaker would crackle with a few choice words as they were told to let go of that rod.

For the first half of our trip to the Philippines, we ran completely blacked out and zigzagged to avoid detection by submarines. About halfway to our destination, VJ-Day occurred and everything changed. By the time we got to Eniwetoc in the western Caroline Islands, we got word that we could end our black out and straighten out our course, heading straight for Manila.

Manila was just a stopping point on our route. They then put us on a "Peanut Roaster," which was a little engine and train, and took us to Clark Field, an Army Replacement Depot. Basically we were going to replace the men who had been in combat. The outfit that I went into was the 51st Field Artillery, part of the Sixth Infantry Division. That was ridiculous because we were infantry-trained and knew nothing about artillery. However, many of us were farm boys so we knew how to drive a truck. That more or less qualified us to at least keep the outfit mobile.

In November, 1945, the Army moved two Divisions to Korea to help rehabilitate that country. They called us MP's and we were there to reinforce the Korean police. For a good many years, Japan had dominated that whole peninsula and the Korean people were given no say about running their own country. The Allied Forces decided that the Japanese should leave and turn the country back over to the Koreans. As a result, the Korean people had to build up their own security structure.

Our biggest problem in Korea was not the Japanese but the Koreans who wanted to get back home. The

Japanese government had enslaved a lot of the Koreans and sent them to Okinawa and other places to work. The Koreans were friendly to us because we were the good guys.

I left Korea for home on October 17, 1946, aboard the Liberty Ship, *Marine Fox*. We came into Oakland Army Base, and boarded a troop train for Fort Sheridan, Illinois (right back where I started). It seemed that every train on the railroad—including cattle cars, had the right of way over troop trains. We sat on a lot of sidings.

Following my military service, I enrolled at the University of Illinois under the GI Bill. I graduated with a degree in Agricultural Engineering and began working for the Soil Conservation Service with the U.S. Department of Agriculture. I started working there in 1951 and continued there until I retired in 1988.

Eileen and I were married in 1959. Both of our first spouses had died about five years earlier, within a month of each other.

Eileen Koch

My parents didn't have a lot of money but I knew I wanted to go to school, so I joined the Army Nurses Corps. They paid most of my tuition for nursing school. I really had planned on going into the Service but the War ended just before I graduated.

I remember the rationing. When I went away to school at the University of Michigan at Ann Arbor, my parents had to send all my ration books with me. The dormitory had to have those in order to feed us. When I would go home to Elkhart, Indiana, for a weekend, I would ride the train to Miles, Michigan, and even though gasoline was scarce, my parents would meet me in Miles and drive me back there when I returned to the University. The trains were so crowded that it was hard to find a seat. We would sit in the ladies' restroom and travel that way.

—Interviewed by George Beggs, February, 2003

Eileen and Paul Koch

ROBERT B. LAMBERT
With
Catherine Lambert

My late husband, Robert ("R.B.") Lambert, was already in the Navy when we met in the early part of 1941. He had entered the Service on November 30, 1940, and had taken his basic training at Norfolk, Virginia. After Basic, he spent about three months at Jacksonville, Florida, before shipping out to Pearl Harbor. His job was in Aviation Ordinance—taking care of planes and loading them with ammunition. He was at Ford Island when the attack on Pearl Harbor occurred.

I have a copy of an article which appeared in the Marietta Daily Journal, in which the writer, Joe Kirby, interviewed R.B. about Pearl Harbor. In the article, Mr. Kirby quotes my husband as saying, "I had no idea for a while that you could get killed. It was like cowboys and Indians... The full realization of what had happened hit me about noon, when I walked through the barracks (where a makeshift hospital had been set up) and saw all the sailors, who had been pulled out of the burning oily waters of the harbor, lying in the hallways... The unsung heroes that day were the Navy wives who were nursing them. They were fantastic."

Kirby goes on to tell that R.B. had written his father the

week before the attack, telling him how mighty the U.S. fleet was. Ironically, the letter arrived in Atlanta on December 7. R.B.'s barracks were a short distance from the battleship *U.S.S. Oklahoma*. The morning of the attack, about breakfast time, he heard explosions and ran outside to see what was going on. "I saw the *Oklahoma* turn over, and I knew then it was not for fun," R.B. said. The sailors in the barracks were ordered to go to the ground-floor mess hall and get under the tables for protection. Only the Navy guards were allowed to leave. R.B. lied and told an officer he was a guard, and managed to get out the door. He went to the Base armory and found the only weapon that was left—a 30-caliber Lewis Gun. When asked if he knew how to fire a Lewis Gun, R.B. replied, "Sure," even though he had never seen one before. He and two others took the gun outside, set it up, and started firing at the Japanese planes. "I've been asked many times if I hit anything," R.B. said. "Who knows? I was throwing everything I could back at 'em. Every time a Jap plane was hit, people would get up and holler 'hooray!' like they were at a football game. I did, too. It was kind of stupid. I don't know why we did it."

Even after the attack ended, many were trigger-happy. "Anything that moved, we shot. Some guys even opened up at some driftwood that night, thinking it was the Japs landing. I grew up pretty fast that week," R.B. said. In succeeding days, R.B. saw many bodies being fished out of the harbor and rescue crews cutting through the hull of the overturned *Oklahoma* in the hopes of reaching men trapped alive inside.

R.B. always said that a lot of the men who would normally be aboard the ships in the harbor, were on shore leave because it was the weekend. Otherwise, even more would have been killed. This happened on a Sunday and it was Wednesday before I got a telegram that he was fine. I think he called me the next weekend. After that, it was three years before I saw him again. We had a long romance by correspondence.

From Pearl Harbor, R.B. was sent to our Naval Air Station on Jackson Island. He just went from island to island, including Midway. Finally, he came to Moffet Air Force Base in Alameda, California. It was during that period that we were married—June 4, 1944. R.B. came to Marietta for the wedding and we had two weeks before he had to go back. A friend lent us her cabin out at Mountain Park so that we could have a honeymoon. I went back to Alameda with R.B., by train. Once out there, we bought a car so that we could drive back to Georgia. Then R.B. flew back to Alameda and went back overseas for about nine months. When he returned, we were sent to Cecil Field, Jacksonville, Florida.

They were looking for men with Service experience to be Station Keepers for the Atlanta Naval Air Station. R.B. applied and was accepted. At that time, the Naval Air Station was out at Chamblee. During R.B.'s time they moved it to Dobbins in Marietta. He was at the Naval Air Station from 1946 to 1959, and was an Aviation Ordinance Chief when he retired.

Following his military service R.B. worked for several different companies then decided that he wanted to drive a bus for MARTA. He did that for thirteen years and loved it. When he retired from MARTA, the men who worked with him asked me if they could give him a Bible as a gift. They said, "Your husband has always tried to give us good rules to live by. He is always telling us how much God loves us, and how much it would mean in our lives if we would accept Him." It is a beautiful Bible.

My husband taught Sunday School at Marietta First Baptist Church for several years. He was also president of the Brotherhood and served as Scout Master and Royal Ambassador (R.A.) Leader for a while. I had joined First Baptist in 1933. Then when we were married, R.B. also joined this church.

All three of our children were born in Marietta. Richard, our oldest graduated from the Naval Academy and served on nuclear submarines but is no longer in the Navy. Our second son, Robert Bradley ("Brad") graduated from Georgia Tech and is a Captain in the Navy. Our daughter Luanne is married and lives near Holly Springs.

R.B. was a member of the Pearl Harbor Survivors Association. There is a monument in the National Cemetery here in Marietta, and a brick walkway with survivors' names on the bricks. On December 7, 1991, we were invited to a Pearl Harbor 50th anniversary observance in Milledgeville, Georgia. On the way home he said to me, "Thank you for sharing my moment of glory."

R.B. Lambert died on May 29, 1994.

—Interviewed by Ruth Miller, August, 2001

The Lambert's wedding.

HUGH LITTLE

In 1944, I was in my senior year at Boys High School in Atlanta and was scheduled to graduate in June of that year. At that time just about everybody was going into the Service. We all took tests to see if we qualified for an officer training program. I qualified for the Navy's B-12 program, in which you would go to college for two semesters and then to an officer training school. If you completed the program you came out as an Ensign in the U.S. Navy Reserve. No telling what would happen to you then.

I was brought up in a time when my parents solidly impressed two things upon me: do what you're told and don't talk back. So, when they told me I was eligible for the B-12 program, I didn't have any idea what it was but I said, "Okay. Everybody has to go someplace."

I graduated from high school one week and the next week I was in basic training at Georgia Tech. Anybody who has gone through the military preference selection knows that you pick one place and they send you somewhere else. I picked Northwestern University because I thought that would get me pretty far away from home. They ended up sending me to Georgia Tech. And the training was very basic.

People who live around Atlanta will remember the old Techwood Apartments. During the War they were used as dormitories to house Army, Marines, and Navy students. Most of us were seventeen or eighteen years old. There were a few nineteen and twenty-year-olds who taught us all the bad things we didn't need to know. But morale was good.

Growing up in the Depression, I didn't feel like I ever got enough to eat until I got into the Navy. Then we got bacon, and steak, and stuff like that—all you could eat. My family was envious when I told them all I had to put up with.

Until I was discharged, my longest trips during my training were by streetcar when I would go home on weekends. D-Day was June 6, 1944, just about the time I went in. As far as the Navy was concerned, they needed Ensigns less and less as time went on. We were supposed to stay at Tech for two semesters but it stretched out. Finally, after two calendar years, the Navy said, "We've decided we don't need you." So, in 1946, they put us on a troop train and took us to Jacksonville, Florida, to discharge us.

When I left the Navy I was an Apprentice Seaman. However, they encouraged us to get into Naval ROTC, which I did. By going to school year round, I had enough credits to graduate in 1947. I got my degree and was commissioned as an Ensign at the same time.

I was proud of my military service. I was never ashamed of it. The Lord blessed me in many ways. The Navy told me to select a major. Without any premeditated dependence on the Lord (but I think the Lord was in it), I selected Aeronautical Engineering. I loved my career in that field. All the years that I worked in it I thanked the Lord for putting me in that place. I think the Lord did nothing but good for me in all that.

When I finished college, I worked briefly for McDonnell Aircraft in St. Louis. Then I worked for eight years with what is now NASA, at Hampton, Virginia. I found Martha, my first wife there, another one of the Lord's blessings. I know a lot of good men who had trouble finding one good wife. The Lord blessed me with two good wives. Martha and I came to Georgia, where I worked for Lockheed until 1991. I retired and began to work for Marietta First Baptist Church.

When my high school class had its 50th reunion in 1994, 80 of us out of the 144 who graduated, were able to attend. Not many 50th reunions get that high a percentage of people back. Out of that class of 1944, I don't think we lost anyone in World War II. We were just a little bit too late for the heavy stuff and just in time to get in on the fringes.

—Interviewed by Marcus McLeroy, March 2001

WILLIAM E. "BILL" LLOYD
With
Catherine Lloyd

Both Bill and I were born and grew up in West End, Atlanta, Georgia. He was born October 21, 1918, and I was born October 17, 1922. Bill graduated from Tech High and I graduated from Girls High. We lived in different school districts but we both attended West End Baptist Church. Although we were in the same Intermediate Department of the Sunday School, I really didn't get to know him well before he went off to war.

Bill was enrolled in Georgia Tech night school and enlisted in the Naval Reserve on May 7, 1941. He was pulled into active duty very soon after Pearl Harbor. He entered at Charleston, South Carolina, and was assigned to the *U.S.S. Hornet*, an aircraft carrier. Bill's main job was to operate the elevators that moved the planes up and down to and from the flight deck. He was on the *Hornet* on April 18, 1942, when Doolittle's Raiders flew their B-25 bombers off the flight deck on their famous bombing raid to Tokyo.

That ship was later sunk at the Battle of Santa Cruz. Bill told his mother how the sailors shot down 45 of the 60 Japanese planes attacking their carrier. Three Japanese pilots made suicide dives onto the flight deck. The guns were still firing away as the ship listed heavily, with the

Captain being the last one to slide down the ropes into the water. Bill swam away from the group because he was afraid the Japanese would bomb any concentration of men in the water. Eventually, the survivors were picked up by the Destroyer, *U.S.S. Mustin*.

Bill then came back to San Diego for R&R. He had shore duty until he was assigned to the *U.S.S. Lexington*, where he served out the remainder of the War. Bill served in thirteen major battles in the Pacific including: Tarawa, Wake, Gilberts, Palau, Hollandia, Truk, Marianas, Bonins, Yap, Ryukyus, Formosa, Luzon, China Sea, Philippines and Japan. His list of medals included the Good Conduct Medal, American Defense Service Medal, American Campaign Medal, Asiatic Pacific Campaign Medal with two silver stars and three bronze stars, World War II Victory Medal, Philippine Liberation Ribbon, and the Presidential Unit Citation. Bill's rank at the end of the War was Electrician's Mate First Class. He never wanted to talk much about his war experience. He did have nightmares about it for years and would wake up screaming.

During the War, I was back in Atlanta, working for the U.S. Army Corps of Engineers. I actually worked for Army personnel in the real estate division. We were acquiring land for practice bombing ranges, hotels for convalescent hospitals, all kinds of things. Our office hours were regulated to provide 24 hour coverage and to spread out the ridership on the crowded bus lines. I was living with my father and my sister and her baby while her husband was fighting in Europe. He was in the Battle of the Bulge. Things were rationed—tires, car parts, paint, maintenance materials for homes, sugar, meat, shoes. One of my jobs was to stand in line to buy canned milk and Karo syrup to make baby formula. I remember the first time I saw an Army convoy driving up U.S. 41.

I would go to the movies and see the news reels of the battles. My friends' husbands were being called up.

Newspapers had daily lists of those killed in action, missing in action, or prisoners of war. I would go to church for Wednesday evening prayer meeting and hear Bill's mother ask us to pray for him. Since he was the only boy I knew serving in the Pacific, I prayed for him every night. At one time more than 170 members of our church were in military service. A friend and I began a prayer time on Sunday evenings for family members and friends of service men to come and kneel at the altar and pray.

My prayers must have gotten through because one Wednesday evening in February, 1945, Bill Lloyd showed up at prayer meeting. He asked his sister if I had gotten married. When the answer was "no," he asked if he could take me home. We rode the bus. It was a short six week courtship before he had to return to San Diego. We corresponded—love letters. When the War was finally over and Bill was to return to Charleston to end his service, they put him on a "floating dry-dock" that had to go down through the Panama Canal and around to San Diego. When he got home three months later, I went to meet him at the train station only to find he had grown a beard. He wanted to go to church like that but I got my scissors and cut off the beard and he shaved before we went to church. We were married in West End Baptist Church on October 20, 1945.

After the War, Bill worked for several companies, mostly in the carpet business. We had five children, Bill, Nancy, Susan, Cathy, and Tommy. Bill had a number of bouts with bad health, some of them perhaps service related. He died, February 12, 1986, while on a business trip to Florida. I have worked as a licensed real estate agent ever since Tommy, our youngest, was in high school.

Among Bill's papers was a letter dated November 1, 1945, from James Forrestal, Secretary of the Navy. It reads in part:

"I want the Navy's pride in you, which it is my privilege to express, to reach into your civil life and to remain with you always ... You have served in the greatest Navy in the world. It crushed two enemy fleets at once, receiving their surrenders only four months apart. It brought our land-based airpower within bombing range of the enemy, and set our ground armies on the beachheads of final victory. It performed the multitude of tasks necessary to support these military operations. No other Navy at any time has done so much. For your part in these achievements you deserve to be proud as long as you live. The Nation which you served at a time of crisis will remember you with gratitude...."

—Interviewed by Ruth Miller, September 11, 2001

Bill Lloyd

NORRIS KEMP MABRY

I was born in Cobb County. My father, wanting a good education for me, paid $5.00 a month in tuition for me to attend school in Marietta for eleven years. I graduated from Marietta High School in 1942 and attended Georgia Tech for two years before I was drafted. After receiving a deferment to finish my sophomore year at Tech, I was drafted into the Army and on April 20, 1944, reported for duty at Fort McPherson. I was eighteen years old.

I spent seventeen weeks in basic training at Camp Blanding, near Jacksonville, Florida. My father, who had served in the Marines during World War I, told me that you had to move fast and grab quick at mealtimes or you would go hungry. Actually, I found the food at Camp Blanding plentiful and the housing adequate. Due to the heat and the rigorous physical training, we had to take a salt pill every day. Our orders were that if a man passed out, to step over him and keep going. I reached my physical limit while in basic training—obstacle course, running five miles before breakfast—I have never since had to exert myself in that manner. I attended radio school and when I had finished basic training I waited for 32 days and nights on KP duty for my orders to come through. I am an unchallenged expert dishwasher.

Following basic training, I was assigned to the 566th Signal Corps, Black Panther Division at Camp Rucker,

Alabama. I lived and trained there for six weeks but was able to go home on most weekends. I made the trip home by either sleeping in the baggage rack on a bus or hitchhiking. People were very kind and were quick to offer a soldier a ride. From Camp Rucker I traveled to a port of embarkation in the Northeast and boarded a British troop ship for Southampton, England.

We arrived in England around 4 AM and disembarked with our duffel bags. Members of the Red Cross put sugar, canned milk, and coffee (in that order) into our canteen cups. It was the best thing I had ever tasted and I have been hooked ever since.

At Christmastime, 1944, I was invited to attend an Episcopal church in the Southampton area. I was surprised in the service to hear "America" being played in an English church. I soon learned it was not "America" but "God Save the King!" An English lady tried to explain the service to me. I couldn't understand a single word she said but I thanked her with a smile on my face.

We had been told that we were going to the Battle of the Bulge. Just before Christmas I was asked if I wanted to go over with an advance party. I was promised "good billets." I declined because I thought it best to stay with the radio team to which I had been assigned. I was soon to be grateful for that decision.

On December 24, 1944, the *S.S. Leopoldville*, a Belgian troopship carrying 2,235 men from the 66th Infantry Division (mostly from the 264th Infantry Regiment) was hit by a German torpedo and sank in the English Channel five and a half miles from Cherbourg, France. The French-speaking ship's crew dropped the anchor and escaped in the lifeboats. The American soldiers, unable to understand the language, and not having been given the order to abandon ship, were unsure what to do. They had to either try to jump into a rescue boat that had pulled up alongside the ship, or jump into the water in the hopes of being pulled out. Eight hundred and two men were confirmed killed, and 493 were never found. My Marietta Troop 2 Scoutmaster, Sherry M. Hamilton, told my father he heard I had been lost in that disaster.

On December 26, 1944, we drove our radio truck onto an LST for the trip to France. When we landed at Cherbourg, we had to move quickly because of a German resurgence of air power. We caught up with our artillery in the middle of the night and learned that our orders had been changed from the Battle of the Bulge to relieve a division on the Channel. Our troops had laid siege to 50,000 Germans in the areas of St. Nazaire, Lorient, and Belle Isle. We held the German troops, not without casualties, and were rotated out every few weeks to different positions.

Once, when in the field at St. Nazaire, my radio team stayed in a little stone house. As it was very cold, we burned tar paper and shingles to keep warm. The fumes made all of us very sick. After a few days, when we were missed, someone was sent to look for us and found us too sick to move.

The 66th Division HQ was located at Chateaubriant in Loire, Inferience. I lived in a tent in the bivouac area and ate in the mess hall, which was located in town. The food was not as good as in basic training but the morale of the men was high. We were American soldiers and we knew we would win and be the liberators of France. While my radio team was stationed at Nantes, we did not venture into town alone. Due to an unfortunate USAF bombing error, Americans were not popular there.

At Vannes, Morbihan, France, I would stroll along the beach when I was not on duty. There, I met a group of cub scouts and their leaders. Having studied French in high school and at Georgia Tech, I was able to talk with them. They invited me to one of their homes for dinner. I took a gift of Coca Cola. At a Boy Scout rally (I am an Eagle Scout) in that community, I made a little speech in French. On one furlough in Paris, walking down the middle of the *Champs Elysee*, I met Milton McLemore, of Marietta First Baptist Church. We went to see Air Force Major R.A. Tipton, our Marietta High School math teacher, in General Eisenhower's headquarters.

On VE-Day, the war in Europe was over for some, but not for me. I didn't have enough points to go home and was transferred to Koblenz, Germany. From there, I went to Arles, in southern France, the seat of the French Popes, where I remained until VJ-Day. Then I was transferred to the Army of Occupation, 42nd Rainbow Division, 132nd Signal Corps in Salzburg, Austria, where I served for nine months. While there, I lived in the servants quarters next to a mansion. The General stayed in the mansion's guest house. I was able to attend the Rainbow University at Zell Am See, studying German, Calculus, and Psychology.

I mustered out of the Army on June 18, 1946, with the rank of T-3 (Staff Sergeant). I received medals for Good Conduct, The Battle of Northern France, and Army of Occupation (Austria). I am very proud to have been one of the many who served our Country.

After my service, I returned to Georgia Tech to complete my degree in electrical engineering. I spent ten years working with YMCA's around the state of Georgia. I married my wife, Evelyn, on March 18, 1959. I then moved into public education, teaching both on the high school and college level. I earned a Master's Degree in Counseling from Georgia Southern, and a PH.D. from Florida State University. I have written/edited nineteen college textbooks. I retired as Professor Emeritus from Georgia Southern University in 1988. I remain active in church and civic affairs in Statesboro, Georgia.

I was converted, October 12, 1935, and baptized soon thereafter. I grew up in Marietta First Baptist Church. My father taught Sunday school and sang in the choir. I was active in Sunbeams, RA's and Sunday School. After the War, I was active in Sunday school and other church programs.

—Information furnished by Norris Kemp Mabry, May, 2002

Norris Kemp Mabry

CHARLES MAHIN
With
Pauline Mahin

Both my husband, Charles, and I grew up in Indiana. He graduated from high school in Brookston, and I graduated from high school in Wolcott—both schools in White County, Indiana.

Charles first went into the Marines in 1925, at the age of eighteen. I didn't know him then. When World War II came along, he was doing aircraft mechanic work. That's what he had been trained to do. Because we didn't have any children, Charles and I, and one other couple, were selected to go out west to Sand Point Air Base in Seattle. Charles was 39 at the time and I was 35. We lived in government barracks on the Base. The apartments were very small—just one room and a bath—and the walls were very thin. Our heat came from a coal-burning stove. There was about a two-inch crack around the door that let in all the cold air. We had people there from every state in the Union and every nationality, all working on aircraft.

We were able to buy some food at the Commissary. Meat was scarce and we had to make do. One time some of the men went fishing and brought back huge salmon which they shared. It was wonderful. The nearest pharmacy was thirteen blocks away. We walked everywhere. Charles didn't talk about his work. Everything was classified. I wasn't even allowed to call him on the telephone unless it was an emergency.

I had a lot of time on my hands and eventually went to work at a bank. I worked there until one day a lady I worked with told me there was a baby available for adoption. She knew we wanted to adopt a child and the adoption of this baby had not gone through. I immediately thought this was the baby we were supposed to have. I called Charles (they asked if this was an emergency and I said it was) and told him we were going to have a baby that afternoon at four o'clock. He said to let him sit down, then asked if it was a boy or a girl. Three days later, we had our baby boy.

Washington state adoption laws required us to stay in that state for six months even though the War had ended. Then we traveled by train, with the baby, back to Indiana. It was a joyous time for us to be bringing our baby home. I believe that Charles came out of the service as a Sergeant. He continued working in the aircraft business after the War. I am 93 years old and I don't remember everything I would like to.

—Interviewed by Marcus McLeroy, November, 2001

JAMES L. "PEPPER" MARTIN
And
Dan Martin

    I was born right here in Marietta in 1923. I went through the Marietta school system and about a year after graduating, I met my late wife, Sarah. I was walking down Atlanta Street near the old post office and she was walking toward me. We both sort of smiled at one another. She walked past me and I turned around and followed her into a restaurant. I asked her if I could sit with her and she said I could. Six or eight months later, on June 6, we eloped to Cartersville. So, I was already married when the War started.

    I was drafted and went into the Navy. After a month of boot camp in Virginia, I was sent to Newport, Rhode Island, for about three months, for advanced training in Gunnery and Radar. If we were under attack, I was to be a gunner. Otherwise, I did radar operating. I then spent four months in Philadelphia. By that time, Sarah and I had a son, Dan. She brought Dan to Philadelphia while I was stationed there.

    I was assigned to a brand new Battle Cruiser, the *U.S.S. Guam*—a "pocket battleship." We sailed down the east coast of the U.S., through the Panama Canal, and out to the south Pacific. We never had a base. For four years we just kept moving. We took on our fuel and ammunition at sea. A small mail boat, which made its rounds of the fleet, brought us mail about once a month. There were 2500 guys on board and we slept in hammocks (we called them racks) stacked four or five high. You just hoped the guy sleeping in the hammock above you didn't weigh too much.

Our ship's first stop was at Pearl Harbor for fuel. Because of the damage to the harbor, we had to anchor outside the harbor. From there, we went to the Philippines. That was our first battle. My battle station was a five-inch anti-aircraft gun. There were five men on each eight-hour shift at that station. I was a loader. I don't know whether our gun ever hit anything or not. They didn't tell us. We were in six other battles after that.

We had a full hospital and four doctors on our ship. Just before the War was over, one of our aircraft carriers was hit by two bombs and started to sink. We went out to take the men off that ship and bring them to our hospital. I was helping bring the men aboard and heard one eighteen-year-old boy say, "I just bought me a new pair of shoes today." There was just one problem, his left foot had been blown completely off. He died that night. I have other stories, but that one stayed on my mind more than anything else.

Iwo Jima and Okinawa were my last two battles. We were in Okinawa one morning, loading ammunition to go to Japan when they called and said, "Guys, it's all over." We ditched that ammunition over the sides of our ship. That was the one of the happiest days of my life. We hadn't had a celebration when VE-Day occurred because we still had a job to do but we did celebrate on VJ-Day.

After that, we went to Inchon Harbor, Korea, to wait our turn to come home. We stayed there about a month, then sailed home on the same ship we went out on. We sailed into New York harbor and dumped the rest of our ammunition there. I can tell you, there's a lot of ammunition in the harbor at New York. Today, the *U.S.S. Guam* is anchored in Charleston Harbor.

I got my orders to be discharged but had to go to Jacksonville, Florida, to actually process out. That was one slow train. It took us four days. I was discharged in October, 1945, and took the train to Atlanta, where Sarah and Dan met me.

At the time of my discharge, I held the rank of Petty Officer, Third Class. I wouldn't take anything for my War experience. It taught me a whole lot about life, what it was and what it means to me. I am proud of the part I had.

When I got home, I took about a month off, then got a job at the Army Service Depot, driving a truck. I did that for about a year and a half. Then I worked for about three years at the Lawson General (VA) Hospital in Chamblee. After that, I came to Lockheed and worked there for 35 years in the planning and engineering division. I also spent 25 years doing sports broadcasting for the kids in Marietta and around Cobb County, on station WFOM.

Meanwhile, Sarah worked as a secretary at Life of Georgia, and then at Potter and Company until she died. We had been married 50 years and she was one heck of a sweet girl. Sarah and I have four children: Dan, Miriam, Freddie, and Sharon.

—Interviewed by Charles Miller, October, 2001

Pepper Martin

JOHN H. MATTHEWS
With
Abbie Matthews

I met my late husband, John Matthews, on a streetcar going to Atlanta to work. John was born here in Marietta on July 16, 1918. He graduated from Marietta High School and attended Draughn School of Commerce. I attended Fulton High School in Atlanta. When John saw me on the streetcar he arranged for a friend to introduce us. We dated for two years and were married, at John's mother's home in Marietta, January 14, 1939.

Even though John was working for the government and we had a six-month-old son, he was drafted into the Navy. On April 11, 1944, after processing at Fort Benning, Georgia, he went to the naval training base in Bainbridge, Maryland. From Bainbridge, John was sent directly to the Pacific, assigned to the *U.S.S. Porterfield*, a Destroyer. He remained on that ship doing office work the whole time he was in the Navy. Of course, he had to stand guard duty, too.

The *U.S.S. Porterfield* was engaged in many of the major battles of the Pacific. John was there for the campaigns on Guam, the Philippines, Okinawa, and Iwo Jima, and a number of other islands. The ship came back to San Diego, in the Fall of 1945, for repairs. John was discharged about in March of 1946, as a Yeoman 2nd Class. He was awarded the Victory Medal, the American Theater Medal, the Asiatic Pacific Medal, and the Philippine Campaign.

Meanwhile, back in Marietta, in our house at 210 Frazier Street, I coped with the baby. I was able to make our house payments by keeping two girls from the Bell Bomber Plant as boarders. When John's ship came back to San Diego, I took the baby and drove out to be with him. I had four recapped tires and another lady went with me to help with the driving. It took about four days.

After John's discharge, we drove back to Marietta, and he returned to working for the federal government. We came to Marietta First Baptist Church in the early fifties. John served as a Deacon, and eventually as Chairman of the Deacons. He was Training Union Director, and also taught intermediate boys. I taught junior girls for several of years.

John died from a heart attack in April, 1962, at the age of 43. His was the first funeral conducted in the Sanctuary. Our son, Mike, was eighteen and a student at Emory University. Our daughter, Polly, was fifteen and a sophomore at Marietta High School.

I worked at McRae Style Shop, doing alterations. I continued to do alterations for people until I turned 80. Then I decided it was time to hang it up.

John never did talk much about his World War II experiences. He just wasn't cut out for military life but he felt that he did his duty for his Country.

—Interviewed by Ruth Miller, June, 2001

John Matthews

PIERCE "BUCK" MCCURLEY
With
Martha Crissey McCurley

My husband, Buck, was raised just up the road from Marietta, Georgia, in Elizabeth. On his eighteenth birthday, April 10, 1943, he and some of his friends joined the Marine Corps. The basic training at Camp Le Jeune, North Carolina, was quite rigorous. The recruits had to crawl under live bullets and all of that. Buck never did learn to swim. He said he would sink right to the bottom, but they kept him anyway.

Buck was assigned to the Third Marine Air Wing. He was in the Identification Friend or Foe (IFF) unit. It was a radar unit. He was shipped overseas on an aircraft carrier. They slept on the deck. He saw action at Bougainville and in the Philippines. His discharge papers indicate he was involved in battles in the northern Solomon Islands and in the Philippine Islands Campaign.

As part of a radar unit, Buck operated mostly behind the lines. One time his unit was shelled by artillery and they shot back but they don't know if they hit anything. Another time he helped recover some survivors from a battalion which had been mortared out of usefulness. He liked to tell the story about being on guard duty one night. He wasn't supposed to be sitting down but he was sitting on the tail gate of a truck with his gun on his lap, watching the trail. He was more worried about an officer catching him sitting down than he was about the enemy. Suddenly he heard a big noise behind him and something coming crashing through. He just knew a Jap had him. It scared him so badly he couldn't even find his rifle. It turned out to be a cow.

Buck served in the Marine Corps until July, 1945. He came out with the rank of Private First Class. He took his GED at Marietta High School and later attended Georgia State College. He worked at various jobs but then went to work for Bell Telephone and worked there thirty-something years.

I believe Buck was glad that he had a part in the War but I think he was glad to get out, too. He wanted to get on with his life. One of his best memories was of a pilot who looked him up to give him a hug and to say thanks for saving his life. He gets a little teary when he tells about that.

I have a few memories of war time in Marietta. We lived across Washington Street from the National Cemetery. They took the stacks of cannon balls from the Cemetery and melted them down for the war effort. They also melted down the cannons that had been in the park (Marietta Square). We saved tin foil and made great big balls of it. We all coped with shortages. Most of the young men my age were gone. We young people would find one person who had a car, pool all of our gasoline stamps and get enough gas to go for a little drive somewhere.

I met Buck on a blind date on Christmas Day, 1945. He was the only blind date I ever had.

—Interviewed by Marcus McLeroy, November, 2001

CLIFTON MOOR

I was born and grew up in Marietta, Georgia. At the age of 23, in November or December of 1942, I was drafted into the Army. I spent my first year of service in Louisiana. Basic training lasted about three months, with lots of drilling, marching, and 25-mile hikes. My second year I was in Gainesville, Texas. After that I went overseas. I was part of the 103rd Infantry Division, 382nd Field Artillery Battalion, Company B.

We traveled overseas in a convoy of ships in October, 1944. It took us about fifteen days. During that time, we were in a storm for three days. The ships were double loaded. One night you would have a bunk to sleep in and the next night you had to sleep on the deck or wherever you could find a place.

I had about six months of actual combat. We were shooting with Howitzers. We were not right up at the front. We didn't have face to face encounters with the enemy. The Howitzers were supposed to shoot about seven miles. We would fire a round and then our forward observer would tell us how to adjust the range and elevation so that we could hit the target the next time.

I was in Paris the day the War ended in Japan. Everybody wanted to celebrate. It took us about two months to get home after the War. Originally we were supposed to come home for thirty days leave and then go to Japan but the War ended so we got to come home to stay. I didn't have quite enough points to get out of the service, but before my furlough was up I had enough points so I didn't go back. Since I was already home, I just drove down to Fort McPherson in Atlanta that day and got my discharge and came back home.

I'm proud to have served in the military service. Almost everybody was. It was the right thing to do. I was awarded the American Service Medal, the World War II Victory Medal, Good Conduct Medal, and the European Action Mid Eastern Service Medal with two Bronze Stars. I came out of the service with the rank of Private First Class. I wasn't interested in advancing in rank. I just wanted to get through and get back home. I had a wife and a baby girl (Clair) who was nearly a year old by the time I got home.

After the War, I had a dairy for seventeen years. Later I had a farm where I raised beef cattle.

—Interviewed by Marcus McLeroy, August, 2001

Clifton Moor

JOE MOOR
With
Pam Moor Gomez,
Eddie Gomez, and
Chuck Miller

Joe Moor was born in Marietta, Georgia, on February 17, 1922. He grew up there and graduated from Marietta High School in 1940. He worked off and on as a soda jerk at Atherton's and Dunaway's drugstores. He was also a lifeguard at Brumby Pool. Joe attended Georgia Tech, where he was on the swim and dive teams.

Joe volunteered for Army duty in 1943. After basic training at Ft. Stewart, Georgia, and airborne school at Toccoa, Georgia, he shipped out to England aboard the *Queen Mary*. As part of the 101st Airborne Division, Joe was assigned to the 501st Paratroop Infantry Regiment, Charlie Company. His unit spent about six months in England getting ready for the invasion of Europe and D-Day. During that time Joe became a Jump Master. The Jump Master was responsible for checking everyone's gear. Sometimes he would be the first to jump but usually he was the last. He would tap the shoulder of each man to signal that the previous jumper had cleared the airplane.

On D-Day, the planes carrying the paratroopers

encountered heavy ground fire. Not only did the pilots start going in all directions instead of to their assigned drop zone, they didn't reduce the plane's speed to "jump speed." Consequently the paratroopers went out at the wrong speed. The shock of the parachute opening at that high speed caused a lot of the men to lose their equipment. Many landed with only a side arm or a bayonet. They were spread all over everywhere and then had to try to find their buddies and their equipment. Joe landed in a canal, waist deep in water, and pitch black. He hooked up with some men from the 82nd Airborne and was eventually able to rejoin his group. Even though they had been dropped at the wrong place, with the wrong units, and with everything else wrong, they did a spectacular job of sealing off the right side of the action (the Cherbourg peninsula) and keeping the Germans in that area out of the battle zone.

Still on the right side of the line, the 101st then advanced through France and made significant progress. After two months of combat they were pulled out and sent back to England for R&R. That's where they were when the concept of "Market Garden" was conceived. By September, 1944, the allied armies had pushed up to the border of Germany and through Belgium to the border of Holland.

Headed by British General Montgomery, "Market Garden" was to be the largest airborne operation ever attempted. It was to liberate Holland. Four airborne divisions would be involved: One British division, one Polish division, and the 101st and 82nd Airborne Divisions. These forces were to take and hold one road across the heart of Holland while armored divisions advanced up that road to the city of Arnhem on the Rhine River and take the town and the bridge. The movie, "A Bridge Too Far" tells the story of this effort.

Joe's unit went into the battle not by jumping, but by glider. With Germans to the north and south of them, the Americans went right into the middle of the Germans. The theory that the Germans would be so disorganized from the Normandy rout that they wouldn't be able to resist turned out to be very wrong.

On one day, Joe's Company was ordered to take out the line of Germans who were dug in behind a levee about a hundred yards back on the opposite side of the river. The Germans were trying to demolish the bridge. The only way across was in canvas bottom boats. They crossed the river, taking fire as they went. When they hit the other side they charged across that flood plain, took the levee and rolled up that whole defensive position. They were able then to come in behind the bridge and save it. When asked what happened after that, Joe replied, "Well we just sat there and did our job and kept the road open. When they decided to pull out in September we were glided out again."

Joe's unit, which had taken a lot of casualties, then went back to France for R&R. During that time the unit got replacements and was filled up again. In December they were reassigned and took part in the Battle of the Bulge. Joe didn't talk much about this Battle, except to say, "It was really bad." The soldiers were in foxholes, with the Germans about fifty feet away. Sometimes you couldn't see because of the fog but you could hear them talking. It was freezing cold. Joe's feet were frostbitten and this damage would bother him the rest of his life. There are those who say the 101st saved Bastogne. Of course Patton did an extraordinary job of bringing his whole armored Army to the rescue. Still, it was General McAuliffe who, in answer to the Germans' asking them to surrender, uttered the words, "Nuts!" That was typical 101st Airborne attitude.

The last jump operation, Joe was involved in was "Operation Varsity." This took place in March of 1945 and involved small units of the 101st. The fighting was intense and Joe was wounded, losing half his stomach. After that he spent time in a hospital in France. It is not clear when Joe was evacuated back to the States but he stayed in the service until December 27, 1945, when he was discharged as a Technician Fifth Grade (T-5).

Joe Moor's awards and citations include the Purple Heart, Senior Jumper Wings with three stars, a Silver Star, two Bronze Stars, Good Conduct Medal, and a number of others. Although he didn't talk about his military service unless asked, Joe was proud of what he had done.

After the War, Joe returned to Marietta and served as a Master Sergeant in an armored unit of the Georgia National Guard. On May 24, 1947, he married Betty Jo Whitlock in Dallas, Georgia. Their only child, Pam, was born January 16, 1950. About that same time, Joe began to work for Marietta Electric Company. In 1958, he bought the company. He was known throughout the Cobb County for the high quality of his electrical work. Joe loved and was faithful to his church.

Joe Moor died in April, 2001. He was predeceased by his wife, Betty, on August 28, 1985.

—Material compiled by Chuck Miller from conversations with Joe Moor, Pam Moor Gomez and Eddie Gomez

Joe Moor

HARRY R. MULLER

My active military service actually took place prior to Pearl Harbor. I graduated from Union Hill High School, North Bergen, New Jersey, in 1933. My goal was to attend the Naval Academy. Since my family didn't have any political clout, I decided the best way to get into the Academy was via the Navy. I joined the Navy and then applied for admission to the Naval Academy, and was accepted.

While the Navy had accepted my inability to distinguish certain colors, the Academy had different tests and standards. Following their first year at the Naval Academy, Plebes are sent out to sea for a tour of duty. Usually about 25 per cent of them wash out because of poor color distinction. I was one of the ones who couldn't distinguish a red dot on a green background. This becomes critical when you are trying to find a red spar or a red buoy on a green ocean. Today, with the electronics, that wouldn't be of concern. Anyway, they took me out of the Naval Academy and put me in the Naval Reserve.

The German submarines were already in the south Atlantic and torpedoing our oil tankers which carried most of the fuel to the northeast. The people in the Miami area would actually come over to the beach at night and watch those ships getting torpedoed and exploding. The Naval Reserve was called upon to operate the oil tankers because the merchant marine sailors considered it too dangerous.

As part of the Reserve, I spent time going up and down the east coast, anywhere from Newport, Rhode Island (where the signs in the public parks read "No dogs or sailors allowed") to San Juan to Havana. We spent a lot of pleasant time in the Caribbean Islands.

This was in the later 1930's, in the period of undeclared war. The war action had already begun in Europe and the U.S. was making supplies for them. We turned our automobile factories over to making jeeps and military equipment to be sent to Europe. The Navy had a co-op program and I got in as a machinist apprentice at Wright Aeronautical, which made small engines. Among others, they made the "Cyclone," a nine-cylinder engine used on most of the bombers that went over to Europe. When the Navy started calling up the Reserve units, they looked over my record and said, "We need aircraft engines more than we need sailors." So they gave me a good discharge and I became a production planner at Wright.

Wright Aeronautical was an American company, financed by the British, using machinery from Russia. The bombing in Europe had put their manufacturing plants in a hazardous position so those countries sent their machinery over here for us to use. Big turret lathes, grinding machines, drill presses, all in metric, and we had to re-calibrate it to American measurements.

Technology back then was so different. At one of the new plants that Wright Aero built, all of the windows were blacked out so we could work at night. The roof was covered with camouflage netting so that if you flew over it, it looked like a field, and you couldn't detect the building at all. That was before radar or sound sensitive equipment and they had these big tin ears, like ear trumpets all around the building with operators sitting on a turret, swiveling those big ears around, trying to pick up sounds of any aircraft.

After Wright Aero got several plants up and running,

my job became boring, and I began to look for something else. I heard about a company called Flintkote that was making building materials. They had started a program to make "plastic onyx," a compound of asphalt, marble dust, and granite, which was remarkably resistant to gun fire. The Victory ships that were put into service had canons installed on the decks and the gun crews had no protection. Steel was in critically short supply and our plastic onyx became the material of choice for protecting the gun crews. Then we also used the plastic onyx to put on the pilot houses of the landing craft. We would get back specimens of the product that had been through battle. One time we got back a panel from a landing craft that had received a direct hit from a German four-inch shell. The shell had exploded, opening up the craft like a blossom, but it never penetrated the pilot house.

Then Flintkote got involved in rubber reclamation. Rubber was scarce and we recycled tires, water bags, inner tubes, douche bags—anything that was mostly rubber. We would grind up the stuff and then reclaim the rubber from all the refuse—the steel bands, the linen and cotton cord—by washing the grind with all kinds of acid. The acids would eat the steel and cotton and the rubber would remain to be made into tires and other things for the war effort.

About that time, the draft board went over our list of military critical people and said to me, "You are not working for a military concern anymore. This is a building materials company." I said, "Heck, we make all sorts of stuff for the military." But they said, "If you are not in a military critical industry a month from now, you're going to be drafted."

Now Bendix Aviation was just across the railroad tracks from Flintkote, so I drove over there and asked if they needed workers. Bendix hired me on the spot and worked out a share arrangement with Flintkote. As a result I spent time at both places. That was in 1942, right after Pearl Harbor. I was in my late twenties by then. Bendix made generators and airplane engine starters and other airplane parts. I was there for the beginning of radar and something called the "air position indicator." Remember technology back in the Forties was nothing.

By that time we were fighting out in the Pacific, and were losing a terrible number of fighter planes. They would take off from the aircraft carriers, and the pilots would get into a dogfight with the Japanese, which might last five to eight minutes. Afterwards, a pilot might not know where he was or where the ship was. The ship could hear the pilot on the radio but could not break radio silence to respond because that would give away the position of the ship. The pilot would be calling, "May Day, May Day. Out of gas, going down!" The ship couldn't go to get the pilot because the Japanese would be listening and send a submarine to cover the spot. You couldn't risk an aircraft carrier to pick up one person. In the beginning, we lost a couple of ships that way. So if a pilot went down he would just have to get out into his raft and pray to God that he would be found. We lost too many pilots that way.

Meanwhile, back at Bendix, we came up with the air position indicator that mechanically coordinated the clock, the air speed indicator, the bank and turn indicator, the rise and fall indicator, and all the planes instruments. Their information was fed into a box which had a reader on the instrument panel, giving latitude and longitude of the plane as it went through the dogfight. With the change of position constantly recorded, the pilot knew where he was and where the ship was. That cut down the loss of pilots.

I stayed with Bendix until after the war ended. From 1946 to 1953, I was in the hotel and resort business in Miami. In 1953, I came to Lockheed, and eventually worked in data processing. I saw the evolution from punch cards, to magnetic tapes, to computers. I retired from Lockheed at age 74, in December of 1987, just short of 35 years of service. After that, I did volunteer work of various sorts for almost ten years. My wife died in June, 1998. We had a mentally handicapped son who lived in a group home because it became too difficult to handle him at home He died as the result of choking on a sandwich.

—Interviewed by George Beggs, January, 2002

Harry Muller

THOMAS MURNER
With
Louise Johnson Murner

My late husband, Thomas Murner, was born in Macon, Georgia, October 18, 1918, the son of Eugene and Mattie Murner. They moved to Forsyth, Georgia, when he was a child. I was born, August 3, 1917, in Monroe County, Forsyth, Georgia, the daughter of Dozier Johnson and Pearl Lunsford Johnson. We lived on a farm and Thomas's father worked as a share cropper for my father.

Thomas's father died when Thomas was ten years old. After that, he and his mother lived with his older sister until he was old enough to be on his own. Thomas then took care of his mother. When he was in his teens he went to Civilian Conservation Corps (CCC) camp for a year. I met Thomas when he joined the same National Guard outfit in Forsyth that my brother belonged to. We dated for several months and were married, November 21, 1940, at the home of a preacher we both knew.

We first lived in Forsyth, and our oldest daughter, Faye, was born there on July 25, 1941. Thomas got a job in Atlanta so we moved there and that's where our second daughter, Phyllis, was born on November 19, 1942. Thomas transferred to the Marietta National Guard when we moved to Marietta. He took basic training at Camp Blanding, Florida.

When World War II started, Thomas's Company was sent to Rome, Italy. He said he walked the same road that the Apostle Paul walked while there. He was promoted to Sergeant, and on March 21, 1945, was awarded the Combat Infantry Badge. He had been overseas since November 27, 1944. While in Italy, Thomas took a course in Specifications, Estimating and Contracts given by the Mediterranean Theater branch of the Armed Forces Institute. He had been overseas eight months when he was awarded the Mediterranean Theater Defense Ribbon with two Battle Starts. He was also awarded the American Defense Ribbon, the Combat Infantry Badge, the Good Conduct Medal, and the Bronze Star for Meritorious Achievement in Ground Operations.

After the War was over, we moved to Marietta. Thomas took a course in architecture and opened an office here. He went back into the National Guard in Marietta and was promoted to 2nd Lieutenant and then 1st Lieutenant. He was selected as leader of the local Tank Unit and later assumed command of the Marietta Ground Force of the National Guard Tank Company 1220, Infantry, succeeding Captain Clarence Delk, who served for two years.

On August 5, 1955, while attending a National Guard Training Camp, Thomas was killed in a car wreck. He had been returning from Savannah Beach to Camp Stewart when his car went over an embankment on U.S. 17 and he was thrown from the car. Our daughters were fourteen and thirteen at the time.

I hadn't had to work while I was married. After Thomas's death, it dawned on me that I had two children to support. I got a job at Lockheed and at the same time went to Massey Business School. When Lockheed had a lay-off, I worked for an insurance company and then in several other businesses. I later took care of Mae and I.B. Hall's grandchildren. I have been active and have held several offices in the Odd Fellows and Rebekah Organization.

Our daughter, Faye, has one daughter who lives in Marietta, and one grandson, who is in military school. My oldest grandson (Phyllis's son), Charles Roan, is a Lt. Colonel, stationed in Columbus, Georgia. I have two other grandchildren and five great grandchildren. I am very proud of them.

—Information furnished by Louise Murner, 2002

Thomas Murner

JAMES NEWSOME

Although I was born in Danville, Virginia, my parents, who were cotton mill workers, moved to Phoenix City, Alabama, in September, 1925. They moved because my father didn't like the way cotton mill people were mistreated. I was three months old when they moved. I played sports in Phoenix City—baseball, football, tennis, and finished high school there in 1943. In June of that year, I signed up for the Navy and was inducted in September.

I entered the Navy at Montgomery, Alabama, and then was allowed to choose where I went to school—either Chicago or Pensacola, Florida. I chose Pensacola because it was warm. Once there, we went through all the standard shots and stuff and I was assigned to Shockley Field.

My father was the Fire Chief in Phoenix City. I would go out with him on calls at night and I had some rescue experience. We did take some people out of burning buildings. When the Navy learned that, they put me in the fire department and gave me an asbestos suit, which I had never seen before. I quickly learned what I was supposed to do. When the planes crashed I was to go in and try to recover the pilots or whoever else was in the plane. The Navy had good equipment. We had the same foam they still use today, and water trucks. They would throw water and foam on me in my asbestos suit to keep it from burning. Later, I was put in charge of training. I spent my days training other people to fight fire, both on airplanes and in buildings. At night I wore the asbestos suit on flights, because we were flying 24 hours a day. There were a lot of runway accidents.

At Pensacola our bedding was hammocks, six high. You got to the top hammock by way of a ladder on one end. Then you laid real still. You slept with one eye open because if you didn't someone would put your hand in warm water, or turn you over, or something. We were always having kids falling out of the top hammocks and hitting the floor. Soon after we finished basic training we got double-decker cots. The food was edible. I did a lot of night duty so I got the better food.

About six months after I entered the Navy, on our way to an alarm, I was involved in an accident. The fellow driving the fire truck was going a little too fast and had a wreck. I was on the side of the truck and was thrown like a slingshot over the truck. I spent three months in the hospital with back and leg injuries.

When I had recuperated, I applied for hydraulics school in Chicago. I spent from January to March there. The cold weather was quite an experience. While I was in Chicago I visited some of the churches. The people were wonderful to us, invited us for dinner, that sort of thing. Then I went back to Pensacola and did hydraulic maintenance. I was there when the War ended.

In the fall of 1945, Admiral Nimitz, Supreme Naval Commander of the Pacific came into New Orleans for a review and celebration. Our unit flew 150 SBD's to New Orleans for the reception. I got to ride in the back seat of one of the planes and see the ceremonies. It was quite a thrill.

Then I went to Quonset Point, Rhode Island. Did I get a shock—snow was six feet deep! I learned what snow is all about. One day I got orders to repair a plane so I went out to the runway in freezing weather. The Chief came out and asked, "Newsome, what are you doing up there on that wing?" I said, "I'm working on this airplane." He said, "No, we don't do that up here. You come into the hangar, and we bring the plane to you." Your hand would freeze to any tool you picked up. But we survived.

I played on the baseball team there at Quonset Point. One day the Captain said, "Newsome, you can't play baseball. We need you here in the squadron." Then the Lieutenant in charge of the baseball team interceded and I was allowed to work nights so that I could go on the baseball trips. The War was over by that time and things had slacked off.

Quonset Point was classified as an overseas assignment, and because of my accident that was as close as I ever got to going overseas. I had a lingering problem with my left leg after it was crushed. It was paralyzed, what they call a "dropped ligament," so I couldn't maneuver very well.

At first I was concerned that I didn't go overseas but after several years I decided that's just the way things fell. I did my part. I volunteered to do whatever had to be done. In the process I was able to do some things that other people had not done. Every time an airplane part went bad they would throw it away. I was able to fix some of those parts.

I was at Quonset Point a year. It was relatively quiet. It was a winding down period. The last month of my duty I had nothing to do. So, I laid on the beach and watched Harry Truman come in on his yacht. I mustered out on November 6, 1946, as an Aircraft Hydraulic Specialist, Second Class. I got some awards but I don't even know where they are. I don't go in for awards. Get the job done and go on about your business.

I went back home and in January, 1947, I went to the University of Alabama. I got a bachelors degree in three years, finished my master's degree, played baseball, and got a job teaching shop and drafting at Tuscaloosa High School. I was making all of $2500 a year. Lloyd Cox had been in some of my classes and one day suggested that I contact Mr. Shuler Antley, who was superintendent of schools in Marietta. That's how I got to Georgia.

I taught drafting and general shop at Marietta High School.

Then I became Principal at Dodd and Allgood elementary schools—two schools at the same time. I went on to Park Street School, where I had a bunch of good men, including Reid Brown and E.M. Funderburk, as teachers. We were able to do a lot of good things at Park Street. I also served Cobb County schools: three years at Hawthorne Elementary, eight years at Daniel Middle School, and four years at South Cobb High School. I retired from the education system in 1981.

After my work with the school systems, I worked at a variety of jobs, finally winding up in the banking business. That's what I am doing now.

I met Sarah through a friend. I needed a date for a fraternity dance and my friend said, "I know a red-headed girl that will probably date you." He fixed us up. We went to the dance but I was busy playing baseball and not interested in women. It wasn't until after baseball season that we got together. We got married in November of 1950. Sarah and I have three children, Jim, Janet, and Robin.

—Interviewed by Charles Miller, April, 2001

Jim Newsome

HENRY ORR
And
Carolyn Orr

Henry Orr

I did not join the Army. I was carried off and put in the Army. I entered at Fort McPherson and was sent to St. Petersburg, Florida, to stay in a hotel for two weeks. This country boy, born out on Stilesboro Road about a mile from Kennesaw Mountain, had never been in a hotel like that before. Nobody had any money back then. We knew we were poor but so was everyone else. I had attended a one-room school at New Salem and when I finished there I went to work as a meat cutter at Dupre's in Marietta. So, I thought that hotel was really something.

Before I even got to Florida, though, I learned not to answer to my name. At Fort McPherson, I had to wash dishes for 24 hours. They had chicken and dressing and those old pans were awful! From then on, whenever they called my name I didn't answer until I saw them packing the bags and getting down to the railroad station. Then I'd join them.

After our two weeks in the hotel, the bottom fell out and they sent us to a tent city about eight miles north of St. Petersburg. I was there about eight weeks. The place was full of briars and sand spurs. The only place to take a shower was on the golf course. From St. Petersburg, they sent me up to Larson General Hospital for a class in anatomy. I was then attached to the Army Air Corps in Orlando.

When the rest of my outfit went to Missouri, I didn't go. They needed a meat cutter down at the mess hall. Since I had done that in civilian life, they kept me there and I cut meat for the hospital for about two years. Then, when the transfer came along, all able bodied men in my outfit transferred to the Infantry. We were shipped to Fort Gordon for eight weeks of infantry training. I was assigned to the cadre to help train the enlisted men coming in. I stayed there until the War was over and they started deactivating the camp.

We were out on bivouac when VJ-Day was announced. One man fired a rifle and they just about crucified him. Our Colonel was sitting there with his steel helmet on. He pulled that thing off and threw it down through a pine thicket, saying, "I'm not going to wear that thing any more!" He had been in Germany and England for two years and said he had never worn a helmet until he came to Fort Gordon, where it was mandatory.

Meanwhile, Carolyn and I were married. That was June 17, 1945, when I came home on a weekend pass. Carolyn would come to Warrenton (about 50 miles from my base) and stay with friends there. That is where we first met I.B. and Mae Hall. I.B. was pastor at Warrenton First Baptist Church.

When the Army deactivated the camp, they sent me to Camp Roberts, California. Carolyn went with me but there was no decent place to stay. After about two weeks, Carolyn came back to Marietta and went back to Reinhardt College.

My meat cutting experience came in handy while I was at Camp Roberts. Instead of having to go on a three-week bivouac up in the mountains, I was assigned to teach men how to cut meat. We would teach 50 at a time. There were

100,000 men at various camps and all the meat was boned and sent out to mess halls around the whole country. When they closed Camp Roberts, they sent the meat cutting, cooking, and bakery schools to the State of Washington. The Colonel told me, "If you go with me, I guarantee you will be First Sergeant by the time you get there." I said, "Colonel, I wouldn't go with you if you told me I would be a Colonel when we got there. I'm going back to Georgia."

They put us on a troop train, across Texas, and I finally got back to Atlanta. That's where I mustered out on February 13, 1946. Since then I have farmed, cut meat, run a grocery store, and hauled hog feed. I would rather farm than do anything else, but just one man farming couldn't make a living so I farmed and cut meat at the same time.

I have no regrets about my military service. I had no desire to go, but after it was over with I was glad I went. In the Army, if you do what they tell you to do and do a good job you have no problems.

Carolyn Orr

I was in my third year at Reinhardt College when Henry called to say he was coming home. I just packed my trunk and called Daddy to come and get me. Mother and I drove over to Henry's mother's house to tell her that he would be home the next day. Stilesboro Road was not paved then and we just drove Daddy's old Hudson, splashing through the mud puddles, telling everybody that Henry was coming home. It was such a happy time.

We joined Marietta First Baptist Church in 1946. We were living on Polk Street and we could walk to the church. Dr. Brown said I had been a Methodist long enough and that he would baptize me any time.

Later, I finished college and taught in the public school system.

—Interviewed by Harland Armitage, May, 2001

Henry Orr

COPELAND J. PACE

I have no war hero story to tell. I was living in Decatur, Alabama, managing a retail grocery store when I was drafted in February, 1943. At the time, I was 26 years old and married (Reba and I had married September 15, 1940).

I was born in Franklin County, Alabama, about three miles from Russellville. I lived there until I was seven years old when our house was blown away by a cyclone. After that we lived on various farms. I attended rural schools through the ninth grade. I had to go four years to complete the fourth and fifth grades because we only had three and four month schools for those four years. There was no money to pay teachers for longer than that. I finished high school at Russellville in 1938.

I entered the Service February 19, 1943. I had eight weeks basic infantry training and I hated every minute of it. I was not used to taking orders. After basic training, because of vision problems, I was assigned to limited service in the Cadre as the mail clerk for the Company. Reba joined me then and worked on Post for the Post Office and the Finance Department of the Army. We lived off the Post, generally in one room, with no cooking facilities. I ate most of my meals at Camp and Reba ate out.

After six months at Camp Wheeler, Georgia, I was transferred to Camp Blanding, Florida, as a Company Mail Clerk, 195th Infantry Battalion. We traveled by troop train, not having been told where we were going, and the journey took twenty-four hours. I was later made Battalion Mail Clerk for four companies. I distributed mail, forwarded mail for those who had shipped out, and kept records on various classes of mail. I was sent to Ft. Rucker, Alabama, for six months to assist in discharging 6,000 service men. Then I was transferred back to Camp Blanding Headquarters as Mail Clerk, Headquarters Detachment Station Complement SC4-1448. About once a year we got a furlough of one or two weeks.

To the best of my memory, there was no big celebration in camp on VE-Day or VJ-Day. We were excited because we knew we would be getting out of the Service soon.

I was separated from the Service at Fort McPherson, Atlanta, Georgia, March 14, 1946. I had attained the rank of TEC-5, Corporal. I was offered a Sergeant rating one month before separation. I declined and asked that it be given to my assistant, who still had a year to serve. Reba and I were able to buy a used car while I was in Service and that's how we got home.

My decorations were what most Service men get: The American Service Medal, World War II Victory Medal, and the Good Conduct Medal. I did not like military service but was glad to do my part.

After the War, I worked for the State Employment Security Agency as Supervisor of the Veterans Readjustment Office and Unemployment Compensation Agency in Russellville, Fort Payne, and Gadsden, Alabama. I was promoted to Specialist III and sent to Montgomery, Alabama, to set up and supervise the Manpower Development and Training Acts training program. After four years, the U.S. Department of Labor asked me to come to Atlanta and take over the Program for the eight state Region. I served in this capacity until the Program expired in 1978. Then I was assigned as Regional Monitor Advocate to carry out a federal court order against the eight state Region, to assure appropriate services were provided to migrants and seasonal farm workers.

After my military service, Reba and I had two children, a daughter who lives in Birmingham, and a son who lives in Dallas, Texas. We have three grandsons, one granddaughter, and one great grandson, of whom we are very proud.

—Information furnished by Copeland Pace, August, 2002

JAMES PARRISH
And
Jo Waldrop Parrish

James Parrish

I was working for Southern Railway in Atlanta when I volunteered for military service in November, 1942. I was born in Quitman, Georgia, but we moved to Cobb County when I was six, so that's where I grew up. I had graduated from Austell High School in 1941, and was working at Southern Railway when I enlisted.

My brother, William "Bill" Parrish, had gone into the Service right after Christmas, 1941, and had become co-pilot on B-24's. He was shot down over Yugoslavia on his third mission. He was led to safety by Yugoslav Partisans and the U.S. then picked him up and took him back to Italy, and ultimately back to the U.S. My sister, Julia, was a registered nurse who served in Korea during World War II. I wanted to be a pilot and applied for the aviation cadet program. My parents had all three of their children serving in World War II.

I began basic training at Miami Beach, Florida. Everybody thinks that's the ideal place to be, but you can freeze to death there in February when you are out marching in the sand. Fortunately that only lasted thirty days and then I was sent to the University of Tennessee on a College Detachment Program. That was to sharpen our education so that we could do better on examinations for pilot training. I served at Maxwell Field, Alabama, and from there was sent to Nashville, Tennessee, for pilot training.

At Nashville, they bid me goodbye from pilot training because I couldn't judge distance well enough to land a plane. Instead, they sent me to Scott Field, Illinois, to train as a radio operator. Then I went to Yuma, Arizona, for gunnery training. We started off firing shotguns. If you fired a box of shells in one day, you ended up with a bruised shoulder. We then trained on 50 caliber machine guns, which were the guns in the waist of the B-24's we would fly.

After gunnery training, I was sent to Westover, Massachusetts, and assigned to a crew. We trained as a crew for three months so that we could operate as a team. While I was there they notified me that my brother had been repatriated and was safely back in the U.S. We flew from Massachusetts to Newfoundland, to the Azores, to Morocco, to Italy. Our base was about 60 miles south of Naples, on the Adriatic side of Italy. We were part of the 449th Bomber Squadron and flew on a periodic schedule.

My main responsibility was to check out the radio before we took off. When we dropped the bombs, I had to send the "Mission Report," telling whether or not the mission was successful and whether it was visual bombing or PFF (radar). The report was very brief. Of course it was in code so that the Germans couldn't read it. We would send the message twice then shut down. No more radio transmission after that.

I went over to Europe in November and our tour lasted seven months. We had to check every day to see if we were scheduled to fly. We bombed targets in Yugoslavia, northern Italy, southern Germany, and Czechoslovakia. One flight was nine hours long—quite a trip with an old B-

24. During that seven month period we flew twenty-five combat missions, which was considered a tour of duty. In May, 1945, when our tour was over they sent us home. We were actually on the ship going home when Germany capitulated.

We were the first ship to put into Boston Harbor after VE-Day. They had bands to welcome us home. On the pier, there was a girl in a shimmering blue dress and all the troops went to that side of the ship. They had to ask us to move to the other side because the ship was listing so badly. They took us to Fort Miles Standish, Massachusetts, and gave us an extended leave before we had to report back. I came back home and found a pretty little girl who had grown up. I had known her sister in high school, but I didn't know Jo as well. We got acquainted quickly, dated for about a week, and I asked her to marry me. That was 56 years ago, August 11, 1945.

When I reported back for duty, they sent me to Greensboro, North Carolina, where I was reclassified as a Power Operator and sent to a Fighter base at Yuma, Arizona. There were so many people there that they had a personnel surplus. I worked every third day, still in radio but in voice rather than in Morse Code.

By the time I got out of the Service, October 3, 1945, I had several medals and awards. I received the Air Medal with two Oak Leaf Clusters. Of course everybody in Europe got the European Medal. Then we got some Battle Stars on that—Rome, Anno, Air Combat Balkans, Po Valley, North Alpines, and the Rhine. I was also awarded the medal for the air raids in Ploesti, Romania, even though that had taken place two or three years before I went overseas. You know how slow the government is in awarding citations.

I went back to work at Southern Railway after my discharge. When we went overseas the government guaranteed that we would have the same job when we came back. That's how it worked out for me. I worked there about ten years and then went to work for the trucking industry. I was involved with motor carrier rate making. Eventually Jo and I went into business for ourselves, publishing tariffs for small and medium sized motor carriers. We worked well together. Since my retirement, I have done delivery work for a number of small firms, including a small blood bank in Atlanta, and Owens Flower Shop. Right now, I drive the courtesy van for Marietta Dodge five mornings a week.

How do I feel about my military service? Considering that we all went over and did what we had to do, with no loss of life, I consider myself very fortunate. Even though we went through some very heavy anti aircraft fire, not one of our crew was even wounded. We went over as a group and came back as a group. The Lord had a hand in that.

We've had a good life. Our children were raised in Marietta First Baptist. Fred Hood was the choir director and the two older children sang with him. They thought the world of Fred; and of Marguerite Borders, who worked as youth director at the church. She is an unusually talented person.

Jo Parrish

I guess I was just going into high school as my sister and James got out. I remember my mother being so worried about her son and son-in-law all in service. It was hard for my mother to get sugar or laundry soap. Of course shoes were rationed—we had to have shoe stamps. Mostly, I remember how hard it was for my mother. James and I have four children: Susan, Buddy, Kim, and Jan. They were all blessings from God.

—Interviewed by George Beggs, November, 2001

James Parish

Jo and Darrell Perkins

DARRELL PERKINS
And
Jo Perkins

My military service began in February, 1944, while I was working as a draftsman at Glen L. Martin Company in Baltimore, Maryland. I had graduated from high school in Salisbury, North Carolina, in 1939. That's where I was born in 1922. Then I worked for a year as an apprentice mechanic at an automobile dealership before entering Wake Forest University in 1940.

It was at Wake Forest that we heard the December 7th announcement about Pearl Harbor. Everybody was excited and patriotic and wanted to go do something. When we came back to classes after Christmas holidays, we found that the school had arranged to offer us a crash course in engineering, blueprint reading, drafting—any kind of work that would help the defense industry.

I finished that course in May, 1942, and with five other fraternity brothers, went off to look for defense work. That's how I ended up at Glen L. Martin. We worked on the PB-3—Navy Patrol Bomber; the B-26—medium bomber, the Big Mars Flying Boat, and another aircraft for the British Air Force. We were expected to work as long as needed and most work days lasted ten to twelve hours.

We all had first class deferments because of the work

we were doing but by the end of 1943 most of my friends at Martin had given up their deferments and had gone into the Service. The two of us who were left decided we couldn't stay any longer so we volunteered for the Air Corps. This was in February, 1944. By the way, the other fellow, Bobby Jones, eventually came to Lockheed and had a career at the Wind Tunnel.

We were inducted at Fort Mead, Maryland, and sent to Keesler Field in Biloxi, Mississippi, for basic training. While there we marched all day in the hot sun on oyster shell roads, with steam coming up. We slept in a city of eight-man tents, most of which had very large holes. Since it seemed to rain every hour we were assured of a wet bed and mosquitoes. We also had wild pigs running around, long lines at the latrines, and lots of KP (Kitchen Police). When you were on KP, you started at three o'clock in the morning and didn't finish until nine or ten at night, after you had washed the last big greasy pot. Then you collapsed.

Morale at Keelser was good. We had a good drill sergeant. He made us sing a lot but he was tolerant and gave us breaks to cool off. The heat was intense. I remember one very hot day, on parade for a visiting General, I passed out while standing at attention. (I'd had three wisdom teeth pulled the day before and had bled profusely.) While I was standing there, I saw stars sprinkle in front of me and I went down like a dead log. My buddies weren't able to catch me and I hit that concrete ramp. They soon hauled me off in the "meat wagon." I should have gotten a Purple Heart for that—shed blood in the line of duty.

After basic training they shipped us to Gunter Field in Montgomery, Alabama, to await flight training. In the meantime, they assigned us all kinds of jobs. I worked as a mechanic on the BT-13 Trainers. We had American and French cadets. We used to get a little upset with the French cadets because they handled the airplanes roughly, never reported problems or necessary repairs. There were two or three squadrons of them and we had a hard time keeping the airplanes in the air.

About the end of July, 1944, we were shipped to Spence Field in Moultrie, Georgia. Still awaiting flight training, I worked as a mechanic again. This time I worked on the AT-7's in the overhaul hangar. I also did some drafting. Then they decided to cut back on flight training and they made me an MP.

One of my MP assignments was to help guard a large group of German POW's. The prisoners got into an argument one night. Somebody had a gun and killed a couple of the others. The MP's had to go in and sort that out.

My only other bad MP experience was when one of the training students crashed and burned at an offsite location. They flew me out in the late afternoon to sit with the plane and the body until the next day. I sat there all night with that young man. A pretty sad time.

In mid-November of 1944 I went home to Salisbury on a three or five day leave. The first thing you did when you got home was go to the rationing board and get your gas allowance—one gallon per day of leave. When I got to the rationing board I saw a very, very pretty girl, and I said, "Um, would you go out with me sometime?" And she said, "Yes." That was Jo.

Jo and I dated until I had to return to Spence. Then we corresponded very frequently. Jo just wrote beautiful letters. Things were pretty serious between us. We decided, by correspondence, to get married. I got a five day leave and we were married on March 21, 1945. We had a three day honeymoon in the North Carolina mountains, then I went back to Spence. Jo was able to join me there after a few weeks. She got a job working with the Red Cross office there.

We were still at Moultrie when VE-Day came. All this time my classification was Air Trainee (AT), sometimes called a cadet. Shortly after VE-Day, we were taken out of trainee status and put into the regular Air Corps enlisted service and I became a PFC. My pay went from fifty dollars a month to fifty-four dollars.

In late July, I was shipped to Scott Field in Bellville, Illinois, to be trained as a radio operator. Jo went back home to Salisbury. Shortly thereafter, VJ-Day occurred. They closed down our radio training and assigned us various jobs. I could type so they put me in the personnel processing center.

I rented a little two room apartment and Jo joined me again. She got a job in East St. Louis and rode the bus everyday. Money was a little tight. One time we ran out of money and had to borrow a dime from the lady next door so that Jo could ride the bus to work and get her paycheck. We really suffered from the cold that winter because you didn't get a coal allotment unless you had been a resident for a year. The furnace was in the basement of our little place. I bought a hatchet and chopped everything I could find that was made of wood, including every other basement stair. But we made it.

In early November, I was typing orders and across my desk came "Darrell Perkins," to be shipped to Las Vegas, then onward to San Francisco and overseas to the Philippines for occupation duty. So Jo went back to North Carolina and I took the train to Las Vegas. When we arrived in Las Vegas, they wanted us to re-enlist for three years. I said, "No sir. Man, I don't want to stay in this man's army a day more than I have to."

Just to show how the Lord works things out, a few days later, I read on the bulletin board that Congress had passed special legislation that all air trainees who had volunteered from civilian life into the Air Corps were now eligible for discharge. Of course the squadron office was flooded with requests. They gave us the choice of being discharged in

Las Vegas or going back to a base nearest our home to be discharged. Another fellow and I decided we'd go back to Goldsboro, North Carolina, to be discharged.

Well, the train and bus workers from Los Angeles to Kansas City were on strike. We would be provided with travel orders, money, and clothing, but no transportation. We decided to thumb our way home. We spent our first night (early December) sleeping on the dam at Lake Mead. From there, we made it to Flagstaff, Arizona, only to find that place full of servicemen. You could see feet hanging out of the hotel windows. All the restaurants had long lines. We sort of napped in a doorway that night.

The next day we caught a ride with two sailors who had bought an old car, a Hudson. They put us in the back seat along with a couple of shotguns, shotgun shells, and half a case of whiskey. We got out in the middle of the desert and the engine just blew up. The piston blew right out of the side of the crank case. Those two sailors got their shotguns and their whiskey and went out and sat down in the desert, drinking and firing off their shotguns. We got out of there as fast as we could.

We finally got a ride with an Indian family, in a two-wheel cart pulled by a donkey. The Indian made us promise that when we got to Winslow we would go into a beverage store and buy him some whiskey. I don't remember whether we bought the whiskey or not. At Winslow, we caught a ride in a Navy Transport to Olathe, Kansas, (near Kansas City). From there we got train tickets to Atlanta and on home. The trains were so crowded that this fellow and I sat out in the vestibule between the train cars. In Atlanta, we got seats to Salisbury.

I don't think I had washed or brushed my teeth or shaved in three or more days. I was so dirty that when I got off the train, Jo didn't recognize me. We went to Goldsboro and in a few days we were discharged and took a bus back home. In time for Christmas.

Our post-war years are another whole story. Briefly, I finished college at Furman University in Greenville, South Carolina, and began working in the fields of drafting, technical report writing, and writing technical manuals. On November 11 (Armistice Day), 1953, we came to Marietta and I began to work for Lockheed. I worked there 32 years, all in the same area and enjoyed it. I retired January 31, 1985.

I feel good about my military service. I wanted to be a patriot. Of course I felt the frustration of not getting into flight training. I felt that I hadn't made any significant contribution toward winning the War. But somebody had to keep the pipeline full for something to come out the other end to go to battle. It took a lot of us to do that. Our contribution was sort of second hand, but I feel good about it. Being able to have Jo with me some of the time helped a lot.

Jo and I have two children, a son, Davis, and a daughter, Sharon Challis.

—Interviewed by Charles Miller, October, 2001

ROBERT ERNEST PYLANT
With
Fred Pylant

Although my older brother, Robert Ernest Pylant (we called him Ernest), died in the Philippines, he is buried in Mountain View Cemetery, right here in Marietta.

Ernest was born in Kennesaw, Georgia, October 19, 1924. He attended local Marietta schools and graduated from Marietta High School in 1943. He was drafted straight out of high school and went into the Army. He was barely eighteen. Following his basic training, he was assigned to the Combat Medics, having never fired a gun in all his training. Before he left for the South Pacific, Ernest was able to come home for three days. When we said goodbye to him at the old train station in Atlanta, we didn't know that we would never see him again.

Ernest went by troop ship to the Pacific. He spent Christmas Day in Honolulu, in an air conditioned sick bay. Then he went on to the South Pacific. He took part in several Pacific campaigns, including the Admiralty Islands; Papua, New Guinea; Luzon, Appa, and Leyte in the Philippines. He was at the liberation of Manila and helped liberate the Santitomosk University. It was there that he met the Bradley family, who later became lifelong friends with our family.

Altogether, Ernest spent about sixteen months in the South Pacific. He was wounded in an artillery barrage in a battle at Leyte but kept on treating people whose wounds were worse than his. For that he was awarded a Bronze Star and the Purple Heart. Ernest was always good about writing to our family and would always say, "I'm doing fine." We still have boxes of his letters.

When Ernest died, May 31, 1945, everything went sour. We didn't find out what happened for two months. Then Washington sent a telegram saying he was in the First Infantry Division. We knew that was in Europe and he had never been to Europe. He had never been in the First Infantry, either. He was in the First Cavalry. We kept hoping it was some other Pfc. Robert Ernest Pylant, but it wasn't. He died in the hospital in Manila from some kind of brain fever—malaria or meningitis? We never did find out what caused his death. The letter from his Commanding Officer reads, in part, "He performed his duties in an excellent manner and always accomplished what would be expected of a first class soldier. He was held in high esteem by all members of his unit and his loss will be deeply felt by his many friends ... The Army Chaplain was called to your son's bedside and the last Rites were administered. He was given a Military Funeral with services held at the grave site...."

After the War, the Army gave parents the choice of taking an expense-paid trip to visit the grave site of your loved one, or of bringing the remains back to the United States. Mother decided to bring Ernest's body home. It was a wise decision.

A few months later, a boy from the First Medical squad of the First Cavalry Division, sent Mother Ernest's Bible and a note along with a photo of Ernest's own ambulance. Ernest had titled the picture, "Tojo's Hearse."

We all loved Ernest. He was always good to his mother and daddy. He was a good son. He bought me my first bicycle. He didn't have to do that.

I was sixteen when VJ-Day occurred. All the sirens and church bells were ringing. I wanted, in the worst way to go to Atlanta but Mother wouldn't let me.

Later, my younger brother, Bill, and I both served in the Army. I was stationed at Fort Jackson and then Fort Bragg, serving as a nursing pharmacist during the Korean War. Bill served later and was sent to Germany.

—Interviewed by George Beggs, November, 2001

Ernest Pylant

HOMER W. RAXTER
With
Wilma Raxter

My late husband, Homer Raxter, was born November 14, 1918, in Marble, North Carolina. He graduated from Andrews High School in 1936 and was working at the Ecusta Paper Corporation, Brevard, North Carolina, when he was drafted. He entered the Army in April, 1942.

Homer took his basic training at Fort Bragg, North Carolina, and from there he went by train to Camp Polk, Louisiana. I remember his talking about how dirty his clothes were by the time he arrived in Louisiana. Homer also trained as a lineman at the Signal Corps school in Fort Monmouth, New Jersey.

Three days before his unit shipped out for overseas, Homer was hospitalized with diabetes. That ended his active part in the War. Homer felt that his military experience was good. He said that all boys should go into service for a year or so before they went to college.

Homer and I met in November, 1943. He wanted to do something to help the war effort so he took a job at the Bell Bomber plant in Marietta. He rented a room in the home of Dr. I.A. White, the former pastor of Marietta First Baptist Church. Dr. White married us in January, 1945.

Following the War, when Bell Bomber closed down,

we returned to Brevard, North Carolina, where Homer owned and operated an appliance store. In Brevard, we had chosen a new doctor, Dr. Julian Sader. On our first visit to the doctor's office, when the doctor's wife (who was also his office nurse) called out Homer's name, she grabbed him and started to do a dance with him. It seems that when Mrs. Sader's brother learned that her husband would be setting up medical practice in North Carolina, he asked her to try to find out what had happened to Homer. Her brother was later killed in the War and she was still trying to find Homer. We became the best of friends.

When Lockheed opened in 1952, we returned to Marietta and Homer worked at Lockheed until his death, at age 52.

We joined Marietta First Baptist Church in 1953, where we both taught in the children's Sunday school classes. I am a charter member of the Parlor Sunday School Class. Homer was active in a number of civic organizations and was a charter member of the Marietta Men's Garden Club. His speciality was roses.

Homer Raxter died on January 17, 1971.

—Interviewed by Marcus McLeroy, April, 2002

Homer Raxter

WESLEY C. REDWINE, JR.
With
Dwayne Redwine

My brother, Wesley, (we called him Red or Junior) was twenty years older than I. He was born in 1924, and I was born in 1944. We all grew up near the little town of Hanford, California. I had not even been born yet when Red went off to war in 1942.

Early in his high school days he had broken his leg. It didn't heal well, and when he was a senior he broke it again, about the time the War started. He enlisted in the Army with a cast on his leg, just a few months before he was to graduate from high school. The Army put him in the hospital, operated on him, put an eight inch steel bar in his leg, and inducted him. At graduation exercises my father went forward from the audience to receive his oldest son's diploma.

Red, quite an airplane enthusiast and builder of model planes, took his basic training at Lackland Air Force Base. He spent some time in gunnery schools at Biloxi, Mississippi, and at Nellis Air Force Base near Las Vegas. He wasn't a big man—about five foot six or seven and 130 pounds. He was barely eighteen when they shipped him off to England, as a tail gunner, with a crew on a B-17.

In England, they were based at Farnsworth, where the government had taken over a girls' school for them to live in. Red, as the tail gunner on a B-17, flew thirty-three missions over Germany. They took part in the Swainfort Raid. The crew was fortunate. It was the first crew to come through the War without a Purple Heart in the crew. They did have to make a crash landing once on a Mosquito Fighter strip in the south of England. They landed wheels up and the plane broke apart but they all got out OK.

One time, thirty-one inches of his fifty caliber machine gun was blown off by a flak shell. It made him so nervous that when they got back to base the entire crew gave him their ration of rum.

Red flew his missions and came back home just before I was born in 1944. (He was quite offended that my mother was pregnant. He thought our parents were too old for that sort of thing.) Red suffered from "battle fatigue." Our mother told me that he had to hold a cup of coffee with two hands to avoid spilling it because he shook so badly. He was scheduled to go to the Pacific theater but did not go. He finished up his time at a small air base near Bakersfield, California. He came back from Europe six feet tall and a 180 pounds, a much different guy than when he left. He had been awarded the Distinguished Flying Cross and a number of other medals.

After the War, Red got a job as a truck driver. He had started going to school to become a veterinarian when the Korean War broke out and they recalled him. He didn't have to go to Korea though. He went back in as a gunnery trainer on the B-29's. He stayed in for two years that time. Basically, he was a truck driver the rest of his life.

My brother loved airplanes. Interestingly enough, he didn't want to fly anymore but he loved model airplanes and built them much of his life. My brother, Wesley, died in 1982.

I am proud of my brother's service. It was something that had to be done. I think it was certainly one of this Country's shining moments.

By the way, my father, Wesley Redwine, Sr., fought in France in World War I. At one point he was missing for ten days. You can imagine what France was like in 1917—no radios, few cars and trucks, mostly mules and horses. The roads were mud. No computers, few telephones. Somehow they lost track of my father. They sent my grandmother a telegram telling her he was missing in action. They took another ten days to tell her that he had been found.

My father didn't talk much about his war experiences. He did tell this one story: When they were boarding the ship to come home, someone made some fairly obscene remarks about the French. They marched them all back off the ship and they had to stay in France for another ten months, working in a quarry. A truck would come by every morning to pick them up. They would get on the truck but by the time the truck got to the quarry the truck was empty. They would just jump off the truck and lay low until night time. No one hassled them about it. It wasn't a terrible punishment but he got none of the parades and hero's welcome that the others got.

—Interviewed by Harland Armitage, November, 2001

Red Redwine

CHARLES "PETE" REEVE

Almost fifty years have passed but many vivid memories of the campaign in the South Pacific during World War II remain. Those scenes never leave one's mind....

My love affair with the U.S. Navy began when I was a senior at Lakeland (Florida) High School. Along with my parents we had gone aboard the *U.S.S. Schenk*, moored at Tampa pier, for Visitors' Day. I was impressed with everything about that ship, especially the cleanliness and the good manners of the men.

After my graduation from high school, my family moved to Calhoun, Georgia, and I enrolled at Georgia Tech. When asked for my ROTC preference, I signed up for the Navy. The summer following my second year at Tech, we had a six-week training cruise on the old World War I battleship, *Wyoming*. We were assigned to the crews of deck guns and slept in hammocks swung from the steel beams around these guns. Every morning, we were up cleaning decks and polishing brass. Part of my polishing included the ship's commissioning plaque, dated 1911. It had been polished so often you could no longer read the words.

By the time my third summer came around, the War had started in Europe. The Navy was reluctant to have us on board a ship in the Atlantic, in the way, in case of submarine encounters. Instead, we spent a month at Charleston Naval Yard, studying ship design and construction.

I started my senior year at Tech as usual. The news reports told of German activities all over Europe. On December 7, the first weekend I had not gone home, my roommate, Austin Brown, and I went to First Baptist Church, Atlanta. After lunch, we returned to our room to read. I had turned on the radio to listen to the New York Philharmonic when H.V. Kaltenborn came on the air and began describing the Japanese attach on Pearl Harbor. The next day, at ROTC class, half the cadets wore their Navy uniforms. We were later told that our graduation had been moved up from June 10 to May 16. By mid-April, I had my orders to the *U.S.S. St. Louis* (CL49), and was to report to the Commandant of the Twelfth Naval District in San Francisco.

I graduated from Georgia Tech and received my commission on May 16, 1942, and on May 17, my fiancee, Ruth Keith, and I were married. Three days later we took a train to San Francisco, where I had to report-in every day, after which we would walk around the city, enjoying the sights. Ten days later, I was told to report at six o'clock the next morning, aboard the *S.S.Grant*, an old Pacific ocean liner. I put my bride on a train for Atlanta and set sail for Honolulu.

It took us a week to get to Hawaii. It was just six months after the Japanese bombing and the place was still a mess. The entire shore line was coated with dry oil. There were overturned ships, burned out and rusting. We spent the next 26 days reporting-in every day, awaiting transportation to our ship. We finally sailed from Pearl Harbor at dawn, July 10, 1942, on the World War I Pipe Destroyer, *D.M.S. Elliott*, which had been converted to a mine sweeper. Our course was zero degrees, due north. After seven days of pitching and yawing, during which I was so seasick the ship's doctor had to give me a shot, we arrived in Alaskan waters. On July 18, we were told to stand by to leave the *Elliott* as it was being refueled from the fleet tanker, *Citron*.

In this situation, the two ships steam along parallel to each other, about 50 feet apart, hoping for smooth water. The hoses are passed, pumps connected and started. To transfer personnel, a rope is run through pulleys at the upper levels of the two ships and a large canvas bag is pulled across on pulleys. One at a time, we stood in that bag and watched the line go up and down while the two ships rolled back and forth—not always in the same direction. You just hoped you wouldn't be submerged in the ocean or slung into the next century. However, as with most things the Navy undertakes, the transfer went smoothly and we enjoyed a nice lunch on board the tanker while waiting for the *St. Louis*.

At three o'clock the *St. Louis* came alongside for fuel, mail, and six green Ensigns. She slipped out of the mist and I saw, for the first time, the ship that was to be my home, office, gym, training school, and a lot more. Captain George A Rood welcomed us and asked about our training. Two of us had ROTC and the others were 90-day wonders. We had a lawyer, an optometrist, a math teacher, an English teacher, an Industrial Management major, and I was the Electrical Engineer. The Captain said he was especially glad to see me because the Electrical Division Officer, Lt. Deterding, was just waiting for a "qualified relief" so that he could be transferred to a new ship. Six weeks later, along with our Marine Captain, and twenty others from commands in the Kodiak area, Lt. Deterding flew out on a DC-3, headed for Seattle, and was never heard from again.

In assuming the position of Electrical Division Officer, I took on responsibility for all electrical repairs on our ship. There were 51 men in my Division. The *St. Louis* was an impressive ship, with fifteen 6-inch guns, eight 5-inch guns, and four quad 40-millimeter guns mounts, and about twenty-four 20-millimeter guns. We could throw up a lot of steel. We carried four spotter planes, which were launched (flung 60 feet into the air) by catapults using a five-inch shell powder can as the prime mover. On return, the planes landed on the water and were picked up by a crane on the aft end of the ship.

Our task force had been sent to Alaska because of intelligence which indicated that the Japanese might make some landings on the Aleutian Islands. The small units they landed were not a real threat but did cause concern because they were there and would be hard to remove. We bombarded Kiska in September, 1942, and were successful. A few days later a submarine landing party reported that they found a deserted, destroyed base.

The last time we left Alaskan waters we picked up some passengers and headed for the South Pacific by way of San Francisco. Coming through Unimak Pass we were tossed around by 40 foot seas and were rolling 49 degrees for five hours. We thought we might not make it. Our destroyers had already turned back as they couldn't make forward progress. Ten days later, after running out of all provisions except canned peaches, spaghetti, and bakery items, we steamed into San Francisco. The Captain had radioed ahead and reserved a large gym and treated the entire crew to a great steak dinner. The caterers told me they served 1,000 heads of lettuce and 500 gallons of milk.

When we returned to the ship, our shore lines had been connected and I put in a call to my wife. She caught the first train to California. I rode a bus to the same hotel we stayed in back in June. I got a room and went and put my bag on the deck, and sat down. In two minutes, Ruth was at the door. We didn't waste much of our leave time. After 26 days, Ruth took the train back to Georgia and the *St. Louis* was off to the South Pacific. A dolphin with a large scar on his head went along with us playing in our bow wake for 4800 miles.

After a fueling stop at Pago Pago, we sailed for New Caledonia, arriving on December 20, 1942. The next day we sailed north to the New Hebrides, where Espiritu Santos would be our operating base for more than a year.

On Christmas Eve, we anchored in a long slip between Espiritu Santos and Aore Island. This channel was a mile wide and ten miles long. Both ends were defended by submarine nets through which we had to pass each time we came in or went out. We had small patrol boats outside the harbor to advise ships where the nets and mine fields were and to pilot the larger ships to safety.

The *S.S. President Cleveland*, a large Pacific liner from peacetime, was coming into the port with army cargo and 5,000 soldiers. Upon being challenged by this little 50-foot boat, the ship's Captain replied, "I've entered this port dozens of times and know where the channel is." He promptly hit one of our mines and started to sink. He had enough sense to run the bow of the ship up on the beach and held it there as long as the engines would turn. They did not lose a man, but when the ship finally slipped off the reef into 600 feet of water she took with her to the bottom of the slip 15,000 new Garand rifles destined for the Marines on Guadalcanal.

When we had arrived at Espiritu the *U.S.S. San Diego* was there. Within a few days she was having abandon ship drills on a full compliance schedule. Our ten mile channel sometimes had a four knot current. When 700 men in life jackets and on cord-and-ball rafts hit the water they flooded the harbor. There were about ten boats picking them up. Some men were five miles away when they were finally picked up.

Guadalcanal was 600 miles north of Espiritu Santos. The twenty-mile-wide channel which separated Guadalcanal and Florida Island was named Sealark Channel, but was later dubbed "Iron Bottom Bay" because of the number of ships sunk there. Beginning in August, 1942, major battles were fought there as Japan tried to provision their troops on Guadalcanal while we tried to destroy those ships bringing in supplies. Eventually the Japanese only used high speed destroyers for midnight runs which had become troop removal efforts as they knew they had lost the Island. Our PT boats did a good job of keeping the Japanese out.

The Japanese had airfields on New Georgia and New Guinea from which they continued to harass our forces. Munda Airfield, very important to the Japanese, was within range of planes, even fighters, so they put in frequent appearances. We bombarded Munda Airfield twice in early 1943. We also made similar runs at their bases on Bougainville. During July, 1943, our patrol planes spotted a cruiser-escorted transport group headed down the "Slot" toward New Georgia. We were ordered to intercept them. This required flank speed (32 knots) for twelve hours, which brought us within radar contact with them at midnight.

We assumed battle formation and closed the range to 7,000 yards. The Admiral sent our destroyers in to torpedo-firing range of 3,000 yards. When they fired their torpedoes we opened fire with our main battery of fifteen 6-inch guns on each cruiser. Within ten minutes it was all over. Our destroyers had good hits. The Japs turned on their searchlights after their spotters saw phosphorescent wakes to portside. When they saw our destroyers their 8-inch turrets were swinging around to blow our destroyers out of the water. As their guns bore down on the destroyers our first salvo struck them full on. They never fired a shot. In a minute or so our torpedoes struck their cruisers. Meanwhile, one of their destroyers had spotted the *U.S.S. Helena*. She was out of flashless powder and was using smokeless powder, which gave off longer lasting flashes. The Jap fired his torpedoes at 2,000 yards. The *Helena* took three hits and broke in half, sinking almost immediately.

Since Munda was only fifty miles away the Admiral left two destroyers on the scene to recover survivors and ordered the rest of our task force to withdraw toward Tulagi, a harbor on Florida Island, 500 miles to the southeast. By daylight we slowed to twenty-five knots and saw 150 of our fighter planes from Guadalcanal headed up the Slot. When they reached the rescue area they found that the Japs had started strafing our sailors in the water. One of the biggest dogfights of the War followed. We lost three planes and the Japs lost all of theirs.

At two or three in the afternoon our speeding destroyers passed us with 1,100 oil-soaked survivors sitting on their decks. When we arrived in Tulagi, just before dark, we steamed by one of the "cans", the *U.S.S. O'Bannon*, at which time their men manned the rail, yelling and waving their hats to thank us for our excellent gunnery when they were in the spotlight. It was a moving experience.

Our gun crews in the main turrets used semi-fixed ammunition, that is, the shell was one piece and the powder was in a can about two feet long. Both pieces were raised from the magazines down below by hydraulic hoists. The first shellman took the shell off the hoist, rotated his body 180 degrees and laid the shell in the gun tray. Each shell weighed 130 pounds. We fired salvo fire—the main control closed the firing circuit every seven seconds and the guns which were loaded fired. In one twelve minute period during one battle we averaged over fourteen guns firing. After twelve minutes the cease firing buzzer sounded and the bedlam ceased. At that moment thirteen of our fifteen first shellmen keeled over in a dead faint, completely exhausted. In that twelve minutes, each man had moved 12,000 pounds five feet. They were great guys. None stopped or slowed down until the fracas was over.

The same kind of battle happened a week later at a point about 50 miles further up the Slot. This time the Japanese left a tail guard five miles behind. When the gunfire started he got a bearing on us and fired all of his "fish" in a spread from 8,0000 yards. In a few minutes they reached us. He had set our speed in his range solution as 30 knots. We were making 28.7 knots at the Admiral's order, so instead of hitting us midships, they hit us twenty-four feet from the bow. We lost some peak tanks but our damage was not serious. We slowed to twelve knots until reaching Espiritu Santos, where they poured some concrete ahead of Turret One and built us a stubby bow under our misshapen nose.

After the damage control parties inspected the forward portion of the ship we got underway at twelve knots for Tulagi harbor. At twelve knots, it took us two and a half days to get there, but we made it. The repair ship mechanics poured a wall of concrete three feet thick, reaching from side to side and from the keel to about eight feet above the water line. We then headed across the Pacific for Mare Island (San Francisco), a 6,000 mile trip that at twelve knots would take a month. When we arrived at Mare Island I called my wife and told her to meet me at the Atlanta airport in two days. My leave papers had been prepared even before we docked. In 30 hours I flew to Atlanta, stopping at Los Angeles, Phoenix, San Antonio, Dallas, New Orleans, and Birmingham. I arrived in Calhoun in mid-September, 1943. I was one of the first war veterans to return to Calhoun. Many others had come home in boxes. God is merciful.

I had twenty-one short days of leave then we headed to California by train. We couldn't fly because of air priorities. Most of our war planes were made on the West Coast. The greatest demand for planes was in the European theater so all west-bound planes were full of ferry pilots going back for more planes. We got an apartment near the pier. I was able to get off every other day at noon and had to be back by eight AM. Ruth came to the ship for dinner on the days I had to stay on board. After about three months for repairs, we headed back to the South Pacific with a completely reconditioned ship under us.

During the late fall and winter of 1943-1944, we bombarded Bougainville, New Georgia, and Munda air base several times. On one occasion, we escorted some landing craft on a mission to install a radar station on Green

Island. To avoid detection of the landing party we were ordered to steam around in the large sea between Bougainville and New Guinea. We spread our task force out and traveled pretty fast until we were spotted by Jap patrol planes. The landing party was successful but we spent the day fighting off Jap planes with no fighter planes for cover. We were too far from our airfields for our planes to reach us. We made a huge smoke screen and kept running in and out of it in order to confuse the Jap flyers. They still managed to get to us late in the afternoon.

A Jap dive bomber came in low over the water toward us headed directly for the after bridge. Every gun on the starboard side was blazing away at him. He was on fire and coming in fast. This was in the days before the Japs started using *kamikaze* tactics. He flew right over us about 40 feet behind the secondary bridge, dropped one 220 pound bomb in the water short of us, dropped one 550 pounder on the deck and one 220 pounder in the water about twenty feet beyond the ship. The 220 pounders were instant fuse but the 550 was armor-piercing. It went through three decks and exploded in the compartment being occupied by the engine room relief crew, killing twenty-three of them. It was the most frightening thing I had ever experienced.

The damaged compartment contained our mail room and the ventilation ducts from the aft engine room to the topside air source. At 28 plus knots a large amount of steam is going though the engines, creating a rather warm place to be. Loss of cooling air quickly made the place unbearable and the crew was ordered to leave the engine room and go topside. The steam at the boilers cannot be cut off without a gradual cool-down. We were stuck with an engine room making 28.7 knots when the Admiral signaled a speed of twenty knots. Our other engine room was completely shut off, down to zero engine turns. The ship slowed to 23.7 knots and would go no slower. So, the

Admiral wisely rang up 23.7 for the task force. As soon as the fires were out we opened all hatches to allow for air ventilation down below. It was about three hours before the machinists could go into number two and cut the throttles back.

When we arrived at Tulagi a couple of days later, my orders to the Naval Architecture school at the University of Michigan were in and a week later, on March 1, 1944, I left the *St. Louis* and never saw her again. Leaving her was a sad day, for I had many friends aboard.

I flew from Guadalcanal to Espiritu, to Fiji, to Christmas Island, to Honolulu, to Detroit. I checked in at the University and arranged for Ruth to join me. The Naval Architecture curriculum was tough but it was a great school. I was allowed to play in the University of Michigan band. Ruth stayed with me until early May, when she returned to Calhoun because she was expecting our first child. On June 4, I received the great call that Peter had arrived.

We completed our class on November 1, and I was assigned to the Norfolk Navy Yard at Portsmouth, Virginia. I coordinated the work for certain types of ships while they were being prepared for sea for the first time. We were on a nine-hour day and while there we began to receive ships which had been hit by *kamikaze* planes. It was frightening to see a large transport or tanker completely burned out on the top deck and rusty. Some had temporary bridges built near the bow so that they could be navigated.

After the atomic bomb was dropped on Hiroshima, we all held our breath. When the other bomb hit Nagasaki it was all over. We got in our car and went into Portsmouth. It was a never-to-be-forgotten moment. Everyone was so relieved and large groups of people praying on the corners and in yards showed how grateful we all were. You have no idea of just what jubilation one goes through when the worlds worst war has just ended and no more bombs will fall, hopefully forever.

By October 1, I was getting notice of my separation from the Navy. I spent two years and a 160,000 sea miles in a box of steel with 1200 men—all wanting to be back home or any place besides the graveyard of the Pacific. Many of our men did die there. A funeral at sea is a tragic event. A man dies, no family anywhere near, not time to send messages or to receive answers, so the hero is sewn into a canvas with a 50-pound dummy shell, laid on a long board and covered with the Stars and Stripes. After a prayer by the Chaplain, the body slides off the board, out from under the flag, and into the endless sea. There is no break in course or speed. The ship steams on as usual, its destination unchanged by the loss of one or more sailors. Such moments are never lost but stay buried in the innermost reaches of one's mind.

Pete Reeve died on August 4, 2000

—Most of this narrative was written by Pete Reeve, and furnished by his widow, Lois Reeve.

DOYLE ROACH

I was born in Cherokee County, Georgia, in 1927. When I was nine years old my family moved to Cobb County and that's where I went to school. I dropped out of school in the eighth grade. Later, I completed my schooling by correspondence courses through American High School in Chicago, Illinois.

My first wife and I were married on June 25, 1944. I joined the Navy on April 6, 1945, and took my training at Great Lakes, Illinois. Basic training lasted about six weeks and was a lot of calisthenics, drills, hiking. The usual. I enjoyed it.

After basic training, I went to the Navy Pier in Chicago. My wife had a serious operation and I got so nervous it made me ill. I was allowed to leave the service and go back home. I was discharged at the Navy Pier, as an Apprentice Seaman on July 11, 1945, We were in Atlanta for both VE-Day and VJ-Day. We were down in the middle of Atlanta at Five Points and there was quite a celebration.

After the War I worked several places. I went to work for Lockheed in May, 1951, and worked there for 38 years.

My first wife passed away in 1997. We had been married fifty-three years and five months and had two children, a son and a daughter. A few months later a friend introduced me to Margaret Boyd. We started dating and after two years, we married. That is when I came to Marietta First Baptist Church. I thank God that He gave me two beautiful wonderful women in my life.

—Interviewed by Marcus McLeroy, July, 2001

ARTHUR THOMAS ROBERTS
With
Dorothy Roberts

Arthur Roberts and I met, in 1938, while we were students at Berry College. Arthur was an excellent musician and the day we met he was playing the piano for the college orchestra. He claimed he looked up and saw me standing near the piano and said, "That's the girl I'm going to marry." Five years later he did.

Arthur was born, December 8, 1919, on a farm near Plains, Georgia. I came from Madison, Georgia, the town Sherman refused to burn. Following his graduation from Berry, in 1940, Arthur taught high school English at Preston, Georgia. I graduated from Berry in 1942, and we planned to be married on August 31, 1942, but Uncle Sam's letter arrived and Arthur had to go into the Army. On July 30, 1942, he reported to Fort McPherson, Atlanta, to become part of the 3505th Army Air Force Unit. I rode the bus with him as far as Macon. That was the last time I saw him until the next summer, the day before we were married. I took over his teaching position at Preston.

After six weeks basic training in St. Petersburg, Florida,

Arthur was sent to Sioux Falls, South Dakota, for Army Air Force radio technical school. Sioux Falls was just a small Midwestern prairie town, The winter temperature was about 25 degrees below zero. When the blizzards came, they ran ropes from one building to another to hold onto, because you couldn't see where you were going. The wind was terrible. Arthur graduated from that training in January, 1943, and was given the choice of Officer Candidate School (OCS), radar school in Florida, or staying in Sioux Falls as an instructor. He actually filled out the papers to go to OCS but on the way to the post office to mail them, he threw them in the trash can. He had decided that he would rather stay in Sioux Falls so that we could get married.

I left Atlanta, for Sioux Falls, on June 7, 1943, for the two day train trip to South Dakota. Arthur had gotten me a Pullman ticket—the only time we could afford one. I had to change stations in Chicago, quite an experience for a little Georgia girl who had only ever traveled to Washington, D.C. for her high school senior trip. I arrived about two o'clock on the afternoon on June 9.

Arthur had been going to the USO at the Episcopal church and when the ladies there found out we were to be married, they wanted to help with our wedding. They did the refreshments. All we had to pay for were the cake ($4.50) and my flowers ($4.50). One of the ladies even sent a telegram to my folks to let them know I would stay the night at her home. So, Arthur in his uniform, and I, dressed in a simple dress purchased from Lerner's in Americus and a mail order veil from Rich's in Atlanta, were married. Following the reception, we took a taxi to the rooms Arthur had rented for us. He had a three-day weekend pass.

We attended the Central Baptist Church in Sioux Falls.

That was where the military couples were made welcome. The two Christmases we were there, the pastor and his wife, instead of giving gifts to each other, held a dinner for the service couples. The pecan pie recipe I still use is from one of the South Carolina service wives who grew up on a pecan farm.

We stayed in Sioux Falls until May, 1945, when Arthur was transferred to Madison, Wisconsin. He traveled by troop train and I, five-months pregnant, rode with some friends. Arthur and I met up at the USO and started hunting for a place to live. I found a listing of someone who was willing to rent out the room of her son, who was in the South Pacific. I went to check it out, trying to conceal my condition by wearing my navy blue suit with a three-inch safety pin holding the waistband together but the woman knew. She let us have the room anyway. We stayed in Madison two months and then Arthur was transferred to Lincoln, Nebraska, and I began the search for an obstetrician and a place for us to live. After several unsatisfactory rooms, we settled, along with 25 other service people, in a house where we all shared the bathroom. Arthur's and my room was an enclosed porch, with a tiny kitchen made from a closet. It had no water so we had to carry the water from the bathroom and take it back there. Linda was born in Lincoln General Hospital, in September. I owe my life and Linda's to the old doctor who had consented to care for me.

All the time we were in Nebraska, Arthur's base was being packed up to be sent to the South Pacific. I was afraid I was going to be left by myself but VJ-Day came six weeks before Linda was born. There was great rejoicing in the streets.

In December, we were transferred to Belleville, Illinois. We were there less than a month when we got word that Arthur's parents had been in a terrible auto accident on New Year's Eve. As soon as Arthur got clearance we drove, in zero temperature, back to Georgia. I had pulled all the blankets and quilts off our bed to pack around Linda. At midnight, the next night, our car broke down a mile from Arthur's parents' house. We walked to the house and used a crowbar to break in. Arthur's father never regained consciousness from the accident and died a few months later, and his mother never recovered fully. Arthur was able to get a hardship discharge and left the Service on February 6, 1946, with the rank of Staff Sergeant.

In March, Arthur answered an ad in the Atlanta newspaper for a teaching position in Cobb Country, at R.L. Osborne School, which had all eleven grades. He taught English there for two years. Reid Brown was a roly-poly seventh grader there at the time. When Arthur moved on to teach at Greenleaf Business College in Atlanta, Ann (Carmichael) Corn took his place. That's where she met her husband, Denver Corn, because he lived across the street from the school.

We came to Marietta First Baptist Church in 1962. Arthur served the Church as a Deacon, co-chairman of the deacon body, Sunday School Superintendent, pianist of a Sunday school department, organist for Wednesday evening services, chairman of the Music Committee, member of the Board of Trustees, and member of the Personnel Committee, the Finance Committee, and the Long-Range Planning Committee.

After five years at Greenleaf, Arthur worked at Lanier Business Products for twenty-one years. He was working there at the time of his death. On December 16, 1974, Arthur died, following a heart attack he suffered while playing the organ at Marietta First Baptist Church.

Although Arthur kept up with two of his Army buddies for a long time, he never wanted to go to the reunions. He said, "I have done my duty . . . ."

—Interviewed by Ruth Miller, March, 2001

The Roberts' wedding.

GERALD "ROBBIE" ROBINSON
With
Bobbie Robinson

Robbie Robinson

I was born in Howland, Maine, August 27, 1920. After completing high school there, I attended business school in Bangor, Maine. I kept hearing people talk about being drafted so I just went down and enlisted in the Army. I was twenty-two when I entered basic training at Atlantic City, New Jersey, in October, 1942.

I was used to working in logging camps before I went into the Army, so I didn't think the food or the physical training were all that bad. Of course, we had some calisthenics, a little close-order drill, stuff like that but I was pretty tough. Following basic training, I went to Nebraska for Aircraft and Air Maintenance School. Then I went to Chanute Field in Illinois for Aircraft Electric Specialist training. From there, I went to a B-29 school in Seattle, Washington. Some of the B-29's were being built in Marietta, Georgia, so I was sent there for a while. That's where I met Bobbie, and married her in October, 1943.

From Marietta, I was sent to Pratte, Kansas, where we got brand new airplanes and flew them to Guam. Bobbie brought our baby son to Harrington, Kansas, so that I could see him before I left the country. As crew chief on airplane Number 9 I was responsible for everything on the airplane except the radios, the bombs, and the machine guns.

Our aircraft flew 47 missions and never had to come back without dropping its bombs. The first crew flew 35 missions. They left and went home and I got another crew that flew thirteen more missions.

My brother, John Derwin Robinson, was a tail gunner in the same squadron. He was assigned to plane Number 11. The last mission they flew, everything went wrong. They got shot up, the radio was out, they had electrical problems. They were late in coming back to the base and everyone had written them off as dead. All the planes came back except that one. I sat there in the hangar for two or three hours waiting for him to come home. I was the only person waiting when that plane finally came in—literally on a wing and a prayer. That plane was beyond salvage and had to be scrapped.

I remember how happy everyone was on VJ-Day— shooting off firecrackers and guns. Everybody wanted to go home. I don't remember how I got home. I know we flew back. I left the Air Force with the rank of Tech Sergeant, having been awarded the Bronze Star and the Good Conduct Medal. I was happy that I had enlisted, and happy to get out.

After the War, I was in the chair manufacturing business. Then I owned a metal stand company in Philadelphia and worked there until I retired.

Bobbie Robinson

I was very fortunate that my small son and I lived with my mother during the War. My oldest sister, Anna Grace Polly, had twins and we all lived together. My mother didn't charge us any rent and we didn't have any expenses so I was able to save enough money for a down payment on our first house when Robbie got out of service.

Robbie and I wrote to each other every day but sometimes the letters came in bunches. Mr. C.E. Crissey (a deacon at Marietta First Baptist Church) was our mail carrier. He faithfully and conscientiously delivered mail to our home every day. I remember the day Robbie came home. I guess he came from Atlanta by train or bus and then took a cab to the house. It was shortly after lunch that day. Everybody was excited and happy to see him.

Gerald Robinson is the brother-in-law of Sarah Goff.

—Interviewed by Marcus McLeroy, December, 2001

Buck Roebuck

REUBEN BRADLEY "BUCK" ROEBUCK

I was born, October 21, 1922, in Wilmington, North Carolina. I grew up there and graduated from New Hanover High School in 1939. I entered North Carolina State University (in Raleigh) at the age of sixteen—too young to even go around the corner by myself. I spent two years at the University. By that time, I was almost nineteen and it was 1941. I had had two years of Junior ROTC Infantry in high school and two years of Senior ROTC Infantry in college. I knew I wasn't cut out for digging foxholes, standing in water, sleeping in the cold, and eating cold food. So, I joined the Navy.

I was sent to Atlanta for a two day battery of tests (physical and mental) to see if I could qualify for the Naval Aviator program. For the physical tests we paraded around stark naked all day from one place to the next. The next day we did mental tests and at the end of the day the Commander said to me, "Mr. Roebuck, you didn't do too well on your verbal but you did excellently on your Math. Really, I don't think you are going to do any English work while you are flying, so I'm going to let you become a Naval Aviator." I took the oath of office in the old Biltmore Hotel in Atlanta in the fall of 1942.

I was one of those red-blooded American boys who really understood why we had the freedoms we had. I had cousins, a littler older than I, who had already been called up. One of my closest cousins—I have problems talking about him, even today—was on that Corregidor march and he never came back. Word was that he died in prison. Heaven knows what George went through. I was ready to go, for George and for our Country.

We went by train to Mercer University near Macon, Georgia. They didn't have any uniforms for us so they put us in surplus Civilian Conservation Corps (CCC) Camp clothing. Our commanding officer was a retired Army Sergeant who had been called up. He booted us out of bed at 5:30 AM for calisthenics and drills. We studied military science and tactics along with our flight training. We flew out of what is now Warner Robins Air Force Base. They bused us down there in the mornings and we flew either the Taylor Craft or the Taylor Cub.

After seven and a half hours of instruction, I soloed. We taxied out to the end of the runway, the instructor got out, and said, "You've got it." I thought he'd lost his mind but I did take off and I did land safely. We were just kids! It was in an elimination system. Some didn't make it but I did.

Our housing was good, clean barracks. The food was good, too. The Navy has always been known for its good food. I remember one morning we had honeydew melon for breakfast and most of the men didn't know what it was. My family was in the grocery business so I knew and I let them have a taste of my melon. Pretty soon they were all up and going back to get some. The Navy always served beans for breakfast on Saturdays, whether you liked them or not.

Our classroom instruction ranged from celestial navigation (using logarithms) to Navy regulations to math problem navigation. All of it was necessary because when you fly off the deck of an aircraft carrier with nothing around you but white caps and wind streaks, and after ten minutes you can't see the ship, you had to know what you were doing. And those around you had better know too.

The instructors were great. We not only had to know how to fly, we had to be physically fit because you never knew if you were going down in a jungle or on an island some place. I'm seventy-nine now and I think my body owes a lot to that physical conditioning.

After eighteen months of training, I graduated at Corpus Christi, Texas, on April 15, 1944. I was then sent to Miami, where I got to fly the Torpedo Bomber (TBF) by Grumman, the plane I was going to fly in the fleet. The plane, when fully loaded with a 2,000-pound torpedo, bombs under the wings, and fifty caliber forward firing machine guns, weighed 20,000 pounds. It had a single engine to take off from the deck of an aircraft carrier. Our course in Miami, consisting of tactical flying, night flying, glide bombing, field carrier landing, and formation flying, lasted six months. About the only combat duty I had was flying up and down the Atlantic seaboard on submarine patrol. I don't know what I would have done had I seen a submarine but I did have two 250 pound depth charges underneath the wings of my plane.

Military training could be just as dangerous as actual combat. Sometimes I think actual combat was easier than trying to learn how to be a combatant. I remember one day we were practicing dropping torpedoes. All of a sudden one kid was too low to the water and clipped his wing. He did cartwheels. He finally slowed down, the plane didn't blow up, and he went down in the water and came out in his Mae West, and the ship picked him up. He was at the officer's club that night.

On another day up at Woodby Island, on Puget Sound, we were making practice runs with live torpedoes on this 35-foot boat. You had to hit the water perfectly with those torpedoes or they would "porpoise"—go deep and shoot back up before leveling out. One kid dropped his torpedo aimed dead right, it porpoised just at the wrong time and split that little boat wide open. The three kids on the boat hit the water. We were lucky that day because another safety boat came by and picked them up. The water in Puget Sound isn't warm, even in August.

We had to learn to fly in formations. There would be sixteen planes, in four groups of four, flying in really close formation. You couldn't see the two planes flying on your wings and you couldn't see the lead plane. You can't get excited; you just have to sit there and sweat it for a few minutes and see what happens.

My roommate was killed while we were in Miami. He was to be married and I had gone with him the week before to downtown Miami to rent an apartment. The next weekend (October, 1944) we had to evacuate to get away from a hurricane. Several of the boys didn't make it that morning. They had midair collisions and they were flying too close to the ground. Les was one of them. I took him home to Connecticut to bury him. He was the oldest grandson. All I had to give his grandparents was the flag.

Another friend, a favorite of my dad's, whom I loved dearly, had a midair collision in a traffic pattern up at Daytona Beach. His name was George. He had been on that first train to Mercer with me. I have cried over many of those boys. When I hang out my flag, it's tough.

Well, we finished our training in Florida and were sent to Chicago to an "E Base", which was an elimination base. The instructors were tougher than any Army Sergeant. They would embarrass the life out of you. Being a Southerner, and short, I really had to just take it. My first experience of actually landing on a carrier was aboard the *Wolverine* in Lake Michigan. They had taken an old paddlewheel lake steamer called the *Wolverine* and had put a flat top on it and equipped it with barriers and cables and everything. One morning, we had to make three landings, then join up with the others and fly back home. Again, we had eliminations and some didn't make it. Providence favored me and I was designated, along with five others, to go back to Miami as instructors. We taught instruments. The other kids went on to the Fleet.

After six months of instructing in Miami, I wound up in San Diego. We joined VC-79, a composite squadron of bombers, dive bombers, and fighters. Then they dropped the two atomic bombs on Japan, so we only went as far as Hawaii and then turned back. By that time, I had enough points to get out. I thought about a Navy career, but I had a young, beautiful rose in Indiana and I wanted to go home to her.

I asked to get out and picked up my discharge papers in Los Angeles. We got on a train called "The Scout," and it was perfectly named because it scouted the whole Southwest before it started going East. It took us seven days to get to Chicago and there were no showers or bathtubs on the train. I was separated from the Navy at Norfolk Naval Station, Camp Shelton. My discharge was official on December 7, 1945 and Dottie and I were married the same day.

I took Dottie home to Wilmington and joined my father in the family business. I soon realized that I just couldn't take the retail business. One of the worst days of my life was when I had to tell my father I didn't want to spend the rest of my life in retailing. I have spent my whole career in the wholesale food business.

Dottie and I had three beautiful children and then I lost her. My second wife, Joyce, and I have two daughters, Kathleen and Claudia.

When we came to Marietta one of the best decisions we made was to join First Baptist Church. The church had a great youth program and our girls loved it too.

Except for what Navy people call "hangar flying," (where Navy people sit around and tell stories), this is the first time that I have talked about how I got where I was, and what I did. I appreciate the opportunity to share my experiences.

—Interviewed by George Beggs, November, 2001

THOMAS ROGERS, JR.
WITH
Pat Rogers Anderson,
Marcia Rogers Thompson,
And Thomas Rogers, III

Our dad, was always proud to be a Marine. He was born and grew up in Dallas, Georgia, and graduated from the University of Georgia in 1941, with a degree in Chemistry. When the War broke out he enlisted in the Marines and went off to Quantico, Virginia, to do his training. He was in OCS (Officers' Candidate School) from February to April, 1942. On October 15, 1942, Dad became Executive Officer of C Company, 3rd Marine Battalion. From 1943 to 1945, he served as Platoon Leader, Executive Officer, and, later, Commanding Officer of the Regimental Weapons Company, 25th Marines. He fought with Company C, at the Battle of Iwo Jima, in February, 1945. We weren't even born then but later he told us a little bit of the things that had happened over there—how hard it was, and how fortunate he was to make it out. What he went through in World War II was literally hell on earth.

Dad married in 1943, right before he went off to fight the Japanese. Our mother was also from Dallas. In fact they lived down the street from one another, but they didn't start dating until college. Mother adapted very well to the military life and got used to having to pack up and move. She and three other girls drove all the way from Georgia to California in an old, broken-down car, to say goodby to the guys before they shipped out. The car kept breaking down and tires kept blowing out. It was a long trip.

One important thing about Dad was the friends he made in World War II. He fought beside his fellow Marines and lived in the foxholes with them. When we were transferred to a new base we would often run into some of those men. Daddy kept up with his friends. We think the Marines stick together.

Because Dad was career military, he was sent to Korea during that War. He was Assistant Chief of Staff, 1st Marine Brigade. Pat was in second grade and she and Mother had to move back to Dallas, Georgia. Dad did a lot to help the Korean people. His company helped rebuild a bombed-out elementary school.

When Dad came back from Korea, we were stationed in Hawaii for three years. Because it wasn't very long after the War, we had to do bomb drills at school, going into the underground bunkers at the officers' living quarters. Mother and Dad had a wonderful time in Hawaii. They enjoyed the social life and the friendships.

After Hawaii, we went to Quantico. That's where Marcia was born. Dad taught in the Marine school there and served as Assistant Chief of Staff, G-4. Then we lived in Washington, DC, where he worked at the Pentagon in Plans and Operations Division, Headquarters, U.S. Marines. He was also Assistant Director for Training with the Supreme Allied Command, a part of NATO.

Dad was very disappointed when he didn't make full Colonel. Apparently they had too many Lieutenant Colonels at that time. After 25 years in the Marines, one day Mother said, "We're waiting for a very important phone call." When the call came, Dad just looked sad and said,

"Thank you for letting me know." He had been passed over for the promotion. That's when he decided to retire.

We all moved to Marietta in the summer of 1964. Dad went back to Virginia and got a master's degree at the University of Virginia. He taught chemistry at Marietta High School, and he worked as a counselor at McEachern High School. Then he went to Kennesaw College as Registrar. Dad had his second career at the College and he helped a lot of students make wise decisions about their education. He worked at Kennesaw College for seventeen years.

Mother and Dad had three children, Pat, Marcia, and Tom, who is an attorney in Marietta. Mother died March 13, 1992.

How lucky our country was to have courageous men like our dad. The world would be different if our Country had not had the men willing to sacrifice their lives to preserve democracy and save the United States. They really put their lives on the line. And Dad did it twice, in World War II and in the Korean War.

Tom Rogers died on December 28, 2002.

—Interviewed by George Beggs, October, 2001

Tom Rogers

DALLAS RYLE

I was born September 18, 1927, in Marietta, Georgia. I grew up in Perry, Georgia, and graduated from high school there in June, 1944. I attended North Georgia College in Dahlonega, and Georgia Tech.

I was drafted into the Army in March, 1946, and did my basic training (Infantry) at Camp Joseph T. Robinson, near Little Rock, Arkansas. I was then assigned to the Adjutant General's Office at Fort Shafter, Honolulu, Hawaii, Headquarters Mid-Pacific.

I shipped out from Camp Kilmer, New Jersey, in July, with winter gear. We spent nineteen days on a troop transport, going through the Panama Canal and on to Honolulu. Needless to say, we had to be issued new clothing upon arrival.

The Army was an eye-opening experience for a country boy from south Georgia. My first meal in a dining car, first airplane ride, first travel away from home, first look at the tropics, first time to have real spending money in my pocket, and my first exposure to Yankees, etc.

Hawaii was a paradise and my assignment was so "cushy" that I'm embarrassed to talk about it, considering the sacrifices which so many of the "Greatest Generation" made in service to their Country. Nonetheless, I'm proud to have worn the uniform.

As the time approached for my discharge, I was pressured to re-enlist. The inducement was that I would be able to keep my rank. I was a T-5 (Corporal) at that time.

I declined the offer and was separated from the Army at Camp Stoneman, California, in May, 1947.

Following my discharge I returned to Georgia Tech on the GI-Bill, earning a bachelor's and a master's degree in Aeronautical Engineering. I graduated in 1950 and went to work for Convair in Ft. Worth, Texas. I came to Lockheed in Marietta as an engineer in 1953, and retired from there in March, 1991.

While I was at Georgia Tech, I met an Agnes Scott student on a blind date. Her name was Nancy Dendy, and I was smitten. We were married in 1951, and recently celebrated our golden wedding anniversary with a trip to Ireland, accompanied by our five children and three grandchildren. Nancy is still the light of my life.

Our five children are: Dixie Minor, school teacher, homemaker, and mother of our grandson, Ben; Patty Clay, Methodist minister, homemaker, and mother of our grandsons, Hank and Sam; Dallas Ryle III, attorney; Katie Ryle, medical technician—ultrasound; Stephen Ryle, engineer and consultant. Our family has been our major interest through the years, followed by gardening, golf, travel, friends, and of course, Marietta First Baptist Church. It's been a wonderful life. God has been good to me.

—Information furnished by Dallas Ryle, 2001

Dallas Ryle

HENRY ELDRED RYLE
With
Bonnie Zimmerman and
James Zimmerman

Henry Ryle was born August 17, 1907, at Ethel, Mississippi. He started his military career in 1927, as a member of Company G, 29th Infantry Regiment, at Fort Benning, Georgia. He mustered out in 1930 and spent the next several years with the Army National Guard of the State of Mississippi. There, he served in Headquarters Company 106th Engineers, 155th Infantry Regiment; Headquarters Company, 348th Infantry Regiment; and Company E, 151st Infantry Regiment.

By the time the clouds of war were over Europe and the Far East, Henry Ryle and his wife, and daughter, Bonnie, were living in Atlanta. Henry worked at the Federal Penitentiary. Bonnie remembers the day Pearl Harbor was bombed. The family were caught in a traffic jam and Henry got out of the car to see what the problem was. He came back to the car, stuck his head in the window and said, "The Japs have just bombed Pearl Harbor."

Henry moved his family back to Mississippi to live with his wife's parents and went back to the Army. This time he was with the 81st Division, 81st Military Police Corps. As an

MP, Henry guarded POW's and also, at times, guarded The Little White House in Warm Springs, Georgia. Sometimes President Franklin Roosevelt was in residence at The Little White House.

The War ended, and the Ryle family moved back to Marietta in 1946. In 1948, Henry joined the 116th Fighter Wing of the Georgia Air National Guard as Mess Sergeant. He was called to active duty for the Korean War. During the Vietnam era, Henry was promoted to Chief Master Sergeant, and the 116th became the 116th Transport Wing.

Henry Ryle retired from his military career, September 29, 1967, after 40 years of service. He died on July 2, 1973.

James Zimmerman, Henry Ryle's grandson, writes:

"He had a brilliant military mind, and had he the opportunity to further his education, there is no doubt in my mind that he would have retired a General . . . For me, Chief Master Sergeant, Henry E. Ryle, is my hero. A man of morals, principles and decency. An example that many would benefit by following today. Thanks, Grandad, for your life, your love of God, family, and your service to our Country . . . ."

Bonnnie Ryle Zimmerman, Henry Ryle's daughter says:

"It was not like a duty. It was a part of his life. He was very much a military man. When he was working at the prison, he was still in the Reserves. He would get home from prison around midnight and they would have an alert and they would call him. Never did I hear him complain. He would get out of bed and put on that military uniform and out the door he would go."

—Interviewed by Charles and Ruth Miller, July, 2002.

Henry Ryle

DONALD SCOTT, JR.

I was born and grew up in Stuart, Virginia. After graduating from high school in 1939, I attended VPI (Virginia Polytechnic Institute). By the time I turned twenty-one events were leading up to Pearl Harbor, and Germany had invaded Poland. I enrolled in the Enlisted Reserve Corps in August, 1942, which was supposed to allow me to finish college before entering the military. It didn't turn out that way. Along about the end of my sophomore year, I was called to active duty. You could say I was drafted. It amounted to the same thing anyway.

I reported to Camp Meade, Maryland, for classification. That included all kinds of testing, and on my papers they stamped in big letters, "Qualified Aerial Gunner." Then we were off to beautiful Miami Beach, Florida. I had never ridden on a train before and had never seen the ocean. We were billeted in the Oceanic Villas. I had already survived freshman hazing at VPI so basic training was a lark. I was given a choice of three schools—armament, aircraft mechanics, or radio operator. I had two years of electrical engineering in college so I chose radio.

They sent me to Sioux Falls, South Dakota, where I spent half of each day taking Morse code, and the other half studying aircraft radio and electrical systems and aircraft avionics navigation equipment. We were supposed to be able to do minor repairs in flight but the biggest job was Morse Code and operating the radio. That was an around-the-clock experience—shift work, seven days a week, and you rotated shifts from day shift to swing shift to midnight shift. You really didn't get a day off. After about six months of that they sent me to gunnery school in Yuma, Arizona.

I barely escaped the severe winter in South Dakota and went to the desert, where it was hot in the day and really cold at night. We slept in tents and dealt with sand and sandstorms. In a way, the training was a piece of cake. I had done a lot of hunting as I grew up. I had a .22 rifle and also used my daddy's shotgun. I knew how to shoot. We started out shooting skeet, then graduated to machine guns—the little 30-caliber guns and then the big 50-caliber guns. We shot colored projectiles at targets towed by the B-26 Martin Marauder. They could tell who got a hit by what color they found on the target.

My next assignment was at Drew Field, Tampa, Florida, for crew training with the B-17's. We started with ten crew members: two pilots, a navigator, a bombardier, the radio operator, flight engineer, ball turret gunner, two waist gunners, and a tail gunner. We also did some cross-training. For example, the flight engineer was cross-trained to the armorer, who was the waist gunner. The ball turret gunner was my assistant radio operator.

As radio operator, I had a room to myself, with a table and chair, and my receivers and transmitters. The top of the radio room was mostly plexiglass and I had a gun there. It was pointed aft. Of course, it was fixed so you wouldn't shoot the vertical stabilizer off. I had more room than any of the other crew members.

We went overseas by ship. This was late in the War and the Germans were shooting down B-17's in large numbers so our Air Force needed lots of replacement crews. We were the replacements. We left from Hunter Field, near Savannah, and went to Camp Kilmer, New Jersey, and departed from New York on July 14, 1944, aboard the *H.M.S. Aquitania*. That ship had been used as a troop transport in World War I and it was fast. The slower, smaller ships had to cross the Atlantic in convoys because of the threat from German submarines. The *Aquitania* was up in the *Queen Mary* class and traveled alone, zigzagging across to keep away from submarine attacks.

We arrived and anchored in the Firth of Clyde, in Scotland, in July of 1944, just a month after D-Day. Allied troops were already on the Continent. We went by train to an airfield at Knettishall, England, northeast of London, toward Cambridge. England was thick with air bases.

We flew a few practice missions with a skeleton crew and on August 11, 1944, we flew our first real mission. Our target was the railroad marshaling yards at Mulhouse, France. The mission report reads, "The weather at the target area was ceiling and visibility unlimited ... Bombs away was a 11:46 hours, from 19,000 feet. Strike photos show good results. Neither flak nor enemy fighters were encountered. All aircraft returned to base at 15:34 hours." On August 30, after our eighth mission, we were awarded the Air Medal. I mailed that thing home and it's a good thing I did. On September 1, I was promoted to Staff Sergeant.

Our eleventh mission, and the last one for me, took place on September 28, 1944. The mission started off on an ominous note. As soon as we were airborne, I plugged in the IFF (Identification Friend or Foe) and the self-destruct charge went off. It was like a shotgun blast. By the time I got the fire extinguisher the flames had gone out. Apparently in the process of repairs to the unit, the inertia switch had been tripped to the destruct position and not reset. I reported this to the pilot on the interphone and he made the decision to continue with the mission. Our target was the IG Farbden Industry Synthetic Oil Refineries at Merseburg, Germany. Our plane was in the lead group, out across Belgium, in enemy territory. There was fog on the target. A dense cloud prevented visual bombing so we used radar bombing. Over the target area, at 27,000 feet, I was busy dispensing chaff (little bundles of metal strips of paper that gave false targets) to confuse the German radar-directed flight guns.

Just after we dropped our bombs, the cloud undercast started to break up and the flak gunners began firing visually. Flak was bursting all around us. We could see black smoke from the bursts. Usually you can't hear the flak because of the engine noise and the headsets, but we began to hear the explosions and knew they were getting close. Then there was one blast louder than the rest, and our plane was badly crippled.

The good news was that we were still under control, flying straight and level, not in a spin or a dive or a bank. We immediately lost two engines and with the third engine crippled we started losing air speed and altitude. We couldn't keep up with the formation so they had to go on and leave us. We were in bad shape. The radios and the interphone were dead and the navigation equipment was shot up. The navigator didn't know where we were. We hoped we were heading west to friendly territory.

My biggest problem was that I couldn't breathe. No oxygen. My mask was connected to the oxygen line on my left, and the pressure needle was down below zero. I looked over to the right side and saw that pressure gauge was not quite down to zero, so I got really busy, and panicky, and transferred my mask connection over to the other side. The same thing was happening to other crew members. The waist gunner came out really fast and got on a walk-around oxygen bottle. So did the tail gunner. Since we were losing altitude we soon got down to where we could survive without the additional oxygen.

Nobody had major injuries. Part of the windshield had shattered and the pilot had little pieces of glass in his eyes, temporarily blinding him. The same thing happened to the top turret gunner. He had his parachute at his feet because the turret was too tight for him to wear a chute. Coming down out of the turret he couldn't see what he was doing and accidentally pulled the handle on his chute and it opened. The extra chute that we always carried had been shredded by the flak. So that was another problem.

We were still going along, trying to gain altitude. The copilot was flying the plane, doing little gentle stalls, and then nosing it down to pick up some air speed. I opened the camera hatch in the bottom of the radio compartment and we threw out everything we could get loose, but we were still losing altitude. We couldn't talk to each other because the interphone was gone. I looked back toward the waist gunner and he looked all right, and I gave him an OK signal. We finally got ourselves a little better organized and got on the emergency interphone by using the side tone off the low frequency command radio. I guess we were broadcasting to the world but we were able to talk to each other.

We had lost hydraulic and engine oil, and the propellers on the three dead engines could not be feathered. They were "windmilling" and the engines began to smoke. The first thing I heard on the interphone was Mike, the pilot, asking Red, the ball turret gunner if he could see any fire under the engines. But Red was long gone from his turret. Then I heard the pilot say, "Hey, fellows, I'm afraid two of you are going to have to go out on one parachute." I had already snapped my parachute onto my harness and was thankful that I had. When we got down to about 4,000 feet and started receiving more ground fire, the pilot gave the order to bail out.

We bailed out, not knowing where we were but hoping we were over France or Belgium. Instead we had bailed out over the city of Koblenz. White, the flight engineer who had accidentally deployed his chute, wound up gathering his open parachute in his arms and jumping. When he turned it loose the chute opened. Then Sweeney, the waist gunner jumped and I could see him down below. He looked all right. Then I jumped, pulled the handle, and my chute opened with a terrific jerk.

It was very quiet without the noise of the plane. I dropped into some low clouds and heard a popping noise. I looked up at the shroud lines but they were taught. Then I realized it was the sound of gunfire. The Germans were shooting at us as we descended. The ground started coming up fast and I was headed toward a tree. I remembered that we had been told that if you are going down in the woods, put your hands up across your face and cross your legs. I did that, and went down through the side of that tree. It didn't feel like the tree slowed me down much because I hit the ground hard. It knocked the breath out of me. I don't know what the diameter of that parachute was but it was designed to let you down fast.

I got up on my feet and was going to go down to where Sweeney had landed. I got out of my harness, one of those quick release British harnesses. I had just taken a step or two when somebody behind me started hollering. I turned around to see a soldier with his rifle pointing at me. I didn't know where I was but when I saw the *swastika* on his helmet, I knew I was not in friendly territory.

Another German soldier had captured Sweeney and they marched us to a nearby building, where we were faced with several military types holding a variety of weapons. I heard someone shouting and a civilian came running around the corner of the building and hit me in the mouth with his fist. The soldiers grabbed him and took him away. They searched us and took my wristwatch, scout knife, escape kit, and my *New Testament*, which had a sheet metal cover on one side of it. By nightfall, the Germans had rounded up our whole crew. No one had major injuries.

We were taken to Dulag Luft, near Frankfurt, for interrogation. Then we were separated and I was taken to a transient camp at Wetzlar. From there, I was transported by train to Stalag Luft IV at Grosstychow, Poland. Fortunately, I was wearing my medium weight flying suit when we bailed out. I was thankful for that. I still have the jacket. Most of the crew members had on their heated suits, which are not too heavy and without any electricity they're not made for cold weather. I had been issued a heated suit but because I stayed fairly warm in the plane's radio room, I didn't fool with it. The one time I decided to try out that heated suit I forgot my extension cord. Anyway, the ones wearing the heated suits when they bailed out suffered from the cold more than I did.

We had been advised, "Have your GI shoes tied to your belt, in case you have to bail out and do some walking, because those sheepskin-lined flying shoes are not meant for hiking." I think our navigator didn't have his shoes tied on too good and when his parachute opened his shoes came loose. But I had mine and I was glad to have them. Eventually I wore them out. We got a few items, I guess. Somehow, I came into possession of a GI blanket, which I sewed up partially on one side to make a sleeping bag. And I got hold of a wool knit cap, the kind you wore under a helmet liner.

Now don't get this prison confused with concentration camps. Germany halfway went by the Geneva Convention, which spelled out the treatment of prisoners of war. We weren't mistreated. The worst part was not getting enough to eat. I stayed hungry all the time. All you thought about was food. We got a certain ration of German food: a portion of a loaf of black bread; potatoes; soup with various ingredients including horse meat; kohlrabi; alfalfa soup;

barley. The Germans let some of the Red Cross food parcels come through and we would divide them up. The American margarine would get so cold that you couldn't spread it. The German margarine you could spread even in sub-zero weather. I have often said that if it hadn't been for the Red Cross food, I wouldn't be here today. You just couldn't subsist on what the Germans issued us and halfway keep your health.

The main German issue was potatoes. They would unload a pile of potatoes for the whole barracks and issue us a knife. We would scrape the skins of the potatoes. We didn't peel them because we didn't want to waste any of the potato. Then we would put them in buckets and take them to the cookhouse, which was a separate building, and someone would cook them.

In the prison camp, we couldn't bathe or shave. We didn't brush our teeth because we didn't have toothbrushes. One of the British men, I think, had some hair clippers, so we got haircuts once in a while. Our latrine facilities and washhouse were in a separate building from the barracks. Through the World YMCA, we got some books and some phonographs along with some phonograph records, You probably have seen the TV series, "Stalag 17," which was a comical presentation of prison life. In good weather we would walk around the compound. We would walk and walk and walk, around and around. There was a little low wire near the fence. If you got across it the guards in the tower would start shooting at you. I was there mostly in cold weather so we didn't get out much.

It got dark really early and the guards counted us. They had roll call twice a day. We had to line up outside and they would count to see if anybody was missing. The British liked to tell the story that there was somebody missing one day, and the Germans turned their dog loose in the barracks to chase out anybody who was still inside. Well, the dog never came out. He was eaten.

There was never enough heat in the barracks. We had one little stove and the Germans gave us some coal briquettes. We stayed cold all the time. I had the sleeping bag I had made and I slept in my clothes. All we prisoners got along very well. There were New Zealanders, Australians, Canadians, Irish, English, and Americans. The British were most congenial and shared their bunks with the Americans. I was in the camp approximately four months.

In early February, 1945, the Russians started pushing toward Berlin. We could hear their guns as they got closer. The Germans didn't want to be overrun or captured, and they didn't want us liberated by the Russians. If they had a choice, they wanted to be captured by the other Allies. On February 6, the German command decided to evacuate our camp. There was snow on the ground. I had gotten a GI wool shirt and I sewed the ends of the sleeves together to make straps. Then I sewed the bottom together and made sort of a back pack to carry what little food I had. That was the preparation I made for the evacuation.

The Germans had a backlog of Red Cross food parcels. They piled them out there and as we marched out of the camp we were supposed to take one. I thought two would be even better so I put one in my homemade pack and carried the other one in my hand, and I had my blanket rolled across my shoulder. They marched us out of there, three abreast. We weren't near any shelter that first night and had to sleep on the frozen ground. That was the coldest night. Most of the time we stopped at a farm where we could camp out in the barn or loft, under the machinery, or on the woodpile. I slept on the woodpiles. I even slept in the stall with a horse one time. I was glad to be in out of the weather. The horse didn't bother me and I didn't bother him. You just get sort of numb as you march along. I don't know what happened to the people who couldn't keep up. We just had to keep moving. They wouldn't let us stop.

Later on, in April it wasn't bad sleeping outdoors. The people who were not able to walk were put on a wagon drawn by a pair of oxen. There were air raids every night. One night, those sick and disabled were in a barn some distance from the rest of us. They must have shown some light, or built a fire, or something. A Mosquito Bomber came over and the crew must have thought that group was a German target because they dropped a 1,000 pound bomb on that barn. That was the last of them. We were in the northen part of Germany, near Stedten, trying to get away from the Russians. We got as far west as Hanover. Then we had to turn around because the Allies were getting closer.

In late March, we were crammed into a boxcar and sent to Fallingbostel, Stalag 11-B. I forget how much time it took but we had to sit in the station all day long because they ran the trains only at night to keep them from being strafed. Prisoners of all nationalities were lying there. We were right against each other and that's when I got body lice. They just crawled from one to the other of us. We weren't bothered with them while we walked but at night when we would lay down we would feel them crawling. I didn't get rid of the lice until I was liberated back to GI control. I guess they dusted us with DDT or something.

I spent about ten days in that camp. Then the Allies started getting close. At night we could hear the German troops. First they went one way and the next day or so they turned around and went another way, trying to get away. In early April they moved us out of that camp. At one point, they decided to move us across the Oder River. They moved us in the early morning while it was still dark because of the strafing situation. They took us across the river on a ferry. As it was getting daylight all we prisoners were grouped around on the river bank. Here came two

Spitfires down the river making a pass. They thought we were Germans, I guess. We couldn't do anything but just lay there. The Spitfires went on, rocked their wings, and left without shooting us.

Toward the end of April the Germans marched us up in a northeasterly direction toward Denmark. We knew it was near the end of the War and the Germans knew it too. Our treatment got better. One farmer butchered his bull and gave the meat to the prisoners. There were times I could have escaped as we marched through the woods but the Germans were guarding us and the civilian "*volksturm*" were everywhere. They were armed civilian patrols and they would shoot first and ask questions later. They didn't go by the Geneva Convention.

I had come by an extra pair of GI pants and carried them with me. At the farms where we stopped, there were conscripted workers—French and Russians. Being hungry all the time, I traded that pair of pants to a French worker for a loaf of bread. I had worn out my shoes and had gotten some British army boots. They were really stiff leather and had hob nails in the heel plates. A lot of the time we were marching over cobblestone streets and those boots just chewed up my heels. They couldn't heal because I had to keep on walking. One German guard kept giving me a hard time about that. After we were finally liberated, I looked for that guy but he was gone.

We knew the end was close and the Germans wanted to be taken by the Americans and the British, not by the Russians. They let one of our people go through to get instructions from the British, who responded, "Well, we'll probably lob a few shells first to see if there is any resistance. Just sit tight, sleep with your clothes and shoes on." Nothing happened that night. The next morning while we were having our breakfast, someone hollered, "They're here!" It was the British Airborne Infantry. We all ran up and shook their hands. That was the happiest day of my life. It was May 2, 1945, in a little place called Zorrentin.

We were told to wait for someone to come get us but a lot of fellows just took off, heading for where the Allies were. When nobody showed up for us by the next day, two other fellows and I started walking. It was some sight to see those German vehicles on the side of the road, out of fuel. Finally, we found a truck with a little gas in it. We drove it until it ran out of gas. Then it was back on foot again. Along came a jeep with a British soldier and he gave us a ride to where there was a small American army detachment. We had our first taste of GI food and stayed a day or two until they sent a truck which took us to Lutenberg, Germany, where I was returned to military control. I filled out the Red cross forms, and the War Department notified my parents that I had been liberated. That's where I was deloused and given a uniform.

I went to a transportation terminal at Bremen and was there on VE-Day, May 8, 1945. They put us on a C-47 to Camp Lucky Strike at LeHavre, France. I was able to put on some weight because I would go through the breakfast chow line twice every day. Finally, two weeks later, we left LeHavre on the *U.S.S. Sea Rocket,* a Victory Ship. I didn't have enough points to get out of the Service. They gave me 90 days leave then sent me to Miami Beach. We were taken off flying status of course. Somewhere along in there I was promoted to Tech Sergeant. I finished my time by working in the Air Inspector's Office at Greenville Army Air Base in South Carolina. I was discharged at Richmond Army Base on November 16, 1945, and went back home to Stuart, Virginia. I received the usual awards; The Air Medal, The Good Conduct Medal, The European Theater of Operations, a Citation with Oak Leaf Cluster. In 1988, they created the Prisoner of War Medal.

After the War, I finished my college work at VPI, earning a degree in electrical engineering. I worked several different places, winding up in Marietta, working at Lockheed. I met my wife, Martha, when we were both singing in the choir at Marietta First Baptist Church. We were married on June 24, 1956, in the First Baptist Church Chapel. I still sing in the choir. Martha and I have two daughters: Ann Scott Willis and Mary Ellen Scott May; and four grandchildren: Ellen and Virginia Willis, and Scott and Samuel May.

—Interviewed by Harland Armitage, May, 2001

Don Scott

J. F. Shaw

J. F. SHAW

I was 31 years old, married to Eleanor Godwin of Acworth, and a partner in the Gulf Oil Distributorship in Cobb County, when I was drafted. That was in July of 1943.

I went by train from Marietta to Atlanta Central Station and spent my entire 34 months of service at Fort McPherson. I was able to go home to Marietta every night. I worked in the medical induction and separation center. We inducted hundreds of servicemen every day. Then, at the end of the War, we also handled separations.

VE-Day was exciting. Everybody wondered when they would get to go home. Then, after VJ-Day, everybody was going to headquarters to find out when they were going to be separated. My separation came on May 14, 1946.

Following my military service, I had several business enterprises. I owned Shaw Barbecue for twelve years. After I sold that business, I went into the insurance business. I've been in that business, more or less, for about 47 years. I also had an interest in home construction. My wife says I'm a workaholic. I retired about twelve years ago but I still go into the office but I don't do any work.

I served on the Marietta School Board from 1956 to 1968. In about 1966 or 1967, while I was Chairman, the Marietta High School was integrated. When the matter came up for a vote, the Board was split three-to-three. I cast the tie-breaking vote. Someone asked how I was able to make up my mind so quickly. I said, "Because I had my mind made up when I got here." It was something that had to be done.

—Interviewed by George Beggs, February, 2002

FRED "JACK" SHIFLETT
And
Jo Shiflett

I volunteered for the Marine Corps at the age of 22. Having been born in Enon, Georgia, and having attended Rome High School, I went in as part of the North Georgia Platoon. I was already married at that time and had to have my wife sign my papers so that I could join the Marines. My wife, Jo, was eighteen when I went off to military service. That was in 1942.

We took our basic training at San Diego, California. A friend and I would get up in the morning and run around the parade grounds once or twice before the others even got out of bed. He was going into the Marine Raiders and wanted to be in good shape. I was hoping to be a sniper, so I wanted to be in good shape too. At boot camp, I went from weighing 123 pounds to weighing 137 pounds. We lived for thirteen weeks in a tent city. Then I was assigned to a Dive Bomber outfit (VMSB 144) at Camp Kearney, near San Diego, and was there until we were sent overseas.

While we were in California we had a Jap sub come up and fire a shell somewhere around San Diego. We had patrol duty all the next day trying to find that shell.

In January, 1943, we went to the Solomon Islands as ground crew. We built a camp for the flight crews. The temperature there was so hot you would nearly pass out. Morale was good but food was bad. You didn't want to put your head over your mess gear when you started to eat because if you did, you wouldn't eat. We had been lent to the Navy to help take care of their planes. They were losing about one plane to mechanical troubles every time they went out. Each of we men had two aircraft (FBD Douglas Dive Bombers) to take care of.

One day, we landed at New Hebrides at a place code named "Base Rose." As we unloaded supplies from the ship, I asked a Navy guy, "Were you one of the first Seabees here?' He said, "Yeah." I said, "Do you know E.T. Shiflett?" He said, "Does he talk like you" I said, "Yeah. He's my brother." He said, "I know him. He's about 20 miles away, down on the other end of the island."

One night, I decided to walk to the other end of the island to find my brother. It was the rainy season and the ruts in the road were knee deep. We didn't have a truck to go down there so I couldn't send a message. Instead I took off walking. I ran into seven wild boars and used a flashlight to run them off. I ran into a tree full of monkey bats. They had about a six-foot wing span. I couldn't leave the road because I didn't want to get lost. Then I walked right into a herd of cattle. One old cow had a calf with her. She made two passes at me. I stepped aside and pulled out my forty-five and told her if she came back again I was going to let her have it right between the eyes. Thank goodness, she didn't come back.

When I got to the camp, I asked the dispatcher about my brother. He said, "I don't know where he is right now, but you can come in and sleep in my bed." I laid down and was no sooner asleep than the guy came back saying, "I know where your brother is." We went over there and he was sleeping. I kicked his sack and said, "Get out of that bed!" He recognized my voice and grabbed my flashlight, which I had been shining in his face. He shined the flashlight on my face and wanted to know how in the world I got there. Two weeks later he got a letter from home telling him I had joined the service.

When I was at Guadalcanal I used to pray that I would get to come back home to see my wife, and that we would have a son. Well, I did get to come back home. We were one of the few outfits that came back to the U.S. to re-form. We were on a ship in the harbor and I asked for leave. I told the skipper, "If I get there and you say to come back, I'll come back right then." He said, "I believe you, Shiflett." So he let me go. Jo was living in California, working in a defense plant at that time. After I shipped back out, Jo decided to go back to Georgia. She rode cross-country on a troop train full of Navy boys—two women on the whole train. She was six and a half months pregnant by that time and they all watched out for her. She stayed in the hospital for two months after that train ride. And we did have a son.

When the Japanese tried to take back the Canal, they sent in ships and everything else. They sent 112 aircraft one morning, and 97 of them didn't go home. I sat there and watched as P-38's shot down one Jap plane after another. We had one Chinese pilot who dropped a 500-pound bomb down the smokestack of a Japanese troopship. He was really tickled.

We were aboard a Carrier, in October, in the East China Sea, when a typhoon hit and tore everything up. I found out later that Harry Hamby was in the same typhoon on a little Destroyer Escort. Those Destroyers were supposed to be taking care of us, but they were under water more than they were on top of the water. I was Sergeant Of The Guard and went to tell the men not to get out if a plane broke loose—just to let it go. I was on the catwalk underneath the carrier deck and a wave washed me overboard. My arm caught on the railing. They pulled me back inside before I ever touched the water. Two of the Navy boys on gun watch came running down through there asking, "Are you hurt, Sarge?" I said, "Nah." I could hardly breathe but I wasn't going to let those

Navy boys know I, a Marine, was hurt. Before we got through with that storm, we rode six live bombs for about forty minutes. They came loose and we catapulted them off the aircraft deck.

Then, when we stopped at Okinawa, I had another encounter with a storm. The smokestack had come off our Quonset hut (which held about 1,000 men). We were on the roof, putting the smokestack back on when the wind hit the stack and it came over on me. I started sliding backward down the roof of that Quonset hut and stopped just at the edge, with my head hanging off. I wasn't afraid because I had already told God that if I got to go home and see my son, I was ready to die.

After the War, I rode a passenger train from Treasure Island, California, to Camp Le Jeune, North Carolina. I came out as Staff Sergeant. Our unit had earned a Battle Star during the Battle of Guadalcanal. We also got a Presidential Citation, and seven of us got a personal Navy Citation for taking care of their planes. I later served a year in the Korean War.

I wouldn't take anything for my World War II service. I don't want to do it again, though.

—Interviewed by Marcus McLeroy, March, 2001

Jack Shifflet working on engine.

JACK MADISON SMITH

I had always wanted to go into the military service but I was only sixteen when I graduated from Cartersville High School, in 1942. So I went off to Berea College in Kentucky for a year. In the fall of 1943, at the age of seventeen, I tried to get into the V-12 unit, which was for officer training, but they said I was too young. So, I went back to college until my eighteenth birthday, when I joined the Navy.

After four weeks of boot camp at Camp Perry in Williamsburg, Virginia, we went to sea on a ship. Then they sent me to Signal School at Baltimore, Maryland. A Signalman does visual communications such as breaker lights, Morse Code, flash, and any other type of visual messaging between ships, or ship-to-shore. From Signal School I went into what they called the "Armed Guard." We were Navy gun and communication crews on merchant ships.

I didn't stay long on my first ship, the *S.S. Lyons Creek*. The ship on which I spent most of my time was the *S.S. Mission Santa Clara*, out of Sausalito, California. Both of those ships were tankers. That ship was not run by the Navy, it was run by the Merchant Marines, but we had 27 Navy men on board including one officer. We were to handle the gunnery and the visual communications. We would load up with diesel fuel down in the Caribbean around Aruba and Curacao, go through the Panama Canal, and head to the South Pacific to refuel the Fleet.

It was kind of like the movie, "Mr. Roberts,"—mostly monotonous sailing and refueling the Fleet wherever they happened to be. We were attacked by aircraft several times. Sometimes we would be refueling the Fleet while a battle was going on, especially up and down the Philippine Sea. The Navy isn't like the Army. We were always on the move, never really knowing where an attack might come from. We didn't feel like the attacks were any history–making situations. Nobody kept any records or made any fuss about it.

I was out of the country for both VE-Day and VJ-Day. On VJ-Day, we were sitting right in the middle of Tacloban Bay. An endless number of ships came down through the Bay and a guy was standing on the fantail of one with a bull horn hollering, "The War's over! The War is over!" I was up on the bridge with the Captain and he said, "Aw, don't think anything about it, he's just a drunk SOB." About an hour later this guy came back down there on a PT-Boat, still hollering at us, so we went up to the radio shack and found out the War was over.

I was discharged from the Navy, as a Signalman Second Class, in June or July of 1946 and I went to Oglethorpe University for a year. Some friends and I tried, first, to get into the University of Georgia but it was so crowded that they were sleeping six guys to a room and broadcasting classes over the PA systems. Well, that was what we had just left behind in the military, so we hitchhiked back to Atlanta and went to Oglethorpe. The lady there said they didn't have room for us but Dr. Weltner, the President, said, "If you really want to go to college, and if you have good grades, I'll put you in this school if I have to let you sleep at my house." Everybody loved Dr. Weltner. He seemed to really care about us.

In January, 1948, I enrolled in Mercer Law School. Right after law school I went to work as an insurance adjuster. One day, I just decided I wanted to practice law. My brother-in-law had been practicing for years and he let me come into his office. I worked with him from 1962 to 1966, then came out to Marietta to practice. I do mostly general law practice. I am old and my clients are old, so I do a lot of wills and estate counseling now.

I married Mona Fae Lankford in February of 1952. She was from Whitfield County, near Dalton, Georgia. We have two children: Sara Frances, a nurse, and Fred Smith, a researcher at King and Spalding Law Firm.

I am very proud of being in the Navy and grateful that my Country let me serve. The men and women of World War II literally saved civilization on this planet. I feel honored that they allowed me to be a part of it. We came close to losing that War. Most people will never know how we hung on by just a thread for a long time. The thing I think of about that War is the American people. They stood up, dug in their heels, and wouldn't let some monster take away their freedom. If every last one of us had lost our lives, we were willing to pay the price. If people don't believe that, just go check the cemeteries.

My grandmother was born during the Civil War. My parents lived through World War I. They told me you have to pay a price to be free, to worship God, and you have to pay for it daily. That was hammered into our whole generation.

Each generation, God seems to come up with one or two people to lead us out of the messes we get ourselves into. Seems like we walk around with one leg over the edge of the cliff. We don't stay diligent. It is the men and women of God who lead us through.

(Jack Smith died on April 16, 2002. He was predeceased by his beloved wife, Mona Fae on December 28, 1996.)

—Interviewed by George Beggs, November, 2001

Jack Smith

K. B. Smith

K.B. SMITH
With
Ann Smith

My husband, K.B. Smith, was born in Lewisburg, Kentucky, January 1, 1917. When he was eight years old, his family moved to Atlanta Street in Marietta. He attended Waterman Street School and then graduated from Marietta High School. For two years, he commuted to Georgia Tech and also worked in the afternoons at the hosiery mill. He transferred to Auburn University for his last two years, earning a B.S. in Textile Engineering. He was working for Callaway Mills in Conyers, Georgia, in 1941, when the War started.

At that time we were engaged to be married. Because the work he was doing at the mill was critical (they were manufacturing heavy duck fabric that went into tires), he was given a deferment at first. We married in March, 1942. One day he came home (we knew by that time that we were expecting our first child) and said, "I feel like I have more to fight for than many of our friends who have no children. I think I will go ahead and enlist." So he went to Atlanta, and when he came home he was in the Marines.

K.B. was called to Officers Candidate School (OCS) in Quantico, Virginia, in December, 1942. He graduated from there on March 1, 1943. Meanwhile, I had gone home to live with my parents in Dothan, Alabama. Our son, Ken was born about the middle of March. K.B. had three days to get from Quantico to Camp Le Jeune, North Carolina. He bought a plane ticket to fly home because he hadn't seen the baby. A Major came along and needed the space so they bumped K.B. and returned his money. He went on to Camp Le Jeune. After six weeks, I took the baby by train from Dothan to Camp Le Jeune. It took us two days because the train had to keep pulling off on a siding to let every military train go through.

After that, K.B. was assigned to a heavy artillery unit and sent to Guantanamo Bay, Cuba. It wasn't a bad assignment but one day a submarine surfaced between Cuba and the United States and they were not allowed to fire on it. They couldn't understand why. They all complained, and they all were sent back to the U.S. and reassigned to Camp Pendleton, California. From there they went through Hawaii, and on to Guam.

The Japanese *kamikaze* pilots chose Guam to commit suicide. One of them hit about ten feet from K.B.'s tent. While they were on night maneuvers K.B. jumped a ditch, injured his leg, and was hospitalized. They had been getting ready to be moved and his unit left without him. When he was well enough, he rejoined his unit in Hawaii and they left for the invasion of Okinawa.

K.B. said that invasion was an awesome scene. Ships were everywhere. Airplanes overhead. It was just amazing how big the Navy was. They had been forewarned that Okinawa had very poisonous snakes. By the time they went ashore, they were more afraid of the snakes than of the Japanese. K.B. stayed on Okinawa until the end of the War.

Ken (our son) and I were at my parents in Alabama on VJ-Day. All of my sisters came in. We were so happy that it was over. Everybody ended up at the church of course. In a small town, it's always the church that you go to. We had a worship service.

K.B. had enough points to be discharged but he stayed on until they had a report of a typhoon in the area when they began to ship out everybody who was eligible. (This same typhoon is mentioned in the stories of Jack Shiflett and Harry Hamby.) K.B. mustered out in Jacksonville, Florida, as a Captain, having been awarded the usual medals and ribbons—Sharpshooter, service in Cuba, the Okinawa invasion.

Our son, Ken, had a difficult time adjusting to leaving my parents' home. I believe he loved my mother and dad better than he ever loved K.B. or me. Even though we had talked about K.B. and had shown Ken pictures, Ken only knew his dad as a picture. Ken learned to sit alone, to walk and talk, while K.B. was gone. He was four years old when K.B. saw him. K.B. assumed that Ken was going to be his son, but Ken didn't want any part of him. As far as Ken was concerned, his family was in Alabama. It was difficult for all of us.

How did K.B. feel about his World War II service? He would always refer to it as not the happiest time in his life because it was against some of his training and some of his beliefs. But he felt like it was a necessary evil. K.B. later joined the Marine Reserves. He stayed a part of them for four years, finishing as a Major. I think he was pleased with it then.

After the War, Ken went back to the Callaway Mills for a while. Then he took a course in Architectural Engineering. When he finished, he went to work for Atlantic Steel Erectors. He worked there the rest of the time we were in Marietta.

K.B. Smith died on April 26, 1990.

—Interviewed by Marcus McLeroy, August, 2001

MILDRED MURRAY SMITH

I was born at Georgia Baptist Hospital in Atlanta and grew up in East Lake. I attended Murphy Junior High School and graduated from Girls' High School in 1941. Then I took a course at Morris Business College and worked as a secretary until I decided to join the Women's Army Corps (WAC).

My friends and I were at the age where we went to the USO and danced with the servicemen. It seemed important that we do that. But we had to wait until we were twenty before we could enlist. Meanwhile, we did volunteer work as Red Cross Nurses' Aides for a year or two. We thought we really were going to save the world. Many people were against our joining the WAC's because they said there were a lot of bad people and bad situations there. Well, I turned twenty in November, 1944, and on Valentine's Day, 1945, a friend and I told everybody goodbye and joined the WAC's. We chose the Army over the Navy because we wanted to be in the medical service and the Navy didn't have that.

Our basic training was at Fort Oglethorpe, near Chattanooga, and lasted about six weeks. We rather enjoyed it—the hiking. We were just a bunch of girls together having a good time. It was a real friendly group. A girl that had the upper bunk in my space taught me how to iron a shirt. I had never known how to do that.

Then the Army decided that instead of our doing

medical training, they would make us clerks. It broke our hearts. In fact, I think if we had known over which hill home was, we would have gone home. Most of us had been secretaries and didn't join the Army to do that. We went through clerk school and I typed as slowly as I could think of. I tried every error I could make on that typing but it didn't work.

We did get to go to Stark General Hospital in Charleston, South Carolina, but we were still clerks. During our off duty hours, we would work on the hospital wards where they brought the boys in from overseas. There were some horrible, horrible injuries. I never will forget one young man who had lost a leg. He wanted us to scratch his foot, but the foot wasn't there. It was heart rending.

I think we were still training in Chattanooga when Germany surrendered. Then after VJ-Day, they brought us from Charleston back to Fort McPherson and I worked in the office there, in the personnel center headquarters.

I wanted badly to go overseas. Working with the personnel records as I did, I found that there was a place open for a secretary so I changed my classification number to secretary. That got me on overseas orders to go to Germany. I was thrilled. After a couple of weeks though, I got a call to report to Third Army Headquarters in downtown Atlanta, at the old post office building. I went and was interviewed by this lady Major, who wanted me to fill in for her secretary who was going to go home on leave. I told her I was on overseas orders and she assured me that the job would not interfere with my overseas plans. After I was assigned to her office, I found that she needed me there because she had removed my name from the overseas orders and put her secretary's name in my place. Her secretary got to go overseas and I didn't. I was very angry with that lady. The only cross I ever had to bear in the Army was with Majors. Somehow, I don't like Majors.

I didn't have to work for her long. I got out of there and worked for the Third Army Assistant Chief of Staff. He was a Colonel, a West Point graduate and a really nice man.

It is amazing how God does work. My mother was very sick that year and couldn't work. I lived at home and rode the trolley to work every day. They paid me per diem because I was no longer at Fort McPherson.

I separated from the Army with the rank of Sergeant. I was awarded the World War II Victory Medal, the American Campaign Medal, and the Good Conduct Medal.

I think my War experience was good. I think we were able to do some good. Particularly when we were in Charleston we were able to help people a little bit. I benefitted greatly from the GI Bill. I was able to get my degree by attending evening college.

Roy and I married and a couple of years later, during the Korean War, he went overseas. I worked for the City of Atlanta until our children came along. I left then but they called and asked me to come back. Roy says the reason they wanted me was that I had everything in such a mess, I had to go back and fix it. I worked part-time and when the children were in high school I went back full time. After I retired from the City of Atlanta, I worked for a tour company and got to do some of the traveling that I didn't get to do during the War.

Roy and I have three children: David, Daniel, and Donna.

—Interviewed by Marcus McLeroy, March, 2001

Mildred Smith

JOHN STEWART

I guess the reason I went into the Air Force was because I couldn't get my father to buy a tractor. Farming by hand and mule wasn't the way I wanted to live.

I was born at noon on June 20, 1925, at Pickensville, Alabama, and spent my first seventeen years on a farm. My father raised cotton and corn and things, and I worked in the fields.

I started school at the age of six. It was a one-room, clapboard schoolhouse, back off a country road, at a place called Lizzard Lope. I remember the two pot-bellied wood stoves and my desk location over a knocked-out knot hole in the floor. Every morning, the teacher drove by our house in an open-top Model A Ford sedan to take us to school. We had to turn off the main road onto a dirt pathway and I soon learned where every rut in the road was. We had about ten or fifteen students and the teacher taught all ten grades.

After four years at that school, I started riding the school bus to Carrollton School. I graduated from there in May, 1943, enlisted in the Air Force, and by June was at Keesler Field, Biloxi, Mississippi.

Basic training lasted six weeks. I don't remember that it was particularly tough, but then I had been farming all my life. After Basic, I went to Amarillo, Texas, for a three-month course in B-17 aircraft mechanics. From there, we were sent to gunnery school at Kingman, Arizona. I was training to be crew chief on a B-17. That is the position just behind the pilot and involved firing two 50-caliber machine guns from a revolving turret atop the B-17. The way they taught us to "lead" targets was to put us in the back of a pickup truck, drive around a curvaceous course, and throw clay pigeons out for us to shoot at with a shotgun. Then we also trained on the actual airplane and we had to be careful not to shoot the tail off the plane.

About that time the war in Europe was coming to a close. I was sent, first, to Romulus, Michigan and then spent some time in Connecticut, where pilots were bringing planes back to the U.S. I would fly with the pilots who were ferrying the planes out to Amarillo to "mothball" them in storage pits Then I was given a choice of one of three army bases to go to. That is the only time I ever was allowed to make a decision. All the rest of the time I was told what to do. I chose to go Homestead Air Force Base in Florida, where I attended a C-54 transport airplane mechanic's school. From there, I went to Miami and then to West Palm Beach with the Air Transport Command (ATC).

I was assigned to the flight crew of a C-54 and we flew to the Panama Canal Zone, Puerto Rico, British Guiana, Belem and Natal in Brazil, Ascension, Liberia, Casablanca, Tripoli, and the Azores. When in Casablanca, we could get a pass to go to some of the nice resorts along the coast.

About 1946, I moved up to Westover, Massachusetts, from where we flew to the West Coast, Canada, Greenland (north of the Arctic Circle), Iceland, Bermuda, France, and Germany. After about a year of this I was sent to Wheelus Field in Tripoli, Libya. That's where I spent my last year. One time a B-17 had crashed near Bahrain. About twelve bodies had been out in the desert for three or four days and we had to fly them out of there. I took all the escape hatches off the side of the C-54 and we flew, at low altitude, with all the windows open.

While in Tripoli, we flew to Saudi Arabia, Asmara, Greece, Italy, France, and Germany. This was during the

Berlin Airlift and in Frankfurt we would have to sit for long stretches of time because the planes flying the Airlift always had right-of-way.

In 1949, after six years in the Air Force, I asked to be sent to some school. They refused to send me and that's when I decided to get out. I thought if I was going to get further education I'd have to do it myself. I held the rank of Staff Sergeant when I left the service.

I graduated from the University of Alabama in 1955, with a bachelors degree in mechanical engineering. I started working for Lockheed, and except for three years at Weyerhauser in Arkansas, and three years at Texatron in Texas, I worked for Lockheed until my retirement in 1990.

How do I feel about my military service? Well, it was part of my duty in a time when it had to be done. It was just another period in my life. That's the way I think of it, just a part of life.

—Interviewed by Charles Miller, August 2001

WILLIAM THOMAS "BILL" SWAIN
With
Barbara Swain

I didn't know my late husband, Bill, when he was in the Service. We met and married later.

Bill was born, and grew up, in Memphis, Tennessee. He graduated from high school there, then left for college at the University of Mississippi. He was only at "Ole Miss" for two months when he was drafted. They even refunded his tuition since he had barely gotten started. All of Bill's friends were being drafted too and a large number of young men left Memphis about the same time.

After entering the Army Air Corps at Fort Oglethorpe, Georgia, Bill was sent to Florida. He spent some time at Melbourne Beach and then was stationed at Miami. Bill was assigned to the 18th Weather Squadron. He really enjoyed the weather work.

We were all overjoyed when the War was finally over. I was in the hospital on VJ-Day and I looked out the window to see what all the yelling and commotion was about. I remember Bill's mother saying how relieved she was that her son wouldn't have to go overseas.

Bill did go overseas right after the War was over. He saw everything had been bombed out and he never wanted to go back to Europe. Bill held the rank of Corporal when he was discharged. He was qualified as an expert with the M-1 Carbine and also with a pistol. He had a number of citations.

Following his military service, Bill couldn't get back into Ole Miss because it was overcrowded. Most of the universities were full of young men who had returned at the same time. He spent a year at Memphis State University then transferred to the University of Kentucky, where he earned a degree in Civil Engineering. Bill accepted a job with Schmidt Engineering. When they merged with Hensley Engineering and became Hensley-Schmidt Engineering, he moved to Marietta. He worked there until he retired.

Bill died November 9, 1993.

—Interviewed by Marcus McLeroy, November 2001

TOM TABOR

Although I was born in Miami, Florida, in 1923, I spent most of my formative years in North Carolina. My family moved back to Miami in 1942, shortly before I was drafted into the Navy. At that point, my only brother was already in the Navy.

I started my military service at Camp Perry, Virginia. The Company Commander asked me to be Clerk for our company. Since part of that job was to assign the duty roster, I didn't put my name on the list.

After twelve weeks of basic training and some tests, the Navy decided I was more mechanical than anything else, so they sent me to San Diego, California. I went straight to the Landing Craft Depot, which was where they repaired and reconditioned all the landing craft to get them seaworthy again. I was in charge of the engine tune-up room. I spent my entire tour of duty right there.

Our housing situation was good—barracks with four-bed rooms, no upper bunks. Food was good and plentiful.

One of the main things we did was train the Civilian Battalion (CB's—also called "Seabees"). Those people were ranked according to their job experience in civilian life, the more experience the higher their rank. We were to make sure they knew all about repairing the engines before going overseas.

We had every night free. We found out that the San Diego Electric Railway Company needed somebody to repair the bus engines. So we helped out. We would go in one side of the building in Navy uniform and come out on the shop floor in coveralls, and work from two to eight hours. They appreciated that. I don't remember what they paid us, but probably about what their mechanics were making.

I was in San Diego for both VE-Day and VJ-Day. There were no big celebrations. The attitude was, "Hey, it's not over until it's over. It's over when we go home." We were mustered out pretty quickly and I went back to Miami.

After the War, I decided to make use of the GI Bill. I started at Middle Georgia College and then finished at Georgia Tech. I started out in Engineering, then switched to a management major. After graduating from Georgia Tech, I worked several places. Jobs were sort of hard to get at that time. When Lockheed opened, in 1951, I went to work there as a Methods Engineer. My salary was 80 or 85 dollars a week.

I met Evelyn in church, in Ellijay, while I was visiting my aunt. Since Evelyn worked in Atlanta we were able to date frequently. We got married in 1949, at Peachtree Christian Church. As of June 18th, we have been married 52 years.

While I was with Lockheed, I worked for a year at Waybridge, England. My family was able to be with me and our children attended an English school for a year. We also lived in Iran for a year, working for Lockheed. That was back in the days of the Shah. I worked for Lockheed for 36 years, and retired in June of 1990.

I enjoyed my time in the Navy. The training of the Seabees was very important. They went overseas and did a good job. I never had any desire to go out in a landing craft when it was being used because I didn't have any desire to have to hit the beaches. I served my Country and if I hadn't been there to do it somebody else would have had to do it.

—Interviewed by Charles Miller, November, 2001

Tom Tabor

JAMES CLAYTON TEAGUE

I was born October 30, 1923. In 1925 our family moved to Cobb County, where I attended Mountain View School. We lived on a farm on Sandy Plains Road and I went to Sandy Plains Baptist Church.

When I was fifteen, I went to work for Holeproof Hosiery. When I turned seventeen I got a job at North Carolina Ship Building Company, where my brother was working. We built Liberty Ships.

I was drafted into the Army in 1943, at age nineteen. I entered service at Fort McPherson in Atlanta. From there they sent me to Camp Gordon, Johnston, Florida. In April, 1944, we went by train to San Francisco, Camp Isthmus, and waited for a ship to take us overseas. We hiked all over those treeless hilltops. Finally, a ship came in and we loaded up for somewhere. They didn't tell us until we were halfway there that we were headed for Australia. A lot of us were very seasick.

We docked at Sydney in May, 1944. Then we went by train to Brisbane. That's about a six hundred mile journey. No berths. We just had to sit on those old benches. We were all about dead by the time we got there.

At Brisbane, we went into Camp Bilinba, near the ship yards. We were to build big barges (sixty feet long and forty feet wide) for the Chinese Nationalists. After about a year we got that work caught up. Then we had nothing else to do, so they gave us basic training all over again—hiking all over those hills in Australia.

One time, at White Beach, four of us tied our boats together and had one anchor. We went to sleep. A wind came up during the night and the next morning we found ourselves about fifty miles out at sea. All we could see in the distance were a few treetops. It took us about an hour to get back to land. We were harshly reprimanded for that.

While we were at Brisbane, I met my future wife, Joan. After a short courtship we got married. Soon thereafter I got military orders to leave.

From Brisbane we sailed to New Guinea and then on to Manila Bay. I was in a Landing Craft Mechanized (LCM) Unit. We had a medium-size landing craft with a crew of four. I was the Coxswain. One day, we landed on a beach where someone had a short wave radio and heard that the atomic bomb had been dropped on Hiroshima. A few days later we heard that the Japanese had surrendered. Needless to say we were very happy.

We spent a lot of time in and around Manila, moving troops and supplies. In August of 1945, we boarded an AKA boat and headed toward Japan. About halfway there we ran into a typhoon. I looked out and could almost touch the water, the ship was listing so badly. Then, suddenly, we moved into an area that was calm, like a lake. We then proceeded on to Japan. We had to wait out in the harbor for about a month until they cleared the harbor of mines. Finally it was clear enough and we stayed there docking the surrendered Japanese ships as they came in and escorting Japanese pilots off the ships.

In January, 1946, we sailed, by way of Honolulu, into San Francisco. We took a troop train through Arizona, Texas, New Orleans, and on to Ft. Knox, Kentucky. It was about June before my wife was able to join me. She goes back to Australia every couple of years but I really don't like to fly so I've never been back there.

I came out of the service as a Technician Fourth Grade (T-4). I was awarded the Asiatic Pacific Service Medal with two Bronze Stars; the Liberation Ribbon with one Bronze Star; the Merit Unit Award and two Victory Medals.

After I got back home, I completed my high school education at night school. I attended the University of Georgia off-campus center in Marietta for two years. I studied business law. I went to work at the U.S. Post Office in Marietta on February 27, 1946 and retired from there on September 30, 1980 as Station Manager. Joan worked for twenty-five years as a Sales Manager at Sally's Beauty Supply in Marietta.

Joan and I have three children, two sons and a daughter.

I am proud to have served in the military. It was what little part I could do to help out. I'd do it again. And I would go earlier.

—Interviewed by Harland Armitage, February, 2002

James Teague

JAMES THOMAS
And
Katherine Thomas

James Thomas

I was born and grew up here in Cobb County, Georgia. I attended Blackwell Elementary School and Acworth High School. I was working part time at the Coca Cola Bottling Company when I was drafted in August, 1943. I had two brothers already serving in the Army so I asked if I could join the Navy instead. I was eighteen years old at the time.

We completed nine weeks of boot training at Great Lakes Naval Training Center. I was in pretty good physical shape before I entered the service. I was handling forty-pound Coke cases—one in each hand—so I handled the physical training pretty well.

After boot camp they put us on a troop train and nobody told us where we were going. We were in Iowa before we found out we were heading to California. It took us five days to get to Treasure Island, California, which was a big processing center. I was assigned to the Naval Air Transport Service, Squadron VR-11, Oakland, California.

I stayed in Oakland until April, 1944, when the whole squadron was shipped to Honolulu, Hawaii, aboard the *U.S.S. Hercules*, a freighter. We were stationed at John Rogers

Naval Air Station. My first plane was a C-54. Later we flew the DC-4's. Our job was to carry mail, passengers, and cargo (which had priority) to the islands of the South Pacific. My first trip was Honolulu, Johnson, Kwajalein, Tarawa, and Guadalcanal. The marines there stole all my food off my airplane. I told the Commander we didn't have any food left and he told me to make a raid on the mess hall and get us something to eat. He mainly wanted coffee, though.

We practiced ditching all the time. Ditching, inflating the life raft, using our life jackets, swimming to the nearest island. We learned how to eat coconuts and stuff. Thank goodness we never had to use that training.

I was flying with different crews each trip. We didn't know where we were flying to or with whom until our name came up on the board. We might be going to Midway Island, or Kwajalein, or Eniwetok. As the U.S. took the islands back from Japan, one at a time, the Seabeas would have about eight or nine days with bulldozers and tractors to build us a runway, that's where we went—Guam, Peleliu, Saipan, Tinian, Okinawa, Samar in the Philippines. We carried cargo and a few passengers. If the island had a MASH unit and there were hospital litter patients, we would convert the plane into a hospital plane and come back with 42 litters. That called for a 1st Lieutenant, a Flight Nurse, and a Corpsman. We would fly them back to the IU Naval Hospital in Honolulu, but we would stop at either Guam or Kwajalein for gas on the way.

I brought back the first quadriplegic case from either Saipan or Tinian. He had both arms and both legs shot off. They had patched him up at the MASH hospital and he was heading home. I guess he was about the saddest one I had. I had a lot of them, though, with no arms or no legs. The Corpsman would help me feed them or hold a cigarette so they could smoke.

We were on a rotation of three trips south, and then one

trip state side—Honolulu to Oakland. You could make that flight in about nine hours if you had a tailwind but sometimes it took eleven or twelve hours. If you got about halfway there and one of the engines went out, you had to turn around and go back. Ah, I hated to see that. Mostly, we didn't have much trouble with that big old R-2800 engine. One time our chief mechanic, Big Red Morrison, changed an engine almost by himself. We had to have the engine flown in and he changed it. He got a commendation medal for that. Another time, we were down at Manus Island and Melanie Bay in New Guinea. They had just served us steak when the Japs flew down that runway just splattering bullets everywhere. We got only a little bit of our steaks. Fortunately, we had parked our big old plane back off the road.

Another time, we were coming from Kwajalein to Honolulu, and needed to stop at Johnson Island for fuel. The pilot asked our navigator where we were and he said, "I don't know." We were running low on gas and the pilot was getting hot and hollering at the navigator. We flew around and around and finally spotted a light down there. That navigator was sweating that one.

On VE-Day, May 8, 1945, Katherine and I were married at the First Baptist Church in Oakland, California. I had a flight coming in to California and I asked the Commander for a fifteen-day leave. He said, "What do you think this is?" When I told him I was getting married, he said, "You sailors will do anything." I reckon he felt sorry for me because he gave me the fifteen days. Then I had to go back.

I was flying about a 100 hours a month. I had about 1900 hours by the time I stopped flying. I was on the island of Guam when they dropped the atomic bomb. We knew the War was going to be over then. I had enough points to get out, so I did. We got back to the States in October, 1945. We had to come back home by ship. After flying all that time, we sailed under the Golden Gate Bridge aboard the *U.S.S. Sergeant Bay*, a baby flattop. Katherine and I, along with my buddy and his wife, caught a train going east the day after we arrived back in California. I was able to separate from the service at Jacksonville, Florida, on December 14, 1945.

I came out of the Navy with the rank of Petty Officer Second Class. I had been awarded the Asiatic Pacific Ribbon and the American Theater Ribbon. I then joined the Air Force Reserves and rose to the rank of Master Sergeant.

I think my Navy service was a good experience, and it was necessary. I don't think they could have won the War without our help. They had to have the supplies coming to all those islands. It was like the Berlin airlift. We had 98 DC-4's flying, one taking off or landing every 30 minutes. I would do it again if I had to. My Navy training helped me with my present job.

When I first came out of the service I worked at the post office for a few months. Then I worked in accounting and finance with the Veterans Administration for five years. I went to Dobbins Air Force Base as the Air Transportation Supervisor, became the project manager, and retired, after 30 years, as the Transportation Officer.

Katherine Thomas

After Jim and I were married, I stayed in California. I lived with one of the other wives in the group. When Jim would come in, we would go to the hotel. Eventually I was able to rent a room for just us. I would have been really lonesome if it hadn't been for one of the wives who was from that area. She had family who we could go visit on Sundays.

We wives would save our sugar ration coupons so that we could make desserts for the husbands when they came home. They could get some things we couldn't get and they would bring us butter, and silk stockings. We didn't have a car so gasoline shortage wasn't a problem.

When Jim and I returned to Marietta, we had a little two-room apartment on Washington Avenue. We have four children, three girls and one boy.

—Interviewed by Harland Armitage, July, 2002

James Thomas

NORRIS "PUG" THORNTON

I was born at Elberton, Georgia, in 1921, and that's where I grew up. I graduated from Elberton High School in 1938 and worked in a drug store until I joined the Army Air Corps in May, 1942.

At that time, my older brother was in the Artillery, stationed in the Aleutian Islands. He stayed there for the whole War. He said their Quonset huts stayed covered with snow the entire time but it provided insulation to keep them warm.

I took my basic training at Keesler Field in Biloxi, Mississippi. Our living conditions were good and the food was fair. This was my first time away from home. At Keesler I never was good at marching. One day when some "big wheels" came in to review the troops, we went out on the apron to march. I thought that I would get on the back of the line so I wouldn't be noticed. Unfortunately, I turned out to be the pivot man. After we marched a little bit, the drill sergeant stopped and said, "Take that man off that pivot and put him on the back of the line where I'll never see him again!"

After six weeks at Keesler, they sent us to Randolph Field to learn how to be Link Trainer Instructors. Link Trainers are flight simulators which allow pilots to practice without having to take an airplane into the sky. In two months, when we were fully qualified, they sent us to Lackland Air Force Base, Waco, Texas, where we trained pilots in the advanced flying school. Three months later, we went to Tinker Field near Oklahoma City where we stayed until we shipped overseas.

We went first to Blackpool, England, then to Northern Ireland, near Belfast. They put us in the 312th Ferrying Squadron. Our Squadron was supposed to receive our planes from the States and deliver them to where they were needed in England, We had a Link unit there and we trained the pilots in bad weather flying, "blind flying," we called it.

Our living conditions in Northern Ireland were quite good. In the beginning, the P-38's were taken apart and shipped to Northern Ireland. There were a group of "Lockheed technicians" who would then reassemble the P-38's. Later they found they could fly the P-38's to Iceland or Greenland, refuel, and then fly them on to Ireland. So the "Lockheed technicians" were sent back home and we got those nice barracks that the civilians had used.

We were still in Northern Ireland on D-Day (June 6, 1944), and a month later we moved to England, near Oxford. They didn't need any more ferrying of aircraft, so they gave our outfit the C-47 transports to haul supplies. They didn't need Link instructors anymore either so they put me on the line as a mechanic. From there, we moved to France (eleven miles outside Paris) in the fall of 1944.

Our quarters in France were good. We were billeted in an apartment building. The only problem was that when the Germans pulled out, they put cement in a lot of the commodes and made them unusable. We had liberty every night until midnight and we had one day off every week. We could go and spend that day in Paris.

Eventually, they made me aerial engineer on a C-47. That is like a crew chief. I had to see that the plane was loaded and maintained properly. Basically, we were supplying the U.S. Armies—Patton in the south and Bradley in the center. We never did get enemy fire because we stayed far enough back behind the lines.

On VE-Day, we went into Paris and celebrated. That was quite an experience.

My job continued until November, 1945, when I came home. I was discharged with the rank of Corporal. I had received several Battle Stars and since you got five points for each Star, that got me home sooner. I had some ribbons too. The British soldiers had to do a lot more than the Americans in order to be awarded ribbons. The English people used to say they saw an American soldier go to see the movie, "Desert Victory" and when he came out they put another ribbon on him.

We sailed back to the U.S. on a Liberty Ship. Those ships weren't very large. We took turns sleeping in the hammocks on the ship. We would have 24 hours below deck, and then 24 hours above. We took the southern route to avoid the rough seas and it took us ten days. Even then, we had some rough seas. One day, I noticed that the Skipper was just steering into the waves and I said, "We're not making any time, are we?" He answered, "I'm not trying to make any time. I'm just trying to keep it afloat."

We docked in Boston and they put us on a train to Fort Gordon, Georgia, near Augusta. That's where I left the service.

Ruth and I had mutual friends in Elberton, and we had been corresponding—just friendly letters. When I got home, we started dating. In November, 1946, we were married at the First Baptist Church of Elberton. We have been married 54 years. We have one daughter.

I worked in the granite business from 1946 to 1951. They call Elberton the "Granite City of the World." Then Ruth's sister, who lived in Marietta, got me an interview at Lockheed when it opened. I was hired and started out in Inspections. I stayed with Inspections for my whole career. I retired from Lockheed in 1984, with 33 years of service.

How do I feel about my World War II service? Well, after I got back safely, I was glad I had volunteered. I had some mixed emotions along the way. Weather was our biggest enemy and we had to fly in some really bad weather. That was the part I dreaded. Still, I'm glad I was a part of it.

—Interviewed by Charles Miller, August, 2001

WALTER UHORCHAK
And
Sarah Uhorchak

Walter Uhorchak

I was born on the lower east side, Avenue A and Ninth Streets, in New York City, the third son of immigrant parents. My parents were from the Ukraine, although my mother's mother was Polish. We moved several times and wound up in Brooklyn, where I went to high school.

I was seventeen and half, just graduated from high school, when the War broke out. My eldest brother, Milton, had been in the National Guard so he was federalized in the 1940's. In June, 1942, my brother, Teddy, and I decided to enlist and convinced our dad to sign the permission papers.

I had been active with the Sea Scouts and loved the sea and the water. I tried to get into the Merchant Marines, the Coast Guard, or the Navy, but I was turned down because I was wearing glasses. Teddy, who would get seasick just spelling the name of his ship, ended up in the Navy and I ended up in the Army. Teddy, as a sonar operator, was deployed to New Caledonia and had to stay in sickbay for a week or two.

I entered the military at Governor's Island, New York, on June 25, 1942. My first meal was a form of stew and I said, "I don't know if I will be able to handle this." A couple of days later I was ordered to report to Camp Upton (on Long Island). My next meal was on a Friday and it was greasy fish. Again, I said, "I don't think I can handle this." I stayed at Camp Upton several months, with no particular assignment, working in administration, receiving new recruits. No basic training, no nothing, just get the recruits lined up and take them through orientation.

Then they shoved me into a train with a couple of thousand other people to open an Army Air Force reception center at Atlantic City, New Jersey. I did some insurance administration work and when that got boring they made me a drill instructor, which I didn't know anything about. I had to learn cadence, and we drilled, and drilled, and drilled. Finally, in early 1943, I was sent to a center in Greensboro, North Carolina, again to do insurance work.

One day a lovely redheaded gal walked through the building and I was determined to meet her. I was a Buck Sergeant, green as beans, with no experience. I walked back to her office and introduced myself to Sarah Elizabeth Hudgins, who had just moved in from Winston Salem. I got brave enough to ask her for a date and we dated seven days straight. Finally, she said, "Stop! Enough!. I've got to wash my hair." We dated for four or five months and got serious. When I got a weekend pass, I took her to New York to meet my mother. After dinner and a show, at two o'clock in the morning, we walked down to the East River, I proposed, and she accepted.

I went shopping for her birthday and wound up buying an engagement ring. We became engaged in September, her birthday was in October, and we were married by the Chaplain at the Base Chapel in Greensboro, November 6,

1943. Sarah's mother wasn't too happy about her marrying a Yankee and a Catholic.

I got transferred out of the headquarter's detachment and into a training company troop as a small arms coach—carbine, pistol, submachine guns, .45's. We had fifteen or twenty thousand recruits in basic training. We drilled them, marched them, did bivouac, and trained them in use of gas masks. Just discipline. At one point we had some air force crew members who had completed their missions and were back waiting for re-deployment. They were kids our own age who had fifty combat missions. Most of them were very humble.

I remember one incident in the mess hall. We had finished eating and were headed to dump our trays. This kid (looked to be about twenty-two) hadn't touched his food. A big fat mess sergeant, standing there at the garbage can, asked him why he hadn't eaten his stuff. "Don't you know that guys overseas are crying for it?" The kid looked him in the eye and said, "Sarge, have you ever been overseas?' The sergeant said, "No, why?" The kid opened his raincoat to expose a chest full of ribbons and said, "I have, and this is slop." Then he dumped his tray and walked out.

Up to that point, Sarah and I had been able to live together. However, as the military was wont to do, they separated us. In the summer of 1944, I had volunteered for crash boat duty. Six thousand of us wound up at Gulfport, Mississippi. They only needed about 500 so the military farmed us out. I ended up at Cochran Field in Macon, Georgia, doing military police duty for a few months. Then they sent us back to Gulfport for reclassification. They asked me what I would like to do and I answered, "How about ordinance school up in Denver?" So, late in the winter of 1944-1945, I went to Denver. From there, I went as a bomb-sight and automatic-pilot technician, to San Angelo Air Force Base, where Sarah was able to join me.

I think I was somewhere between Denver and San Angelo on VE-Day. I remember feeling relieved that my brother would no longer be exposed to combat. Then I was put on a list to be sent to Japan. I had ten days pre-overseas-shipment leave so Sarah and I took a train to New York. We were on the train on VJ-Day.

Early in the fall we ended up at Camp Stoneman, California, ready to go overseas. Then the departure was canceled. We heard a rumor that the merchant marine crew hadn't had shore leave in a long time so they let the water out of the boilers. Next, they sent us to Wichita Falls, Texas. I got a two week furlough and went home to see Sarah and her parents. When I got back to Wichita Falls the barracks were empty. Everybody with 36 or more points had been discharged. I had 38 points so I said, "Where do I apply?" Then I called Sarah and told her I was coming home.

I don't have any war stories to tell. I never did get attached to any particular unit, I just floated the whole time. I've met one or two other guys who had the same experience. I came out of the service a "three striper" (Buck Sergeant). I was awarded three medals, Good Conduct Medal, Service Medal, and I don't remember what the third one was.

I volunteered for military service because I felt it was my obligation as a citizen of this country. By volunteering, I thought I had a better chance of doing what I wanted to do. It didn't work out that way. I guess God just planned out all this stuff and said, "OK, I'm going to watch you and I'll intercede every so often when you get in trouble."

Sarah Uhorchak

I came from Hendersonville, North Carolina. I had been working in Washington and when the War started we were moved out to Winston Salem. After Wally and I were married we found a room in a private home, where we lived until he was sent to Mississippi. Shortly after that I was transferred back to Washington to work at the Pentagon. After Wally was transferred from Denver to San Angelo, I joined him there. At first we couldn't find a place to live. You could only stay in the hotel three days and then you had to find another place. We would go to the USO every day and wait for someone to call in a vacancy. Later, we found a house which we shared with another couple. Wally worked nights and I worked days. We met coming and going. Sometimes we had breakfast together.

The time we took the train from Texas to New York (over VJ-Day) there were just mobs of people. We had to stand from Kansas City to St. Louis. Wally would get close to the gate, and we would hold hands and he would try to pull me through the crowds. It was a mad race.

—Interviewed by Charles Miller, 2001

Sarah and Wally Uhorchak

JAMES "UPPIE" UPSHAW
And
Eleanor Upshaw

    I was born in Cobb County, Georgia. My father had a farm out on the Canton Highway. I went through the ninth grade at Elizabeth School. That's as high a grade as any of the County schools (except Acworth) had at that time. If you wanted to get a high school diploma you had to go to Marietta. I went to Marietta High School and played football there. Shuler Antley was the high school principal at the time. He helped get me a job at the Piggly Wiggly so that I could afford the five dollar a month tuition that non-Marietta residents had to pay. After I graduated I got a job at the A&P Store just north of the Marietta Square. I have worked in several A&P stores in Atlanta and Decatur.

    While I was at Marietta High School I was in the National Guard and one evening about October or November of 1940, I ran into the First Sergeant of that group. He said they were going to be mobilized. They would all go together, and take all of their recreation and musical equipment. He said they would serve a year and be able to come home. He talked me into it. So we all went to Fort Stewart to be in an Anti-Aircraft Artillery unit. I started out as a Private.

    It was while I was at Fort Stewart that I met Eleanor,

who was from Ludowici. We had all been out with a group and I thought she sounded like somebody that would be interesting to get to know. It went on from there.

Early in 1942, our unit went to Newfoundland for six months. By that time the Draft had started and we knew we wouldn't be getting out. When we got back to Georgia, they asked for volunteers to go to officer candidate school at Ft. Benning in Columbus, Georgia. I volunteered, and that's how I ended up in the Infantry.

I was commissioned a 2nd Lieutenant and assigned to the west coast of Oregon. When that division was transferred to Arizona, I applied for a ten day leave to go home. I asked my mother to invite Eleanor to come to Marietta as our house guest. She did and the second night we were together, I proposed. Eleanor accepted my proposal, went back to Brunswick to work, and I went to Arizona.

I hadn't been back in Arizona a month before they decided to send me to motor maintenance school at Fort Benning. I arranged to have two extra days leave and went to Brunswick. The next day Eleanor and I went to the courthouse, got our marriage license, and got in touch with the preacher. Dr. Warren Cutts, pastor of Second Baptist Church (now Crestview Baptist) married us in the pastorium.

After my training at Fort Benning, my division was sent to Carson, Colorado, for three months. Eleanor came out by train (sitting on her suitcase most of the way) to be with me.

On September 7, 1944, we left Carson to go to Camp Kilmer Embarkation Center. From there, our unit was sent to France—the first to land directly in France after the D-Day invasion. We landed at Cherbourg. I was leader of the third platoon (a mortar platoon), M Company, 414th Battalion, 104th Infantry Division.

That was about the time when Patton needed supplies

at the front. They took everybody out of our company who could drive a two and a half ton truck and had them driving supplies for Patton. They called it the "Red Ball Express." The rest of us stayed back there in the hedgerows and played football, and did close-order drill.

We moved, then, up through Belgium. During that time we were attached to the Canadian Army. Our first combat was to clean out those pockets of resistance that Patton had sealed off. We did that for about a month and then moved to Aachen, Germany, right after it had been secured. By that time, we were part of the U.S. Seventh Army, with General Collins as Commander.

Our living conditions were good. In the mortar platoon, we would go in, when we had cleared out a town, and set up until the next time we would be needed. We'd just pick out a house and say to the occupants, "Vamoose!" They would go stay with their neighbors or kinfolks. We would try to take good care of those houses. Other times, we just stayed in bombed-out buildings.

I realize everyday how lucky I was. As part of the mortar (81 mm) platoon, we stayed behind, like artillery, and fired overhead. There were very few times when we were closer than a thousand yards to the Germans. I carried a carbine and I never did have to fire it.

One time we were up in Holland, hiding among the dikes and banks in the sand and it had been raining. As we crossed a little foot bridge over a canal, I looked down at my carbine and it was just coated with sand. I though, "That thing wouldn't fire if I needed it to." So I aimed it down toward the water and pulled the trigger. It did fire, and that's the only time I pulled the trigger the entire time.

I told that story right after the war ended. One of the men who was up there and knew what happened said, "Yeah, but think about all the men who were killed by those mortars that you gave the orders to fire."

About the middle of November, 1944, the fighting got

heavy. By that time we were down in Germany, in the industrial heartland called the Ruhr Pocket. I was wounded near the little town of Weiswaller.

When we would set up the mortars, an observer would go out following the front line and adjust the aim for our guns. I usually sent a Sergeant out to do that but that time I decided to go myself. I took two men with me and we strung telephone line until we ran out of wire. I told the men with me to splice the wire and I would drop back four or five feet and clip in to see if it was working. About the time I clipped in and put the telephone to my ear, I heard a tank coming down the road. I was about four feet from where the tank was going by. That's the last thing I remember.

It seems that some advanced troops had found a mine field. Headquarters sent a crew who had taken out the mines, stacked them up beside the road, and had gone to get a vehicle to haul them off. They didn't get back up there right away and that night the Germans came back and put the mines back in their holes. To everybody concerned, that mine field wasn't supposed to be there but I have evidence that it was. That tank ran over a mine, it exploded and sprayed me with shrapnel. I got eighteen different penetrations, including through my helmet. That one is still in my head.

I spent the next two and a half months in a hospital in England. Then I went back and took over the same platoon I had commanded before. The first time I saw the Battalion Commander when I got back, he asked, "Why are you wearing those gold bars?" I answered, "Sir, I don't know. Last time I heard, that's what a 2nd Lieutenant is supposed to wear." I had been promoted and didn't know it. About three weeks after that the promotion order came through.

From the Ruhr, we went down and crossed the Rhine at Remagen Bridge. We were the last ones to cross before that bridge fell into the water. We used the tunnel to go through the mountains on the other side of the Rhine. In the Hartz forest we ran across a gas chamber. It hadn't been used recently and was cleaned up just spick and span.

We moved east then as fast as we could. We got to the Mulde River and met the Russians. One of their generals came across the river in a touring car, driving about 50 miles an hour. The only guard he had was someone in the car with him. But following his car was a pickup truck with a 50-caliber machine gun mounted on its bed. The person manning it was holding onto those dual handles with both hands. I stood there and laughed. Going 50 miles an hour, I don't know what he would have hit if he had shot the thing.

We stayed in that area until the war ended. When our troops got ready to leave, our engineers took out that bridge. One day the Russians came up, a bunch of them riding on the back of a stake-body truck. They stopped there across the river. They grabbed an axe and a saw and started cutting down pine trees. They made their own lumber right there on the spot and built a bridge.

VE-Day ended the war in Germany. We were brought back to the U.S. and given a thirty-day leave. After that, we were supposed to go to the south Pacific, but during our leave, the atomic bomb was dropped. As soon as we reported back in they started sending people home. I was discharged on October 7, 1945.

Most of the decorations I received were just because I was in the right place at the right time—the European Theater of War. I was awarded the Bronze Star, the Purple Heart, the Good Conduct Medal, and the Combat Infantryman Badge.

I feel like I was lucky with my military service. I did not have the experience some of the others had. Sometimes I think they contributed more than I did. But did their service amount to any more than mine? I don't know. It's pretty hard to say. Somebody had to cook; somebody had to keep things going. When you got down to it, somebody had to be President. I don't give a whole lot of thought to it.

After the War, jobs were hard to get and I did a variety of things, including trying to sell ladies jewelry door to door. I finally went back with A&P and stayed with them until I retired in 1980.

Eleanor Upshaw died on May 21, 2001. James Upshaw died on February 17, 2002.

—Interviewed by Charles Miller, March 2001

Uppie Upshaw

MARVIN PAUL WABLE
And
Louise Wable

Paul Wable

Although I was born in West Virginia, I moved to Georgia when I was thirteen, and attended school in Sonoraville. After I left school, I worked in a cotton mill and then in Civil Service in Marietta. From there, I went to work at Southeastern Ship Building Corporation in Savannah and that's where I was when I first volunteered for the Navy. I was seventeen years old at the time. The Navy said I had a swollen foot and rejected me, so I went back to the shipyard. When I turned eighteen, the Navy called me back. That was September 27, 1943.

I had three weeks of boot camp at Pensacola, Florida. I stayed there throughout the winter, then they put us all on a train to San Diego, California. We went with the shake down crew of a new Aircraft Carrier, the *U.S.S. Solomon* CVE67. We sailed to Hawaii and back, then put on a full crew, airplanes and all. We left San Diego and cruised the Pacific for a long time.

German submarines were sinking a lot of merchant ships in the North Atlantic so they sent us through the Panama Canal to do submarine patrol. We spent the rest of the War doing that. I was a Seaman Second Class. We manned the guns, kept the guns clean, cleaned and painted the ship. Whatever needed to be done, we did. I was part of the deck crew. We didn't have anything to do with the aircraft. Those involved with the flight operations had their own area.

There were about 2500 of us on that ship. Most were between the ages of eighteen and twenty-five. Shipboard life was good. The food was good. The only thing I didn't like was having baked beans for breakfast. I loved baked beans but they were served only for breakfast. We had a good commander and he would let us off to go ashore when we reached a port. We pulled into some interesting places like Casablanca, Recife and Rio de Janeiro, Brazil.

Our ship was not attached to a fleet and we moved solo, with two Destroyers or Destroyer Escorts, one on each side of us. We often saw other American vessels. Although our ship was never hit, one night we had a near miss. I was back on the fantail, where we were manning two five-inch guns. About two o'clock in the morning, I looked down and saw a torpedo headed for our ship. We had a long cable which we would drag behind the ship every night. That was supposed to detect torpedoes and keep them from hitting us. Anyway, the torpedo didn't hit us but we could see the wake as it went by. Talk about your heart in your mouth, that will do it.

Other than that torpedo, our ship was never fired on. We fired two or three times but we never fired on airplanes. In one of our biggest engagements we sank a big supply sub. Another time, a submarine came up and was firing on our aircraft. We could see it on the horizon. That thing shot down three of our planes. The Squadron Commander said, "We can't have this." So he flew out over the submarine, dropping depth charges, using everything in the world. He got so close down there, he ditched his own airplane. Of course he didn't come back. We lost three other airplanes and their pilots, but they got that submarine.

I stayed in the Navy, at sea the whole time, until my discharge on December 9, 1945. I went to work for Lockheed in 1951 and worked there for more than 36 years. I spent my whole career there in quality control, rising to the level of inspection supervisor. I received seventeen commendations and a ten-year perfect attendance recognition. Then I got another five year perfect attendance commendation.

I wouldn't take anything for my World War II experience. I sure wouldn't want to do it again, though.

Louise Wable

I remember when Pearl Harbor was bombed. I was ironing at the time. Our family had a dairy farm and so we didn't have anyone directly involved in the military.

I worked for 28 years at Kennestone Hospital. I pioneered the first personnel program there. I was Director of Personnel Administration for eighteen years Then I helped set up the department for volunteers. I came to Marietta First Baptist Church from Lost Mountain Baptist when Earl Stallings was pastor.

—Interviewed by George Beggs, September, 2001

Paul Wable

ERNEST J. WESTER

I will never forget December 7, 1941. It was a quiet sunny Sunday afternoon. About 2 PM, as my brother and I sat daydreaming and listening to our old battery powered Philco radio, the announcer suddenly interrupted the regularly scheduled program to announce that Pearl Harbor had been attacked. My brother, home for a weekend pass from Camp Stewart, Georgia, was wearing his army uniform. Twelve months earlier, he, along with some one hundred other local National Guard boys had been mobilized, supposedly for twelve months active duty. They were expecting to be deactivated within a week. Pearl Harbor changed all those plans. Instead of being deactivated, they were to serve another four years on active duty, mostly in the Pacific theater. Before the War ended all four of my brothers would serve in the military.

I had graduated from Cedartown High School in June, 1941, As a high school graduate I thought I knew everything, but I had no clue as to where Pearl Harbor was. Neither did my brother. At age eighteen, I thought it would be exciting to be in the Service, travel, and see far away places, unaware of the danger involved. As we listened to the frequent war announcements, we thought surely that a powerful nation like the U.S.A. could defeat a small country like Japan in just a few months. We didn't realize how ill equipped we were to fight a war.

Realizing that I would be drafted soon, I joined the

Army Signal Corps Reserves on November 25, 1942, at Fort McPherson, Georgia. As a civilian I received training in listening to, sending, and receiving international Morse Code, several hours a day for five months. On March 26, 1943, our unit was called to active duty, processed, and sent to Camp Crowder, Missouri, for basic training.

Following basic training we were given several more months of intensive training in International Morse Code. Some of us underwent a battery of tests for screening to determine eligibility for the Army Specialized Training Program (ASTP) to study engineering at a designated university. I managed to pass, even though I had no high school background in engineering. But here was my chance to go to college at Uncle Sam's expense. The examining officer in charge warned me that without high school chemistry or physics I would have a tough time. I was elated just to get on a college campus and was willing to "dig."

A few of us were sent to the University of Wyoming, at Laramie, arriving on October 21, 1943. We were taking basic engineering courses but they were tough, and at times I thought I wouldn't pass the tests. Supervised by military officers, we studied and ate with the civilians and were encouraged to participate in campus social affairs. After five delightful months, our entire class of GI's was called back to active duty.

While at the University of Wyoming I met one of the most delightful families that I have ever known: Horace and Vanda Moore, both originally from the South. I, along with several other GI's from Georgia, met them at the First Baptist Church of Laramie. They invited us to their home for Sunday dinner, and we went there almost every Sunday for the duration of our stay in Laramie.

Vanda started a newsletter, sending it to GI's who had enjoyed the Moore's hospitality in Laramie and later scattered all over the world. In that way we were able to get news from our buddies. She corresponded with us regularly when we were overseas. Vanda, now around 93 years of age, still has all the GI letters that she received throughout the war years. I had the opportunity to visit with the Moores in 1996. Vanda and I sat up most of the night reminiscing.

On February 7, 1944, the Army put us on a train to Camp Kohler, near Sacramento, California, for the purpose of forming the 3187th Signal Service Battalion, known as "The Ramblers," being organized at that time. During the organization I was sent back to Camp Crowder, Missouri, for Advanced Signal Corps School. There we trained to increase our speed sending and receiving code to at least 25 words per minute. We were trained as Fixed Station Operators, using equipment such as the automatic key and teletypewriter. After two months, and a week furlough at home, I rejoined the 3187th at Camp Kohler. On September 5, 1944 the Army sent us by train, back across the United States to Fort Monmouth, New Jersey to the Port of Embarkation, Camp Edison.

On November 30, 1944, we marched down to the New York harbor and boarded the *Isle de France*, a former french luxury liner converted to a troop ship. The next morning, when the ship sailed into open water, I learned what sea sickness was all about. The officers would not allow us to stay in our bunks but ordered us to report on deck for fresh air and boat drill. After three days, I was finally able to force down a piece of freshly baked bread. Then the sea settled down and so did my stomach, and I actually enjoyed the rest of the trip.

Our ship docked at Prestwick, Scotland, on December 7, 1944. We went by troop train to Leominster, England, where we were put up in whatever buildings were available. Some of us were housed in an ancient dwelling heated only by fireplaces. It was cold and we had no heat. Before long, our Yankee ingenuity showed itself as GI's scoured the neighborhood for any scrap of wood-old barrels, even old buildings—to burn for fuel.

We spent Christmas, 1944, at Leominster. War news from the Front was dismal as the Battle of the Bulge was taking place. The Army was moving replacements into Germany as fast as possible. After a few weeks we moved to Southampton and on January 4, 1945, we boarded a ship for LeHavre, France. As eighteen to twenty year old kids, we didn't think of danger. Everything was an adventure. Years later we learned that one of the ships carrying some of our group was torpedoed and sank in the English Channel without loss of life.

At LeHavre we could still see the effects of D-Day in the bombed–out seaport and sunken ships, even though D-Day was long past. We were expecting trucks or trains at LeHavre to take us to our next destination. Instead, we heard the order, "Fall in." With full field packs and duffel bags we hiked about nine miles to a snow-covered hillside on which some tents had been pitched. One of my buddies, Bill Mace, and I scrounged some pine straw and broom sedge from a nearby hillside to put on the ground under our blankets. Then, by placing our sleeping bags side-by-side, and sharing our allotted blankets we stayed warmer.

After about a week of this "luxury living," we boarded an unheated "Forty and Eight" troop train. It was a World War I train car used to carry forty men and eight horses. We didn't have to worry about being cold because we were packed in like sardines—each man with his duffel bag, rifle, and gas mask. We slept on the floor of these railroad cars four days and nights, and finally arrived in Verdun, France, shaveless and bathless. At Verdun we were housed in an old French military academy and, although our beds were just wooden platforms, they seemed plush compared to where we had been sleeping.

The Battle of the Bulge was in full fury not far away. We could hear the cannon fire. Some of our Battalion went in to assist with communications but most of us didn't have to go. While at Verdun, we did little but await further orders, stand guard duty for the gigantic motor pool, and perform KP duty. It snowed and I recall making snow cream from new-fallen snow and milk, sugar, and cocoa that we slipped out of the kitchen. Mickey Rooney, an American entertainer, came and put on a show for us there and Bob Hope put on his show not far away at Freiburg, Germany.

On April 21, 1945, we left Verdun for Biebrich, a suburb of Wiesbaden, Germany. I was assigned to "Rambler" headquarters in a nice facility formerly used by German SS officers. We actually had modern plumbing at last. We were in Biebrich on May 8, 1945, when VE-Day was declared. There was great celebrating throughout the day and night involving confiscated German beer and Schnapps. After that, most of our battalion was used as occupation forces until we could accumulate enough points to be discharged.

While awaiting another assignment, I and about twenty other GI's volunteered for a program called "Training Within Civilian Agencies" (TWCA) in which we spent three weeks touring in Scotland. In an agricultural-based program we visited farms, colleges and research stations, and enjoyed visiting many castles and other tourist attractions along the way. In Edinburgh, I watched a parade down Princes Street, led by the King and Queen and the Princesses of England.

Returning back to Wiesbaden at the conclusion of the TWCA tour, my radio team was sent to Munich, Germany. We manned a communications station from a small farmhouse out in the country. Finally, the time arrived when I had enough points to go home. We sailed, from Antwerp, Belgium, to New York, aboard a Victory Ship. I was discharged at Fort Bragg, North Carolina, April 27, 1946. My rank was Technician Fourth Grade (T-4), about equivalent to Buck Sergeant. Five us from the Atlanta area hired a taxi to drive us back to Georgia. It felt strange to be making our own transportation arrangements after having had Uncle Sam do our planning for us for three years.

I attended the University of Georgia on the GI Bill, and by packing four years into three, I received my BS in Agricultural Engineering in 1949. I taught Veterans Farm Training in Polk County, Georgia, two years, and in 1951, came to work with the Georgia Extension Service in Cobb County. I retired as Interim District Agent Chairman for the Atlanta Metropolitan Area in January, 1978.

Through the Internet and by telephone, I have kept in touch with many of my World War II buddies. Piecing together their notes and mine, I compiled a book entitled "Rambling With The Ramblers." It describes some of the events, places, and experiences the guys most remembered.

Uncle Sam colored our lives in a lot of ways. Without my World War II service, I would not have been able to get a college education

I joined Marietta First Baptist Church in 1959 and have served as a Deacon, as a superintendent in the young peoples' Sunday school department, and on several committees.

—Interviewed by Marcus McLeroy, July, 2001

Ernest Wester

JAMES BRYANT WESTER, JR.
With
Amy Wester

My late husband, Jim, and I knew each other before he went into the Service. He was born near Cedartown, Georgia, January 29, 1923, and we went to the same high school in Cedartown. However, when Jim went off to war, I was engaged to someone else, and Jim was married and had a little boy.

While Jim was stationed at the Panama Canal, his wife died of a brain tumor. Then my fiancé, who was a tail gunner on a B-17, died when his plane was shot down. Jim and I began to correspond and continued to do so until the War was over.

Jim was sent from the Panama Canal to Europe. He and a lot of others crossed the Atlantic on the *Queen Elizabeth*. They were packed in like sardines. Jim took part in the D-Day invasion of Europe and then was stationed in Germany as part of the 29th Infantry, Army. The only wound he ever received was a burn from a lamp someone knocked over in their little tent or hut.

After Jim's return from the War in the Fall of 1945, he persuaded me to marry him. I had fallen in love with his little boy, Michael. Jim and I were married on February 17, 1946. We had one daughter, Sheila.

Jim worked at several jobs and in 1956 we came to Marietta so that he could work at Lockheed. We came to First Baptist Church at that time. Dr. Griffin Henderson was our pastor. Jim loved the little children and worked in the church nursery for many years. He developed a painting business while he was on lay-off from Lockheed and eventually did not return to Lockheed. I worked as a stenographer at Lockheed from 1956 to 1986.

In his later years, Jim developed Alzheimer's Disease. He died March 10, 1998.

—Interviewed by Ruth Miller, March, 2002

Jim Wester

SAMUEL DORSEY WHATLEY
With
Jean Whatley Baldwin

My father, Samuel Dorsey Whatley, born January 30, 1915, was named for his uncle, Hugh Dorsey, the Governor of Georgia. The sixth of seven children, he grew up in the West End area of Atlanta, and graduated from Commercial High School. After working for a steamship company a short time, Daddy went to work for the railroads and worked for them forty years.

Daddy and my mother, Charlsey Isabelle Johnson, met in the neighborhood. When Daddy discovered that Mother's house was on his paper route, he arranged to have the route terminate at her house. That way he could sit on her front porch and visit after the papers were delivered. Mother and Daddy went together several years, off and on, and were married in November, 1938, in Washington, D.C. At the time of their marriage, Mother was finishing her nursing training at Baptist Children's Hospital in Washington. Following Mother's graduation, they moved back to Atlanta, and were living there when the War started. I was born in 1939.

With a wife, a baby, and a job with the railroad, Daddy could have gotten a deferment from military service. However, his office was on the second floor above the recruiting office. He went to work in a suit and tie everyday and the soldiers would tease him and ask why he wasn't in uniform. It hurt his pride, so he joined the Navy.

During his basic training at Williamsburg, Virginia, the Navy found out that Daddy was good at typing and shorthand, so they immediately put him in an office. He did that kind of work for his entire military career.

Mother and I rode the train to Williamsburg to join Daddy. Even as a very young child, I remember the chivalry extended to us. The train was full of people and here was this precious little doll with this little baby girl. They were very good to her. Mother's first task was to find us a place to live. She walked down a street in Williamsburg and saw a lady with a little girl about my age. Mother spoke to her. It turned out the lady was the wife of the doctor who was head of the hospital there. They had a spare bedroom they were willing to rent to us. The hospital was desperate for nurses so Mother got a place for us to live and a job all in one afternoon, just by walking down the street. We stayed there fourteen months, until Daddy was sent to Mechanicsville, Pennsylvania. We couldn't join him there because Mother was expecting my brother, Sam, Jr., so we came back to Atlanta.

As a result of his clerical skills, Daddy never had to go overseas. From Pennsylvania, he was transferred to Jacksonville, Florida, where he worked at the Navy Personnel Separation Center. Part of his job was to process the paperwork for people to get out of the Service. One day his Commanding Officer said, "Son, don't you a have a wife and kids? Don't you want to go home?" Daddy said, "Yes, sir!" Within twelve hours, he had his own paperwork completed to go home. He was discharged from the Navy on February 14, 1946, with the rank of Yeoman Second Class.

Daddy returned to work for Atlantic Coastline Railroad. During his employment, he was transferred several times.

He and Mother lived in Louisville, Kentucky; Cincinnati, Ohio, and Washington, D.C. Daddy retired in 1980 and my parents moved to Cobb County.

In 1994, Daddy was diagnosed with lymphoma. He was treated and trained hard to get himself back in good physical shape. He swam and used a rowing machine and fought back to the point where he was able to win another tennis championship. Then, in the Fall of 1999, the lymphoma returned and he died in the March, 2000. My mother lived just a short time after Daddy died. They were very close.

—Interviewed by Ruth Miller, September, 2001

Sam Whatley

JAMES B. WILSON
With
Shirley Olmstead

"Big Jim" Wilson (he was six feet, six inches tall) was born in Fulton County, Georgia, in 1913. He grew up in McRae, Georgia, and entered the Army at age 28.

We don't know where Jim served, but we know he was wounded and was awarded the Purple Heart. He met Lillie Bell Hocutt at a USO dance in Raleigh, North Carolina, during the War. They corresponded and married about two weeks after Jim was discharged in 1945.

Apparently Jim was not a Christian before he entered the Army. We have his Certificate of Baptism, showing that he was baptized by the Army Chaplain in May, 1944, at the Tyrannean Sea on the coast of Italy.

Jim and Lillie came to Marietta in 1951. They both worked at Lockheed and retired in the early seventies. Jim kept up with his World War II buddies. Every year, he and Lillie would go to the reunions. Jim was very proud of being part of the War effort.

Jim Wilson died in 1999.

—Interviewed by Marcus McLeroy, February, 2002

Printed in the United States
19990LVS00001BA/111